Classroom Keyboard

Classroom Keyboard

Play and Create Melodies with Chords

Patricia M. Bissell
With Brereton W. Bissell

National Association
for Music Education

ROWMAN & LITTLEFIELD
Lanham • Boulder • New York • London

Published by Rowman & Littlefield
A wholly owned subsidiary of The Rowman & Littlefield Publishing Group, Inc.
4501 Forbes Boulevard, Suite 200, Lanham, Maryland 20706
www.rowman.com

Unit A, Whitacre Mews, 26-34 Stannary Street, London SE11 4AB

Copyright © 2017 by Patricia Melcher Bissell and Brereton Wadsworth Bissell

All rights reserved. No part of this book may be reproduced in any form or by any electronic or mechanical means, including information storage and retrieval systems, without written permission from the publisher, except by a reviewer who may quote passages in a review.

British Library Cataloguing in Publication Information Available

Library of Congress Cataloging-in-Publication Data

978-1-4758-3541-0 (cloth : alk. paper)
978-1-4758-3542-7 (pbk. : alk. paper)
978-1-4758-3543-4 (electronic)

♾️ The paper used in this publication meets the minimum requirements of American National Standard for Information Sciences—Permanence of Paper for Printed Library Materials, ANSI/NISO Z39.48-1992.

Printed in the United States of America

CONTENTS

Notation Category

Keyboard key names, hand positions, pre-notation repeating, stepping, skipping, and simple melodies played by ear with finger numbers are introduced (along with their letter names).

Much of the information about meter and rhythmic notation is presented in this category and practiced by counting beats.

Four octaves of white keys are shown aligned with the treble and bass clef lines and spaces to orient keyboards to staves.

The intervallic direction and distance between pitches when reading and playing is emphasized (also when improvising).

Initial melodies are played hands together to aid coordination.

Ten authentic compositionally sequenced core melodies are initiated that usually contain repetitive phrases with only four measures that recur in three keys with further arrangements.

Two composition exercises utilize CDE in a mini AABA form.

Chords Category

Harmonic, melodic, and rhythmic ear training occurs in class.

Pitch intervals generated by the overtones are illustrated and explained along with their naming and improvisation.

4th and 5th intervals are introduced in fingering and notation.

Keyboard graphics use finger numbers (and letter names) to illustrate chord structures, inversions, and progressions.

To play chords, the seven pitches are reached from a single hand position by extending the thumb and pinkie fingers.

Students begin practicing left hand chord progressions with inversions (or the right hand further on), and reading/playing melodies with chords from both notation and lead sheets.

Accompaniment advances from root note, partial, broken, and block chords to improvised endings, arpeggios, singing, rock styles, 12-Bar Blues, and Heart and Soul progressions.

The composition exercises involve the creating of melodic patterns from chord progression pitches, and trying out chord accompaniments that complement melodies.

F and G Major Categories

These categories review the elements of the first half of the course and continue in small steps to add more challenging melodies, progressions, and treble/bass polyrhythms as well as some finger extensions and hand position changes.

Whole and half steps, the major scale structure, the black key names, and notated accidentals are depicted and explained.

Keyboard graphics show transposition of C, F, and G major (with key signatures) followed by the keys of F or G chord structures, inversions, and I, IV, and V7 chord progressions.

Seventeen secondary melodies in diverse styles are offered throughout the course (teachers may introduce other content and present performance examples from YouTube, etc.).

The composition exercises demonstrate repetition, contrast, sequence, retrograde, and inversion stemming from CDE.

Minor Category

Major/minor 3rds, the four triad types, four 7th chord types, and chord alterations are depicted, defined, and practiced.

The C major and A minor mode structures are contrasted and upper/lower case numerals show major/minor scale degrees.

Minor chords are practiced, and the harmonic minor scale that allows the playing of the dominant V7 chord is illustrated.

Perfect 5ths and the Circle of Fifths are depicted and defined, the detection of sharp and flat key signatures is explained, and all of the major key signatures are notated and identified.

Six major scales with flats (F, B♭, and E♭) and sharps (G, D, and A) add to the C major and A minor scale fingerings.

Students notate their own compositions, and conclude with a 16-measure A-A1-B-A1 form that illustrates the basic melodic alterations with an arrangement of a chordal accompaniment.

ELEMENTS

NOTATION

1
Musical Sound
White Key Names
The Keyboard
Octave
Middle C
Posture and Hands
C position
Playing Keyboards
Step, Skip, and Repeat
Pitch Motion

2
Hand Positions
Changing Position
Playing Music
Composition One

3
Rhythm
Notes and Rests
Treble Clef and Staff
Beats and Notes
Lines and Spaces
Notated Pitch Motion
Playing Melodies

4
Time Signatures
Notes and Beats
Bass Clef and Staff
Beats and Notes
Note Stems
Grand Staff
Composition Two

5
Dots
Ties
Partial Measures

6
Shorter Notes and Rests
Composition Three

CHORDS

7
Overtones
Intervals
Notated Intervals

8
Chords
Notated Chords
Chord Progressions

9
Chord Structure
Chord Inversion
5 Fingers, 7 pitches
Improvised Endings
Composition Four

10
Lead Sheets
Composition Five

11
Chording Styles
Song Accompaniment
Rock Styles

F MAJOR

12
Half and Whole Steps
C Major Scale
Black Key Names
Notated Accidentals
Scales
The Blues

13
Transposition
Key Signatures

14
Scale Degrees
Chord Structure
Chord Inversion
Key Change
Composition Six

15
Chording Styles
Hand Changes
Partial Chords

16
Song Accompaniment
Composition Seven

G MAJOR

17
Transposition
Key Signatures

18
Scale Degrees
Chord Structure
Chord Inversion
Ledger Lines

19
Dotted Quarter Notes
Composition Eight

20
Chording Styles
Song Accompaniment

21
Hand Changes
Expression
Composition Nine

MINOR

22
Major and Minor Chords
Chord Symbols
Scale Degrees
Key of C Chords

23
Three Pitch Chords
Any Triad, Any Key
Four Pitch Chords
Seventh Chords
Dominant Seventh
Basic Chord Types
Key of C 7th Chords
Altered Chords

24
Major and Minor Modes
Minor Chords
Scale Degrees
Harmonic Minor Scale

25
Perfect Fifths
Key Signatures
Circle of Fifths
Keys with Flats
Keys with Sharps
Composition Ten

**Course:
116 pages.**

MELODIES

Title	Category Source	NOTATION (Sections 1-6)	CHORDS (Sections 7-11)	F MAJOR (Sections 12-16)	G MAJOR (Sections 17-21)	MINOR (Sections 22-24)
★ Hot Cross Buns	i	1, 4	8 (■), 10	14 (■)	17 (■)	
★ Old Ark's a-Moverin'	s	1, 2, 3, 4	8, 10 (■)	14 (■)	17, 18 (■)	
★ Ode to Joy	c	1, 2, 3, 4, 5, 6	8, 10 (■), 11	12, 14 (■), 16	17, 18 (■), 20	
★ When the Saints Go Marching In	s	2, 4	10 (■)			
★ Freedom	s	3, 4, 5				
Mary Had a Little Lamb	a	4	8		17, 19 (■), 20	
★ French Lullaby	i	4	10	12, 14		
Theme from the New World	c	3	10 (■)	14 (■)		22
French Shop	i	5	8, 10		17, 18 (■)	
★ Aura Lee	a		8		17	23
Jingle Bells	a		8, 10 (■)		17	
Alleluia	s		8		17	
Southern Roses Waltz	c		8		17	
Frère Jacques	i		10	16	20	
He's Got the World in His Hands	s		10			
Row, Row, Row Your Boat	a		11			
★ Marianne	i			13, 15 (■)		
Skip to My Lou	a			14 (■)	17, 18 (■)	
Happy Birthday	a			15, 16	19	
Amazing Grace	s			15		
Chorale	c				17	
Morning	c				17	
★ Mozart Melody	c				19	
★ Czerny Melody	c				20	
German Folk Song	i				20	
Song of the Volga Boatmen	i					24
Sideshow Tune	a					24

★ 10 Core Melodies
17 Secondary Melodies

a = 7 American pop sources c = 7 classical sources
i = 7 international folk sources s = 6 spiritual sources

Lead sheets = ■.

See last page for **INDEXES** and **YouTube** use.

PROGRESSIONS

	CHORDS	F MAJOR	G MAJOR	MINOR
Swingin' Skips	8			
Rock Styles	10			
The Blues	11			
Surfing			20	
Heart and Soul				23

viii

Dedicated to the
hands-on understanding of
keyboard musicianship

Dedicated to the training and teaching of up to two dozen students with divergent interests, abilities, and preparation ranging from complete novices to well advanced.

Hands-on training for the rhythmic integration of chord progressions with melodies and an emphasis on reading and playing the pitch intervals in melodies and chords.

Understanding teaches perception of rhythm symbols, pitch locations, expression markings, scales, and chord structures. A variety of styles can also be experienced.

Keyboards are the unique instruments that support melody, harmony, and rhythm. The selections and arrangements in this course are suitable for keyboards or pianos.

Musicianship is more than sight-reading, tone production, and recital. It embraces harmonizing from lead sheets, ear training, improvising, and composing new music.

Musicianship involves knowing how music works the way it does from the inside out.

Implements the
Harmonizing Instruments Strand
of the Core Music Standards

NOTATION ~ 1 a

> This symbol "♫" means to play or do other activities
> as instructed on a **keyboard or piano**.

MUSICAL SOUND
has these qualities:

Voice

♫ **1: Set the instrument voice**
(tone color or timbre)
to **"piano"** on a keyboard
(check the manual).

Volume

softer  L O U D E R

♫ **2: Use less or more finger pressure
to control the volume of a single key**
on a keyboard or piano.

On a keyboard, also adjust the
master volume control.

---

shorter   **Length**   l-o-n-g-e-r

♫ **3: Hold a white key for shorter, then longer periods.**

---

lower, down to left   **Pitch**   up to right, **higher**

♫ **4: Play lower white keys, then higher white keys.**

> Musical sound is organized into patterns of:
>
> melody   harmony
>
> rhythm   ensemble

Following the **Section Number,** the left side pages are labeled
"a, b, or c" and the right side pages are labeled "aa, bb, or cc."

WHITE KEY NAMES

The seven letters **A B C D E F G** are used to name the **white key pitches.**

These pitches repeat, like the seven days of the week, across the keyboard.

Groups of **2 and 3 black keys** are placed between the white keys on a keyboard.

(The names for the black keys will be explained later.)

 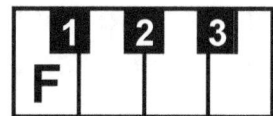

C is to the left of the 2 black keys.

F is to the left of the 3 black keys.

Learn the **Cs and Fs** first,
and the names of the other white keys will fall into place.

♪ **5:** Find and play **Cs to the left of any 2 black keys**
with the left or right **index fingers** "👆👆" (next to the thumbs).

♪ **6: Improvise** (make up as you go along) lower and higher Cs.
Hold the **pedal** down to sustain the sound (the right pedal on a piano).

♪ **7:** Find and play **Fs to the left of any 3 black keys** with the left or right
index fingers 👆👆. **Improvise** lower and higher Fs holding the pedal down.

♪ **8: Improvise** Cs and Fs (any order, lower or higher) holding the pedal down.

THE KEYBOARD

The lowest key on a piano is A. Electronic keyboards often start on other keys.

♫ **1: Play** the white keys stepping up from the lowest key on the left using a left or right index finger 👈👉. **Say** each letter name as you play.

OCTAVE

The **distance** between **eight white key pitches** is called an octave. Octaves are like weeks, Monday to Monday, F to F, etc.

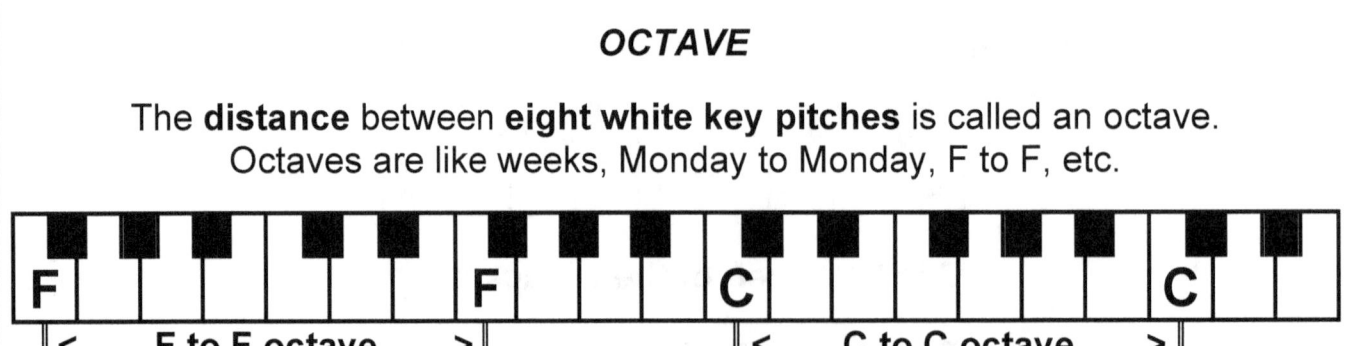

♫ **2: Play** octave pairs: Fs, next Cs, then other pitch pairs with index fingers 👈👉.

MIDDLE-C

The **C to C octave** in the center of the keyboard is usually under the brand name. The C on the left is called **middle C**; the middle C is **checked "✓"** below.

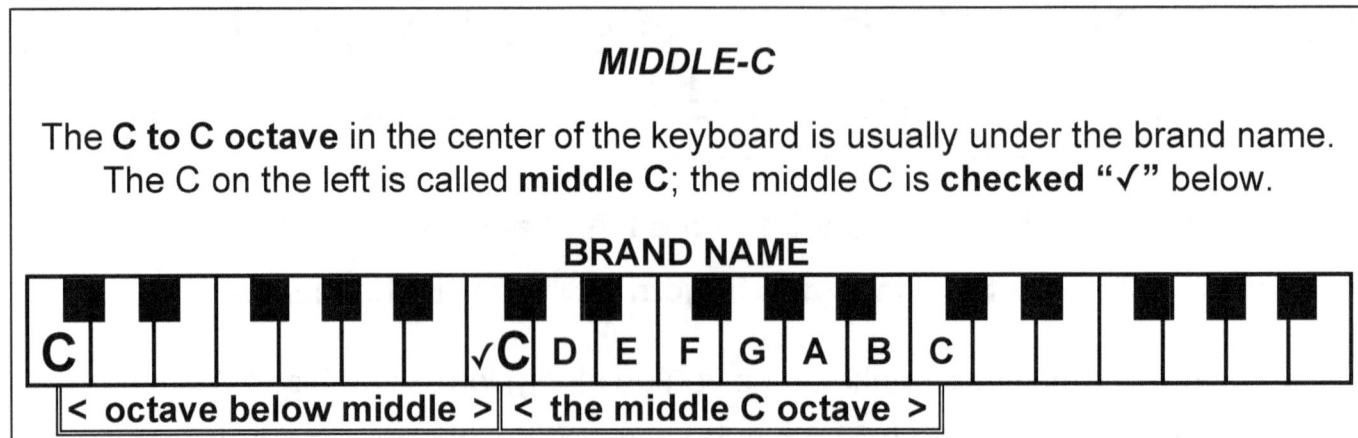

♫ **3: Find middle C** on the keyboard; also find the **C below middle C**.

♫ **4: Improvise** (in any order) on the white keys with the left or right index fingers 👈👉; begin and end on the same pitch.

POSTURE AND HANDS

♪ **5:** Sit directly in front of the keyboard at a distance that allows free movement of the arms. Lean slightly forward with your feet on the floor. Avoid tension in the wrists and shoulders. **Relax!**

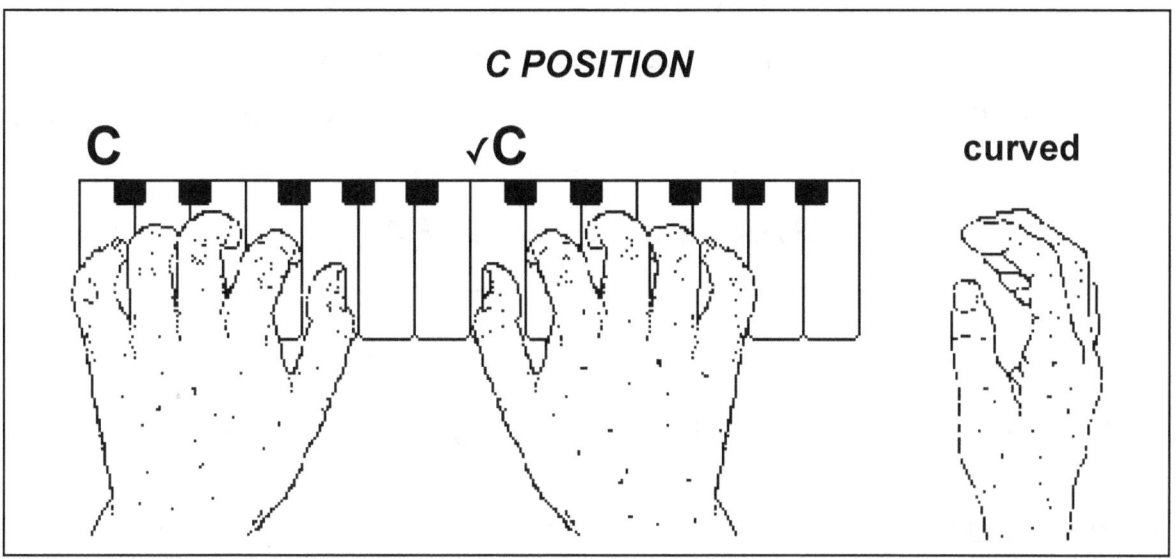

♪ **6:** The fingers of each hand can cover five white keys. **Curve the fingers,** and play C D E F G with the **fingertips.**

Hand Positions are named after the **lowest pitch** covered by the hand. **Finger numbers** are used to identify the fingers of each hand; left and right fingers are numbered in the OPPOSITE DIRECTION!

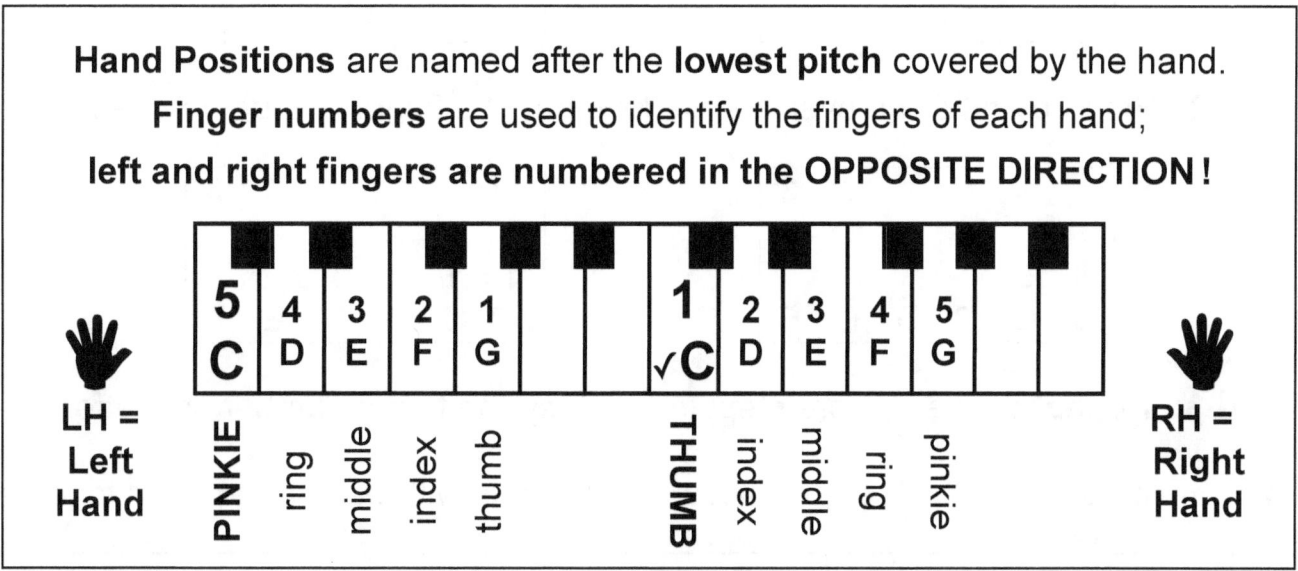

♪ **7:** **Practice** placing the hands and fingers in C position, **left pinkie finger 5 on the C below middle C** and **right thumb 1 on middle C.**

PLAYING KEYBOARDS

Lower pitches are to the left and higher pitches are to the right.
Keep five fingers on the keys. Stop flyaway fingers. Gently press the keys.
Press each new key **before** releasing the old key to connect smoothly.

Play slowly and steadily on the white keys with a medium volume.
Look at the page, NOT your hands!
Think ahead. Anticipate the direction and distance between the keys.

STEP, SKIP, AND REPEAT

```
                3                                    3
LH         4        4                           2        2          RH
fingers   5          5                     1              1      fingers
          C  D  E  D  C                   √C  D  E  D  C
```

♪ **1: Step** up and down key to key with each hand separately, then hands together.

```
                3                                    3
          5          5                     1              1
          C     E    C                    √C     E        C
```

♪ **2: Skip** up and down over a white key; **say** the finger number and letter.

```
                   3 3                                  3 3
             4 4                                   2 2
          5 5                              1 1
          C C D D E E                     √C C D D E E
```

♪ **3: Repeat** the key before stepping up; **say** the finger number and letter.

♪ **4: Improvise** (try) C D E steps, skips, and repeats with each hand, then together.

Practicing is the habit that develops playing skill and an understanding of music.
Several **short sessions** each week are the most effective way to practice.

PITCH MOTION

Play these melodies by pitch motion,
the **direction** (repeat, up or down), and **distance** (step or skip) between pitches.

Play the pitch lengths **by ear** ("hold" = twice as long and "faster" = half as long).

♪ 5: Hot Cross Buns

Begin with right-hand finger 3 on E above middle C.

							faster							
3			3								3			
	2			2				2	2	2	2		2	
		1 ~			1 ~	1	1	1	1					1 ~
E	D	C hold	E	D	C hold	C	C	C	C	D	D	D	D	E	D	C hold

Hot cross buns! Hot cross buns! One a pen- ny, two a pen- ny, hot cross buns!

♪ 6: Old Ark's a-Moverin'

Begin with right-hand finger 1 on middle C.

			3	3			3	3			3	3			3	3		
					2	2							2	2		
1	1								1	1					1 ~
C	C	E	E	D	D	E	E	C	C	E	E	D	D	E hold

Old ark's mov- in', mov- in', mov- in, old ark's mov- in', I thank God!

♪ 7: Ode to Joy

Begin with right-hand finger 3 on E above middle C.

				5	5								
			4			4							
3	3					3				3	3		
							2		2			2	2	~
								1	1				
E	E	F	G	G	F	E	D	C	C	D	E	E	D	D hold

continue

				5	5								
			4			4							
3	3					3				3			
							2		2		2		
								1	1			1	1 ~
E	E	F	G	G	F	E	D	C	C	D	E	D	C	C hold

♪ 8: Look at the **repeating pitch motion patterns** in each of these melodies.
Then play them again with the left hand (LH 5 on the C below middle C).

NOTATION ~ 2 a

HAND POSITIONS

```
| LH        1                       |   | RH          5                     |
|         2   2                     |   |        4         4                |
|       3       3                   |   |      3             3              |
|     4           4                 |   |    2                 2            |
|   5               5               |   |  1                     1          |
|   C  D  E  F  G  F  E  D  C       |   | √C  D  E  F  G  F  E  D  C        |
```

♪ **1:** **Step** up and down key to key with each hand separately in **C-position,** then play hands together. **Keep your eyes on the page. Do not look at your hands.**

```
| LH        1                       |   | RH          5                     |
|       3       3                   |   |      3             3              |
|   5               5               |   |  1                     1          |
|   C    E    G    E    C           |   | √C    E    G    E    C            |
```

♪ **2:** **Skip** up and down every other white key; **say** the finger number and letter.

```
| LH                    1  1        |   | RH                      5  5      |
|                   2  2            |   |                      4  4         |
|             3  3                  |   |                3  3               |
|       4  4                        |   |          2  2                     |
|   5  5                            |   |    1  1                           |
|   C  C  D  D  E  E  F  F  G  G    |   | √C  C  D  D  E  E  F  F  G  G     |
```

♪ **3:** **Repeat** each key before stepping up; **say** the finger number and letter.

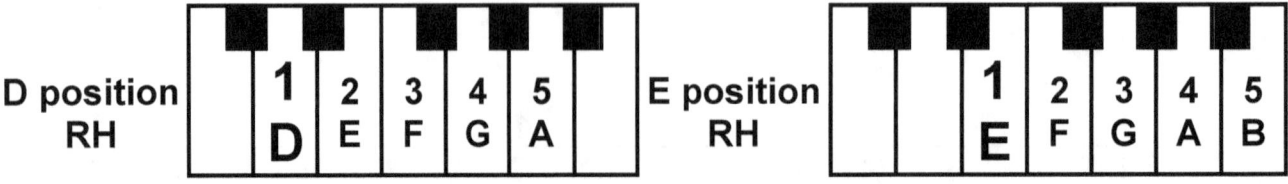

D position RH: 1-D, 2-E, 3-F, 4-G, 5-A
E position RH: 1-E, 2-F, 3-G, 4-A, 5-B

♪ **4:** **Move** the hands up to D position, next E position, then F, G, etc. **Improvise** steps, skips, and repeats in these white key positions (you may look at your hands).

CHANGING POSITION

Melodies can be played or sung higher or lower.
Think of singing **"Happy Birthday"** higher or lower.

PLAYING MUSIC

Once the hands are in position,
DO NOT look at them again.
Focus on the pitch motion
(direction and distance),
NOT the letter names!

Focusing on pitch motion
develops **listening skills** and the **basic mechanics** of playing.

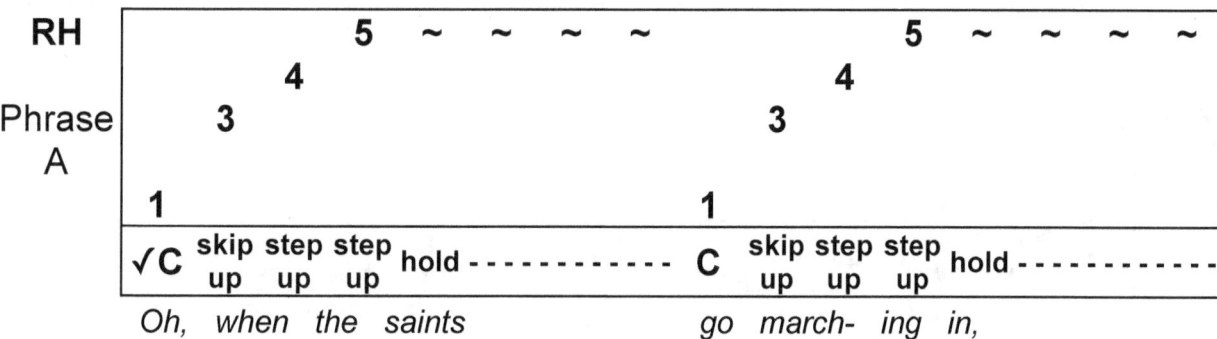

♪ **5: Play** Phrase A of **"When the Saints Go Marching in"** in C position.
Phrases are the shorter parts within melodies,
like sentences in paragraphs.
**Think about the stepping and skipping patterns,
and playing the pitch lengths by ear.**
The "~" suggests the length of longer pitches.

♪ **6: Look** carefully at the phrases in **"When the Saints"** on the next page.
What makes the phrases **similar**?
What makes the phrases **different**?

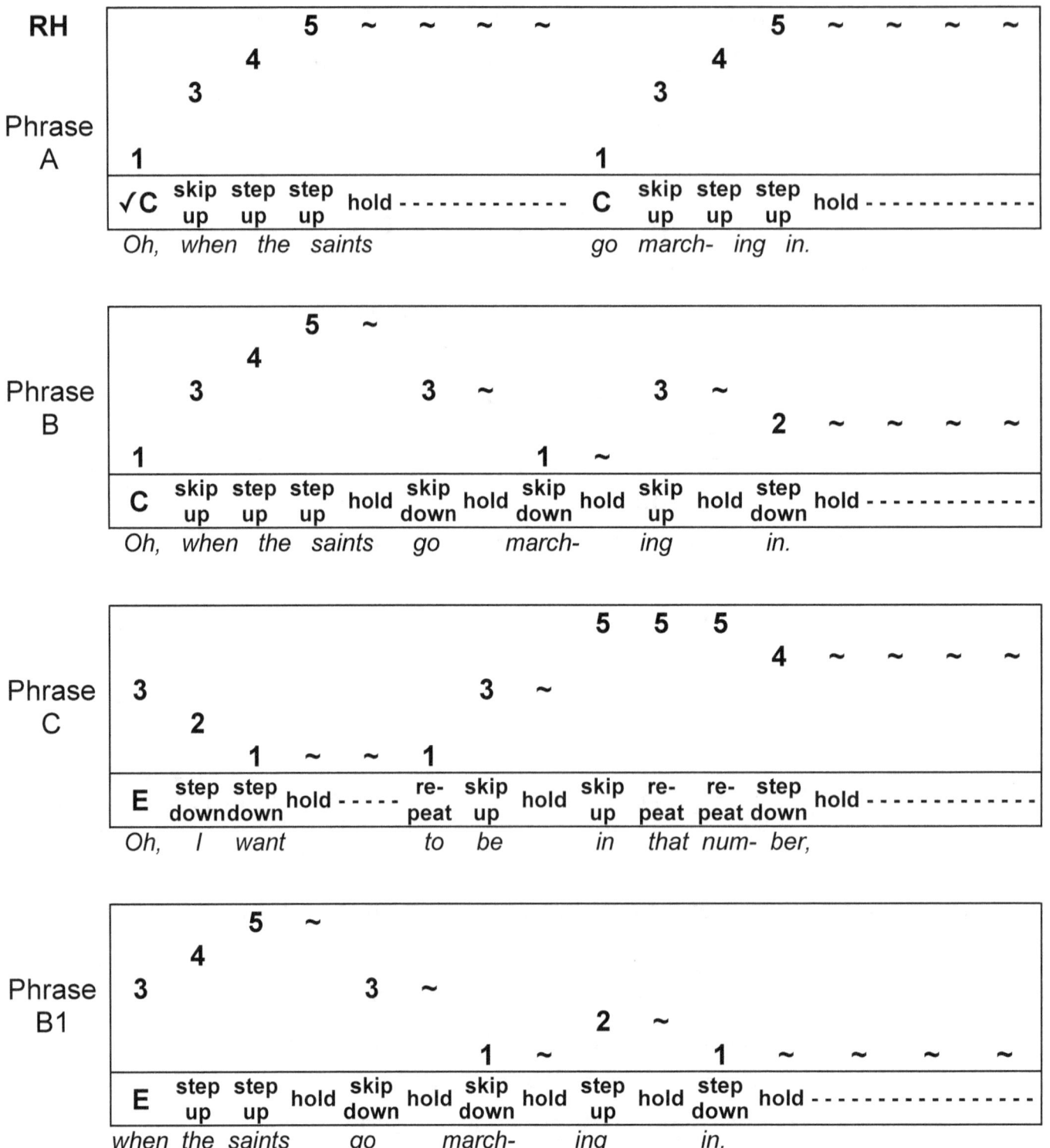

♪ 2: **Play** right hand first, next left hand, then hands together.
Move up to G position and play by finger numbers or pitch motion.

♪ 3: **Improvise** (experiment) with **C D E F G** and different **pitch lengths**.

♪ 4: **Old Ark's a-Moverin'**

Begin with right-hand finger 1 on middle C.			3	3			3	3			3	3			
					2	2							2	2	
	1	1							1	1					1	~
	✓C	C	E	E	D	D	E	E	C	C	E	E	D	D	C	hold

Old ark's mov- in', mov- in', mov- in', old ark's mov- in', I thank God!

♪ 5: **Look** at the repeating pitch patterns in **"Old Ark"** and **"Ode to Joy"** (see 1cc).

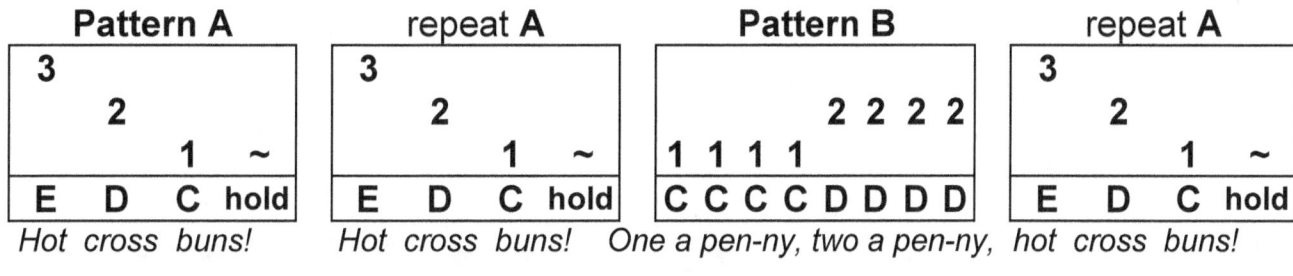

COMPOSITION ONE

Repeating and contrasting **pitch patterns** (groups of notes)
are used to compose the parts of melodies.

♪ 6: **Look** at the patterns in **"Hot Cross Buns"** (see 1cc).

E D C, E D C **(repetition)**; CCCC, DDDD **(contrast)**; E D C again **(repetition)**.

♪ 7: **Compose** (make up) **Pattern A** with 4 pitches using only **middle C, D, or E**, (or right fingers 1, 2, or 3). Fill in **Pattern A** below in **three places**:

♪ 8: **Compose** a contrasting **Pattern B** using only **C, D, or E** (or 1, 2, or 3). **Fill in** Pattern B above, then **play** the melody.

NOTATION ~ 3a

RHYTHM

Rhythm is based on the division of time into **beats** (like the pulse of a heart).

Tempo is the slower or faster **pace** of beats. **Measures** are groups of beats separated by **bar lines** "|" in written **music notation.**

An **accent** is an emphasis that is felt on the **first beat** of each measure.

♪ 1: *Count* each beat: | 1 2 | -- | 1 2 3 | -- | 1 2 3 4 |
    Clap each "**X**"   X X   X X X   X X X X

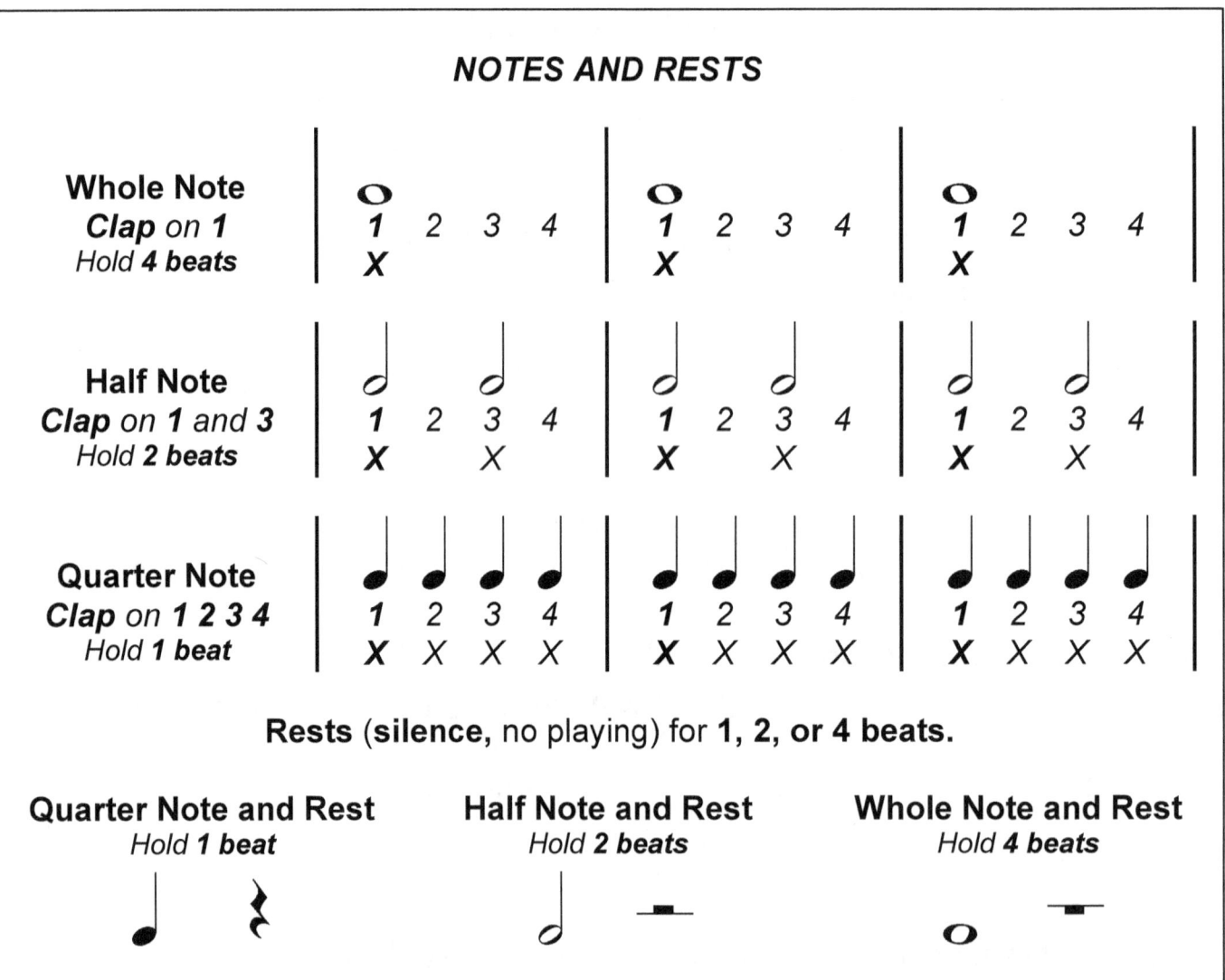

♪ 2: **Count** the beats aloud, and **clap** the Xs for the common note lengths above.

TREBLE CLEF AND STAFF

Each white key is matched to a **certain line or space** in musical notation.
(The notation of the black keys will be explained later.)

A staff " ≡ " for musical notation has **five horizontal lines**. Ledger lines
"-o-" are added **below or above** a staff to show other **lower or higher** notes.
Notes are written on the **lines and ledgers** and the **spaces** between these lines.

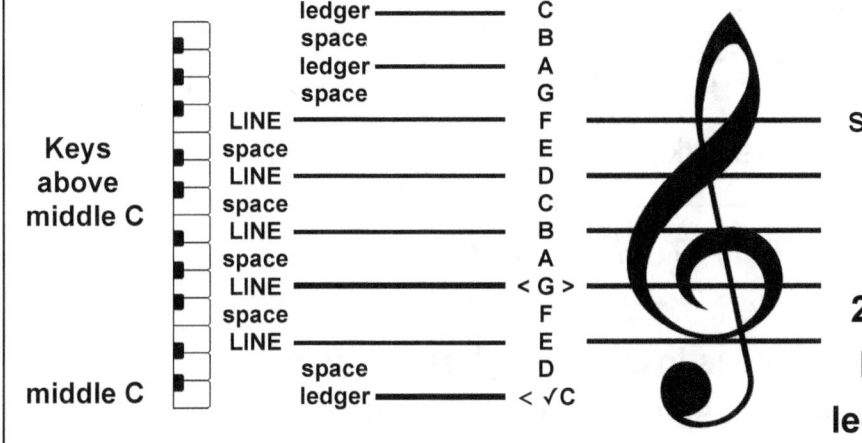

A treble "𝄞" or G clef sign shows the **higher notes** (keys) played with the **right hand**.

This sign circles around the 2nd **line up** where **G** is located.
Middle C is located on the **1**[st] **ledger below the treble staff.**

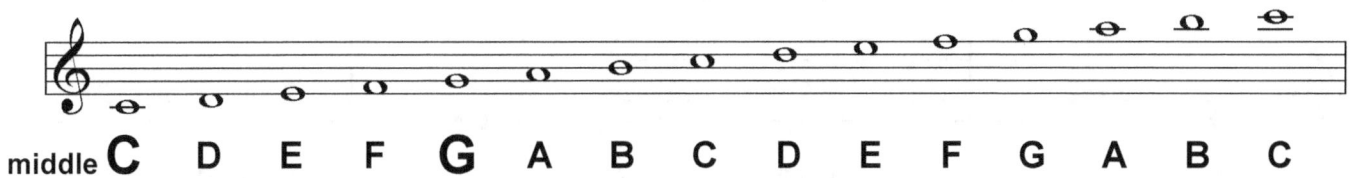

middle C D E F **G** A B C D E F G A B C

♪ **3: Say and play** each note with the RH 2 ♭ starting on **middle C**.

BEATS AND NOTES

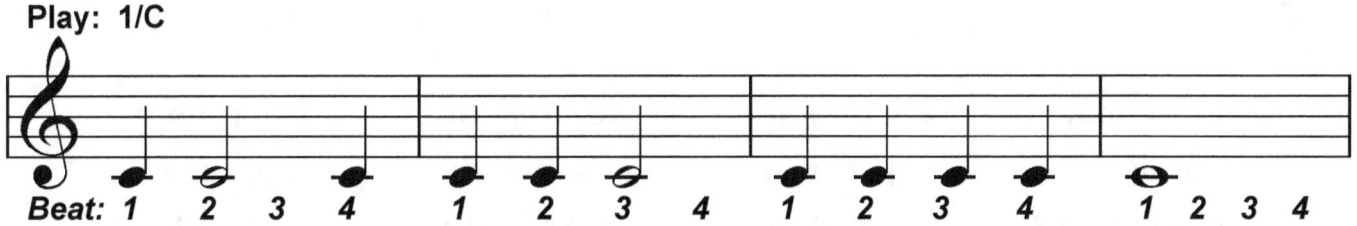

♪ **4:** Cover middle C position with the right hand, and **play C only with the RH 1**.
Count the beats aloud, and keep a slow and steady **tempo** as middle C is played.

LINES AND SPACES

1/C 2/D 3/E 4/F 5/G F E D C

♪ **1: Play** five **stepping notes** with the right hand starting on middle C and **say** line or space with the note name: "ledger **C**, space **D**, line **E**, space **F**," etc.

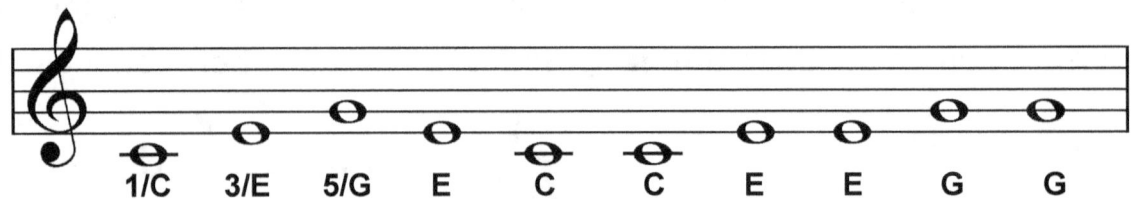

1/C 3/E 5/G E C C E E G G

♪ **2: Play and say** with the note name: "skipping up, skipping down, repeat," etc.

NOTATED PITCH MOTION
Repeat ~ the next note is on the **same** line or space.
Direction ~ the next note is **lower or higher** on the staff.
Step ~ from a line to the next space **or** a space to the next line.
Skip ~ from a line to the next line **or** a space to the next space.

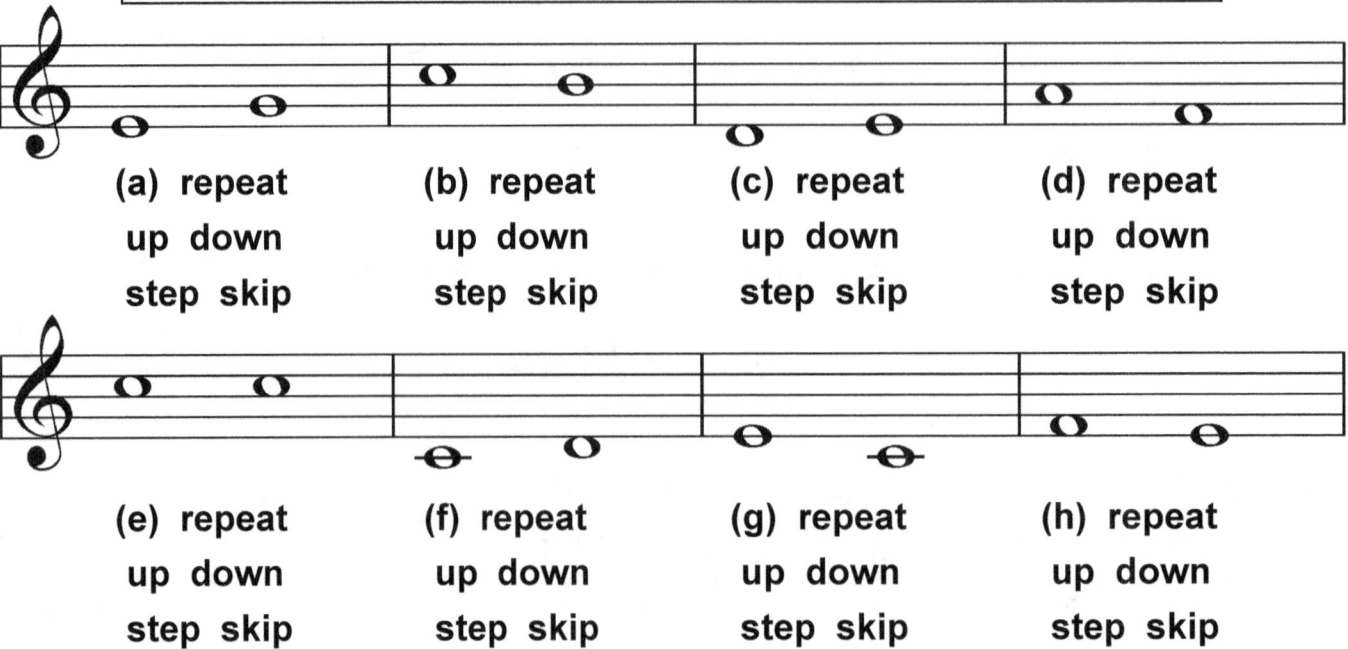

(a) repeat / up down / step skip
(b) repeat / up down / step skip
(c) repeat / up down / step skip
(d) repeat / up down / step skip

(e) repeat / up down / step skip
(f) repeat / up down / step skip
(g) repeat / up down / step skip
(h) repeat / up down / step skip

♪ **3: Circle** (don't play): "repeat, up or down, step or skip" under each pair of notes above.

PLAYING MELODIES

Keep five fingers on keys. Press a new key down before releasing an old key to connect notes smoothly. Play slowly. **Look at the page, NOT your hands!** Think about the **pitch motion** between the notes, **NOT the note names!**

As a guide, **finger numbers** with **pitch names** may be placed above or below the first note or the other notes on a staff such as "1/C" or "3/E."

A **"double bar"** marks the end of the music.

These melodies have **4 beats per measure**.

♪ 4: **Old Ark's a-Moverin'** ~ **play and say** the pitch motion.

♪ 5: **Freedom** ~ **play and count** the beats.

NOTATION ~ 4 a 15

TIME SIGNATURES

Time signatures following the clef signs have **two numbers:**

Top shows the beats per measure

$\frac{4}{4}$ 4 beats per **measure**

      quarter note gets 1 beat

Bottom shows the note getting 1 beat

NOTES AND BEATS

4/4	♩ ♩ ♩ ♩	♩ ♩ ♩ ♩	♩ ♩ ♩ ♩	♩ ♩ ♩
Beat:	1 2 3 4	1 2 3 4	1 2 3 4	1 2 3 4
Clap:	X X X X	X X X X	X X X X	X X X

	♩ ♩	♩ ♩ ♩	♩ ♩ ♩ ♩	𝅝
	1 2 3 4	1 2 3 4	1 2 3 4	1 2 3 4
	X X X	X X X	X X X X	X

♪ **1: Count** aloud "*1 2 3 4*" to keep a steady **tempo,** and **clap** the X below the quarter, half and whole notes.

3/4	♩ ♩ ♩	♩ ♩ ♩	♩ ♩ ♩	♩ ♩
Beat:	1 2 3	1 2 3	1 2 3	1 2 3
Clap:	X X X	X X X	X X X	X X

♪ **2: Clap** the quarter and half notes above, and **count** aloud "*1 2 3*" to keep a steady tempo.

♪ **3: Improvise** quarter, half, and whole notes on any of the **five black keys** with the index fingers ♩♭. **Count** "*1 2 3 4*" and hold the pedal down.

BASS CLEF AND STAFF

Each white key is matched to a **certain line or space** in musical notation.

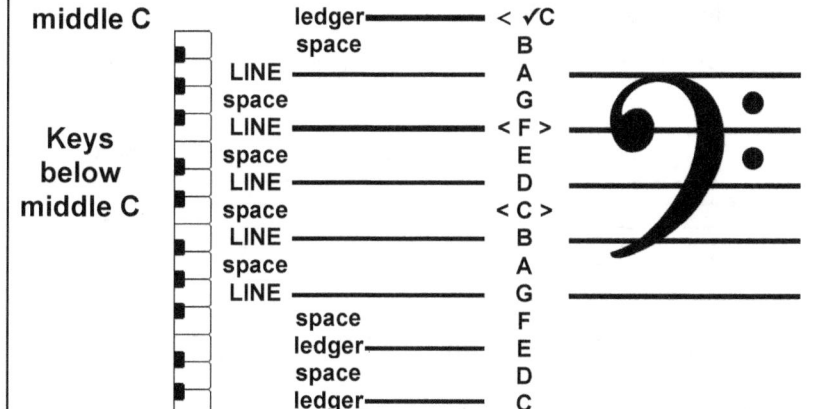

A staff with a **bass clef "𝄢"** or **F clef sign** shows the **lower notes** (keys) usually played with the **left hand**.

This sign circles around the **second line down** on the staff and is the location of the F below middle C.

Middle C is on the ledger line above the bass staff.
C below middle C is in the second space up from the bottom on the bass staff.

C D E F G A B **C** D E **F** G A B middle C

♪ **4: Say and play** each note with LH 2 ♩ starting **two octaves below middle C**.

BEATS AND NOTES

Beat: 1 2 3 4   1 2 3 4   1 2 3 4   1 2 3 4

♪ **5:** Cover C below middle C position, **play C only with LH 5; count** the beats. Notice the time signature grouping of the beats and the length of the notes.

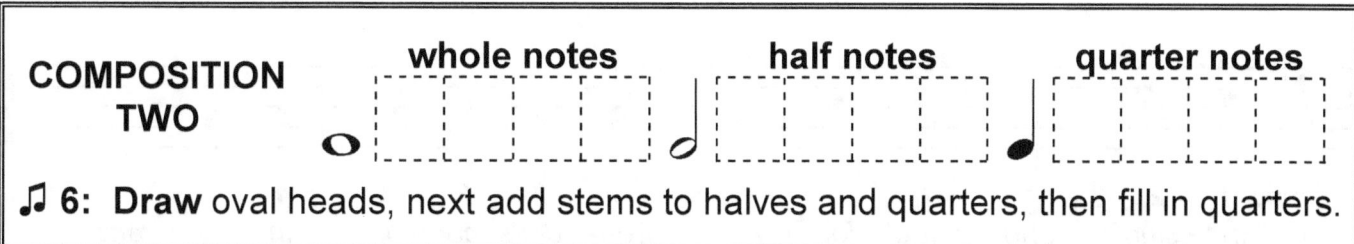

♪ **6: Draw** oval heads, next add stems to halves and quarters, then fill in quarters.

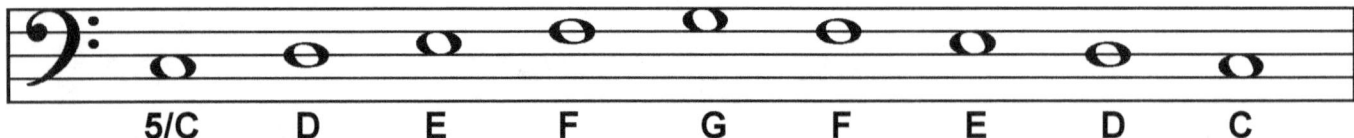

♪ **1: Play** five stepping notes with the left hand starting on C below middle C, and **say** line or space with the note name: "space **C**, line **D**, space **E**, line **F**," etc.

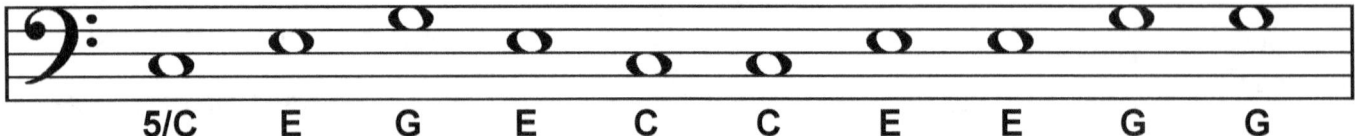

♪ **2: Play and say** with the name: "E skip up," "G skip down," "C repeat," etc.

NOTE STEMS

The note heads below the staff center line have stems that **point up,** and heads above or on the center line have stems that **point down.**

♪ **3: Old Ark's a-Moverin'** ~ **say** the pitch motion.

Old ark's mov-in,' mov-in,' mov-in,' old ark's mov-in,' I thank God!

♪ **4: Freedom** ~ **count** the beats.

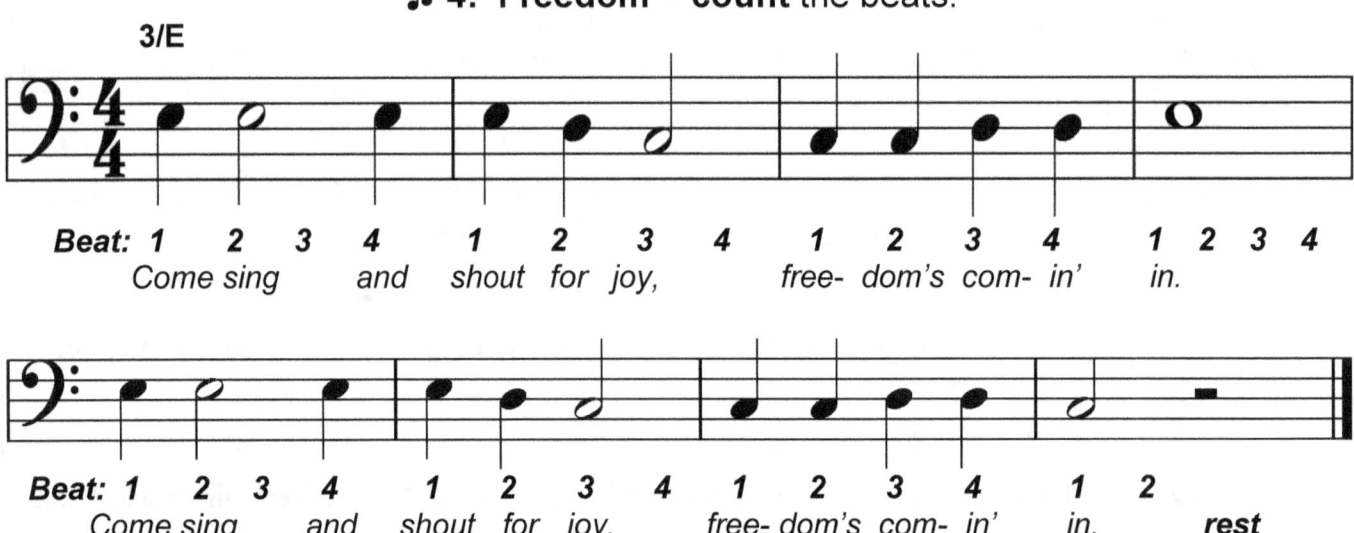

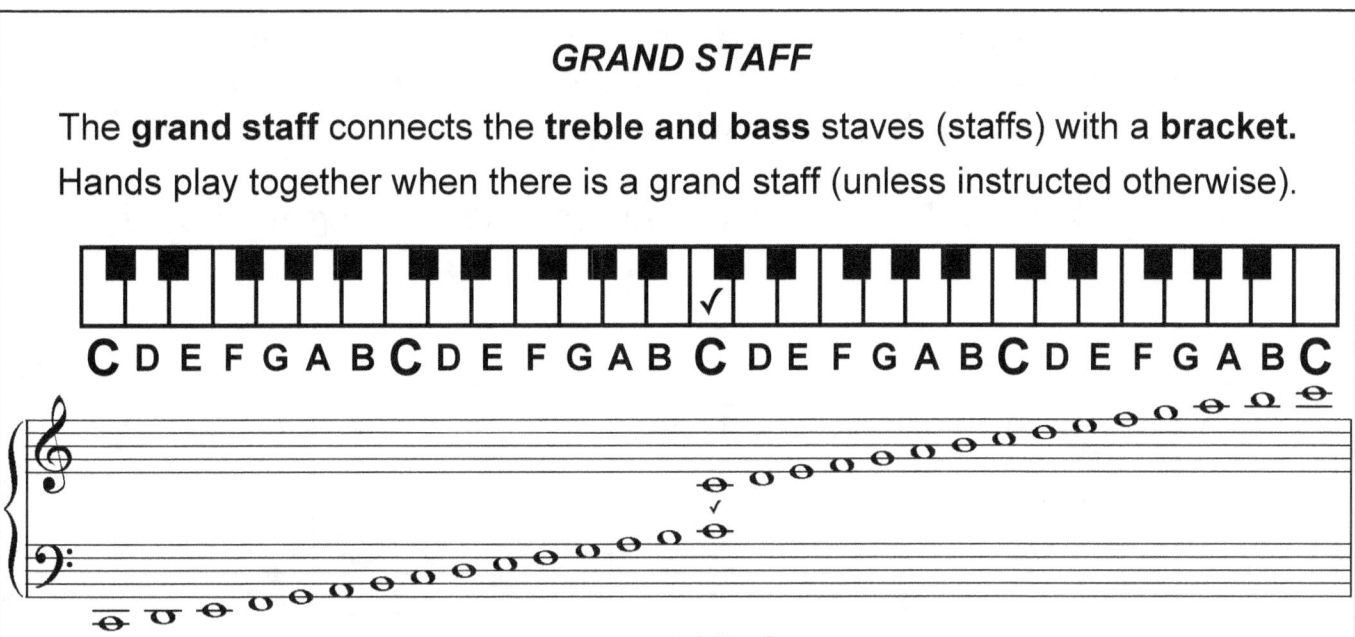

♪ 5: **Play** ♪♪ **and say** the grand staff notes starting two octaves below middle C.

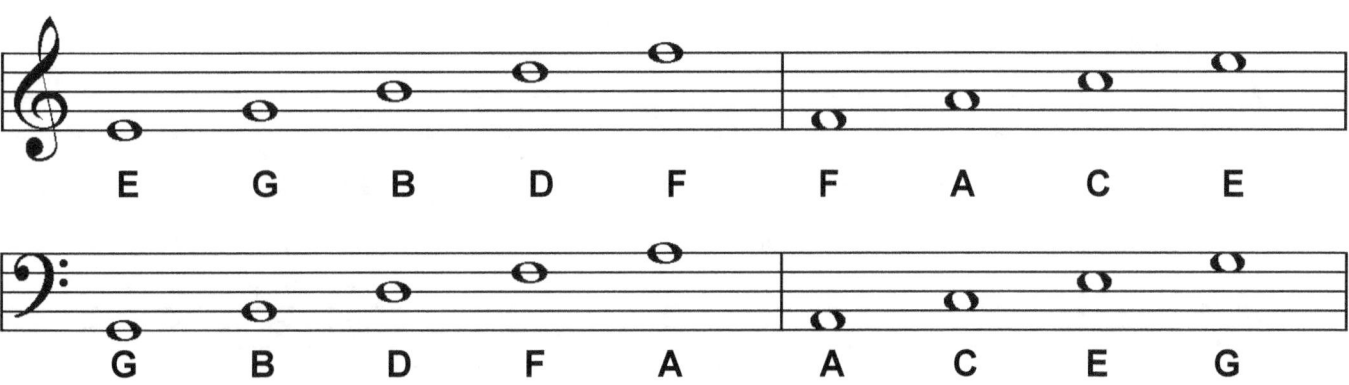

♪ 6: **Play** ♪♪ **and say** the line and space names for the treble clef, then bass clef.

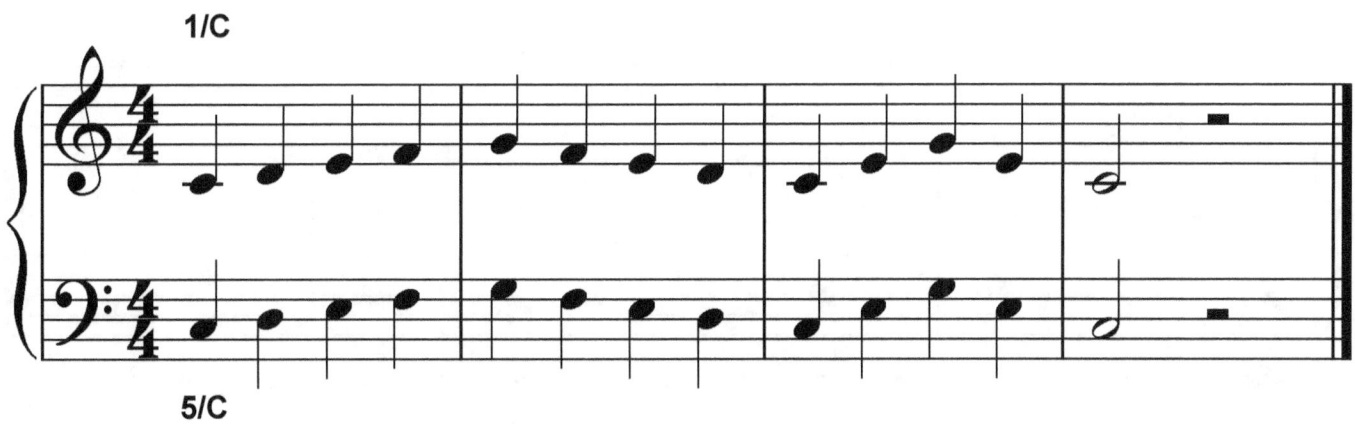

♪ 7: **Play** the hands together in C position, and **say** "step or skip, up or down."

♪ 1: **Look** at the repeating and contrasting **melodic patterns** in these melodies. Clap the note rhythms. Practice each hand alone slowly (phrase by phrase). Play hands together by preparing the LH note followed by the RH note.

♪ 2: **Old Ark's a-Moverin'** ~ **say** the pitch motion looking at the page.

♪ 3: **Freedom** ~ **count** the beats aloud to keep a steady tempo.

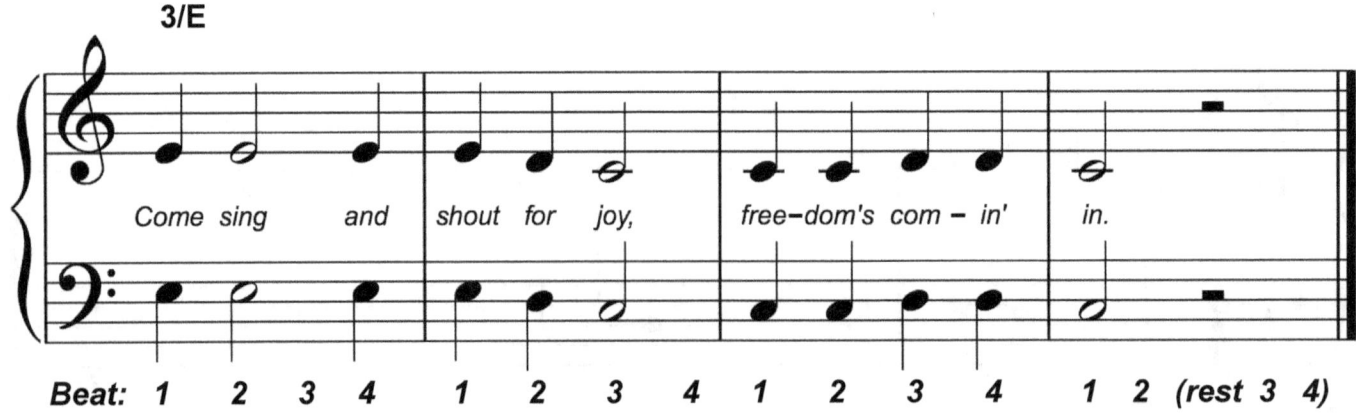

♪ 4: **Play** these melodies in F, then G position with the same pitch motion (fingers).

♫ 5: Ode to Joy

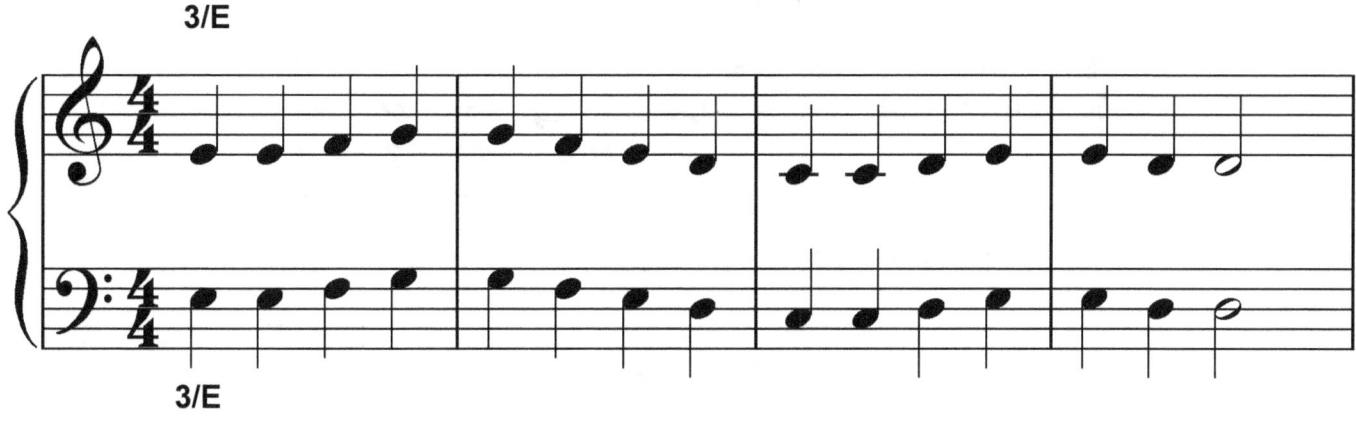

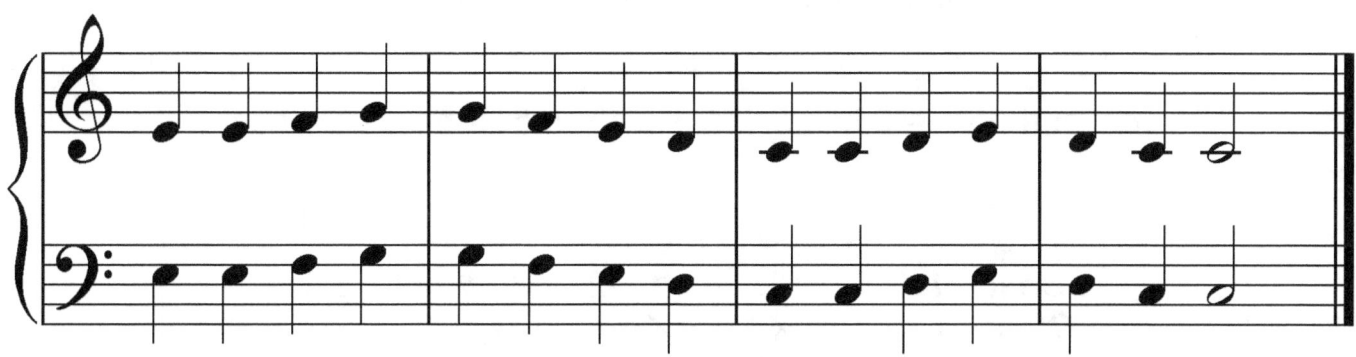

♫ 6: Mary Had a Little Lamb

NOTATION ~ 5 a

> **Time signature review:**
>
> **3** 3 beats per **measure**
> **4** quarter note gets 1 beat
>
>
> Beat: 1 2 3

♪ **1:** **Count** aloud and **clap** the beats above; **repeat** several times.

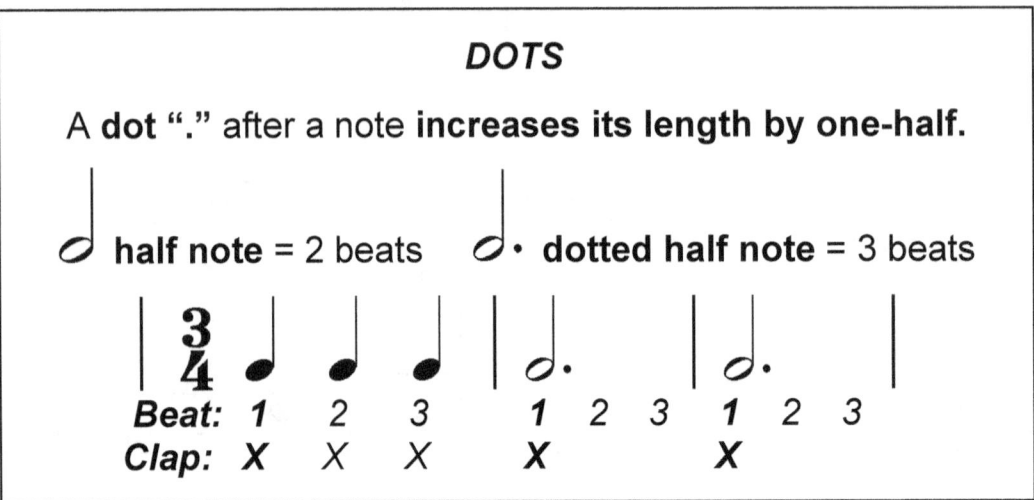

♪ **2:** **Count** aloud and **clap** the quarter and **dotted half notes** above.

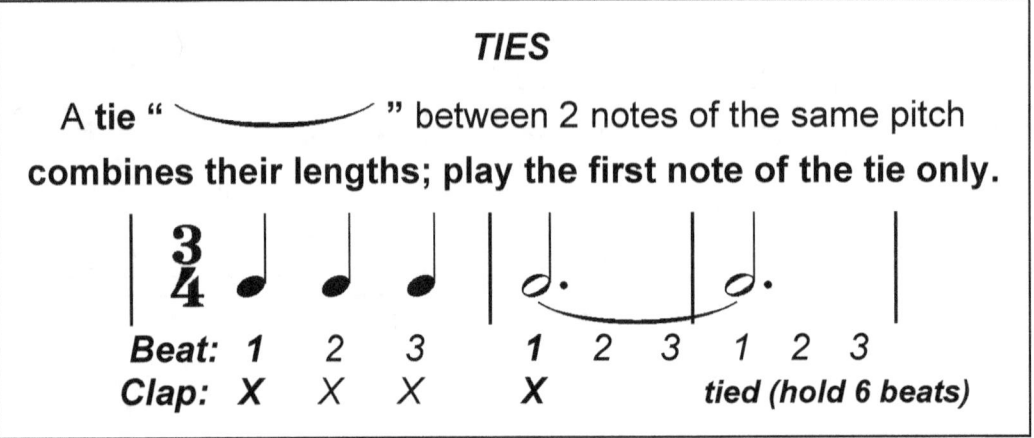

♪ **3:** **Count** aloud and **clap** the quarter notes and tied note above.

> In **"French Lullaby"** measure 15, *"ritard"* (Italian *ritardando*) means to slow down. In measure 16, *"D.C. al Fine"* means to return to measure 1 and repeat to *"Fine"* in measure 8.

♫ 4: French Lullaby

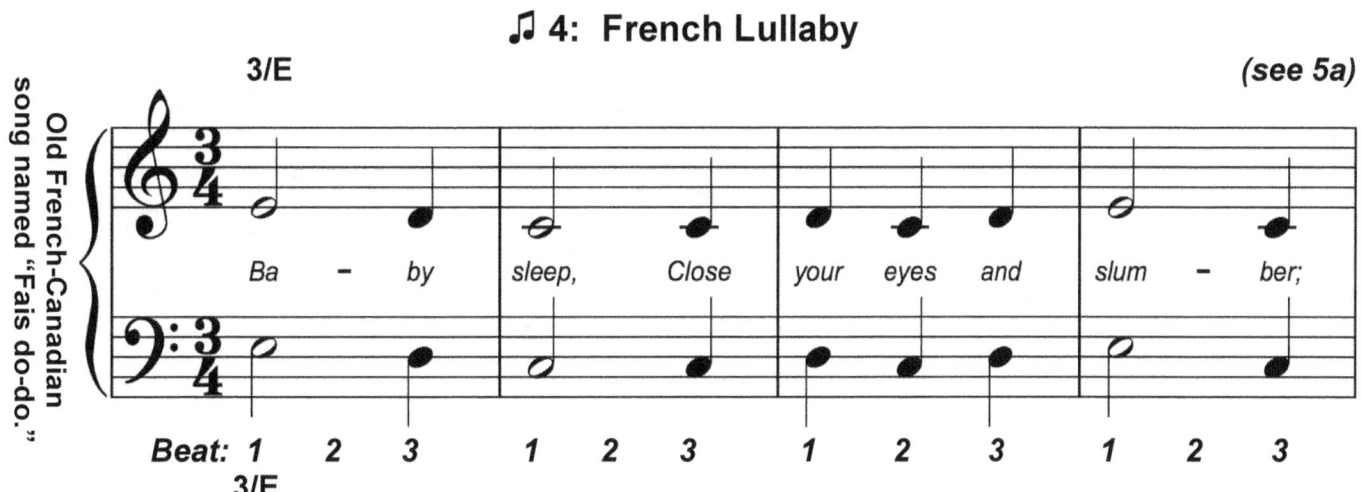
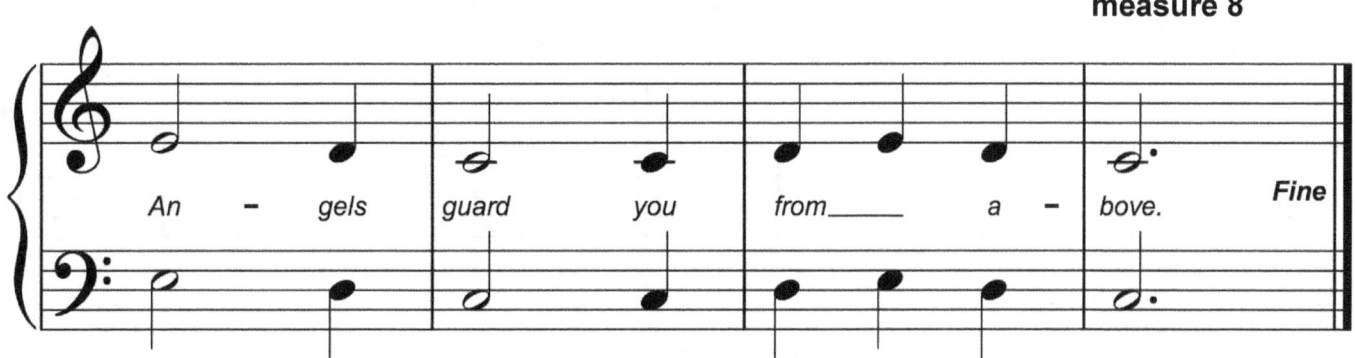

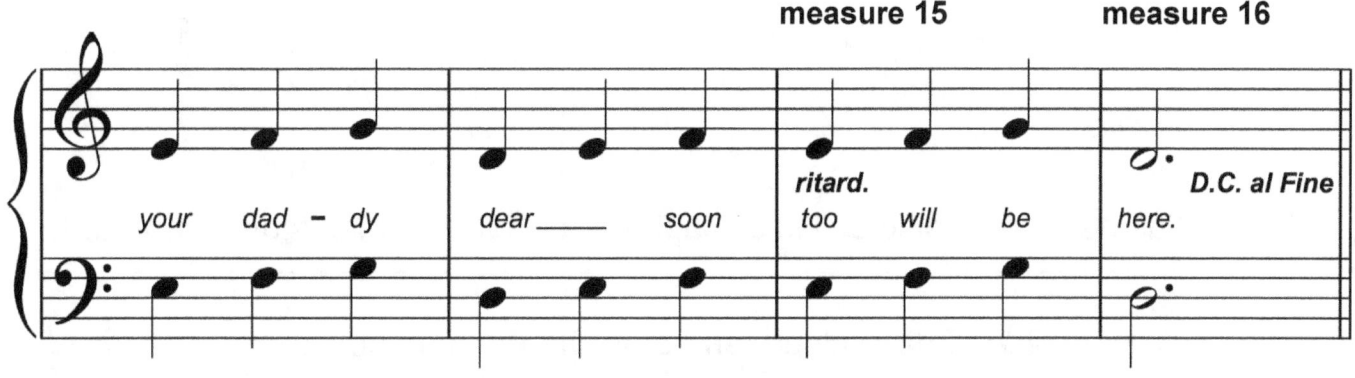

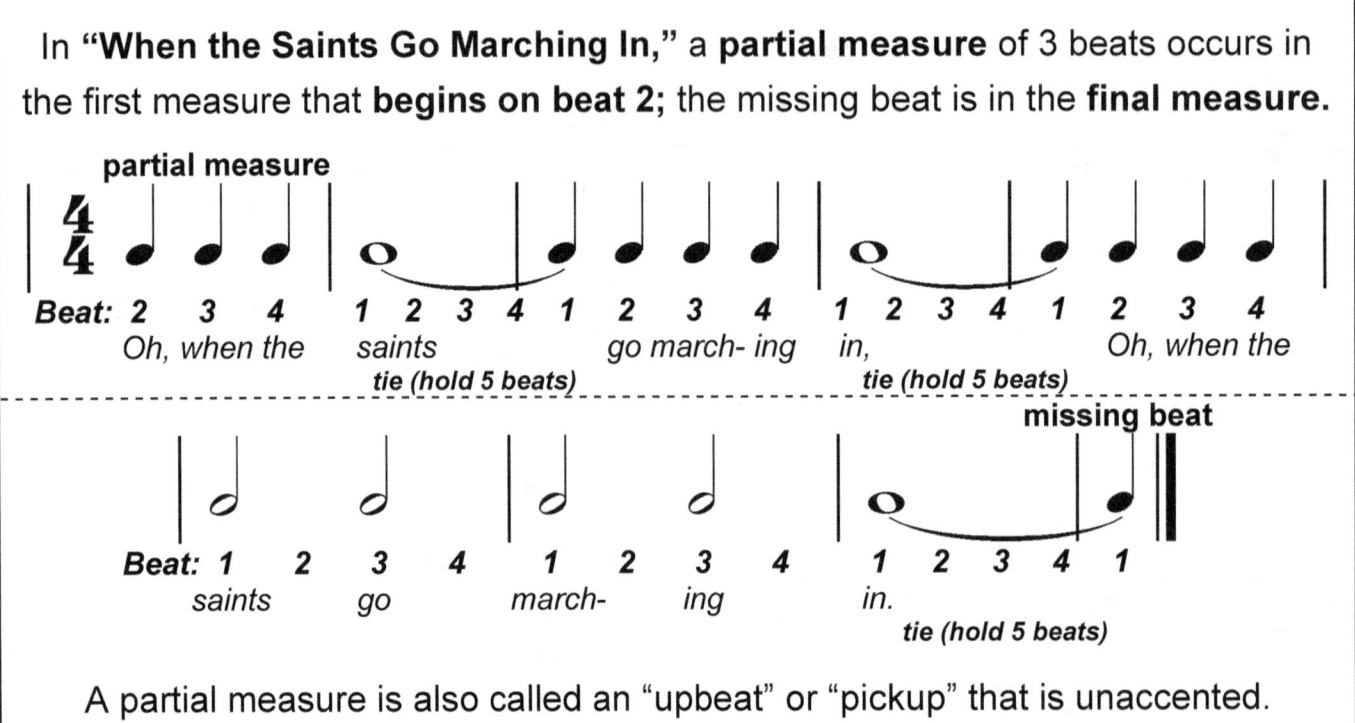

♫ 2: **Count** aloud, and **clap** the rhythm above.

♪ 3: When the Saints Go Marching In ~ **count** the beats.

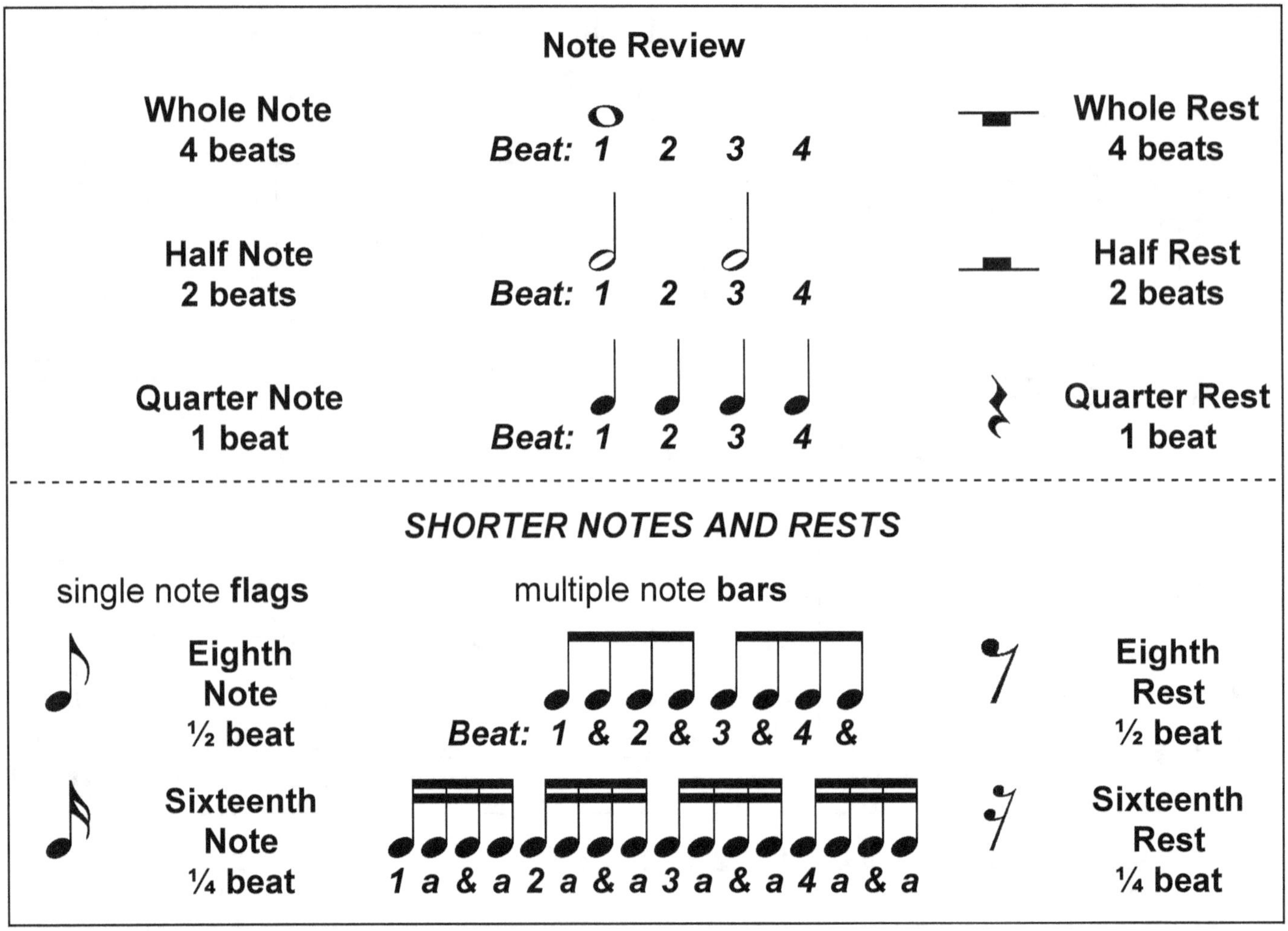

NOTATION ~ 6 a

Note Review

Whole Note 4 beats	𝅝 Beat: 1 2 3 4	𝄻 Whole Rest 4 beats
Half Note 2 beats	𝅗𝅥 𝅗𝅥 Beat: 1 2 3 4	𝄼 Half Rest 2 beats
Quarter Note 1 beat	♩ ♩ ♩ ♩ Beat: 1 2 3 4	𝄽 Quarter Rest 1 beat

SHORTER NOTES AND RESTS

single note **flags**   multiple note **bars**

♪ Eighth Note ½ beat	♫ ♫ ♫ ♫ Beat: 1 & 2 & 3 & 4 &	𝄾 Eighth Rest ½ beat
♬ Sixteenth Note ¼ beat	♬♬ ♬♬ ♬♬ ♬♬ 1 a & a 2 a & a 3 a & a 4 a & a	𝄿 Sixteenth Rest ¼ beat

♪ **1: Count** eighth **notes and syllables** as: "1 & (say 'and') 2 & 3 & 4 &," etc., and sixteenth notes as: "1 **a** (as in d'**a**'y) & **a** (as in c'**u**'t) 2 **a** & **a**," etc.

♪ **2: Improvise** whole, half, quarter, and eighth notes on the black keys using index fingers 👆👆 while holding the pedal down.

♪ **3: Hot Cross Buns**

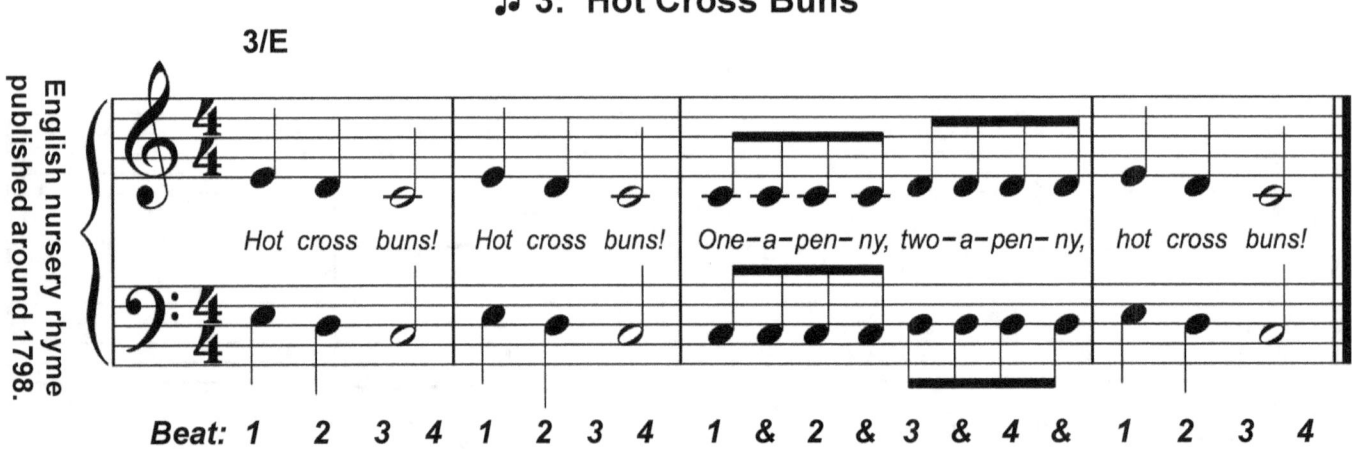

English nursery rhyme published around 1798.

3/E

♫ 4: Freedom

Adaptation of "Standing In the Need of Prayer."

♫ 5: French Shop

Fill in the beats below.

1/C **Count** and **clap** the rhythm. ***(see 5a)***

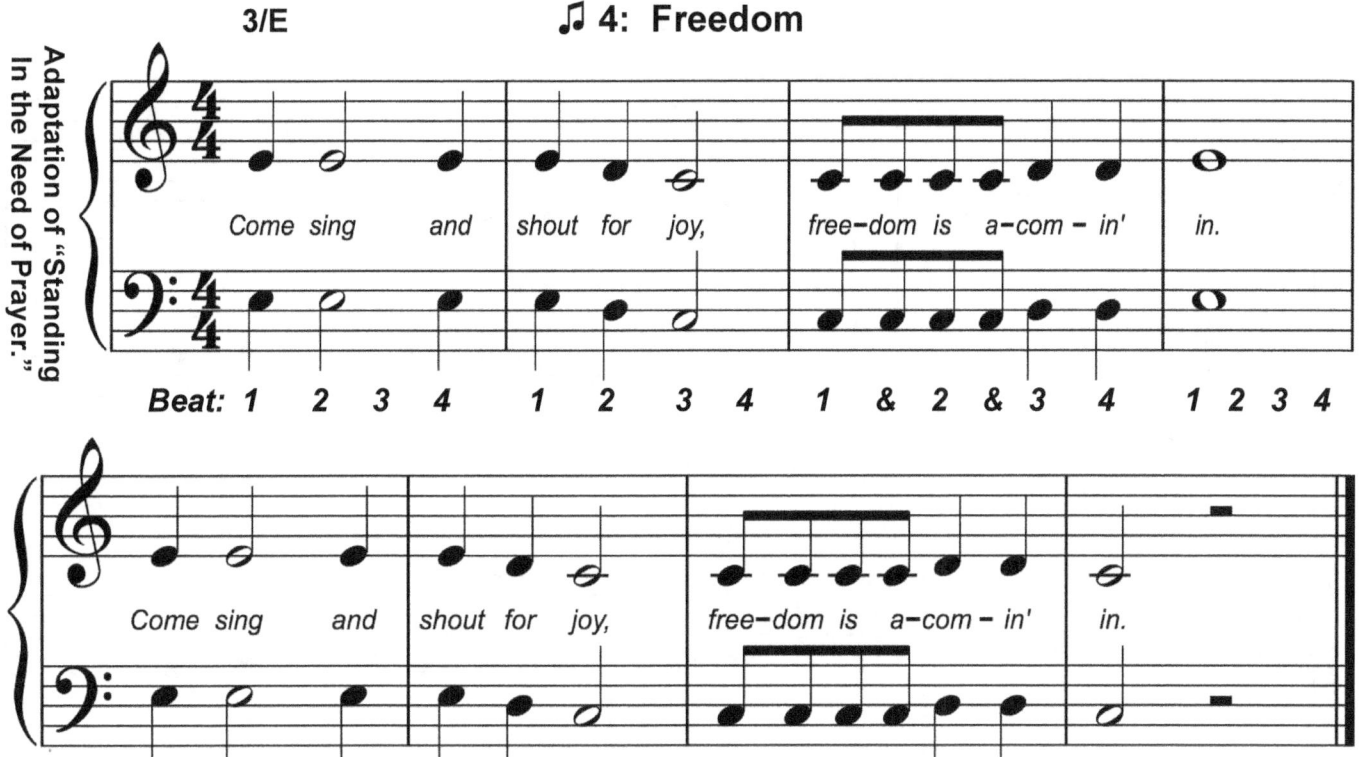

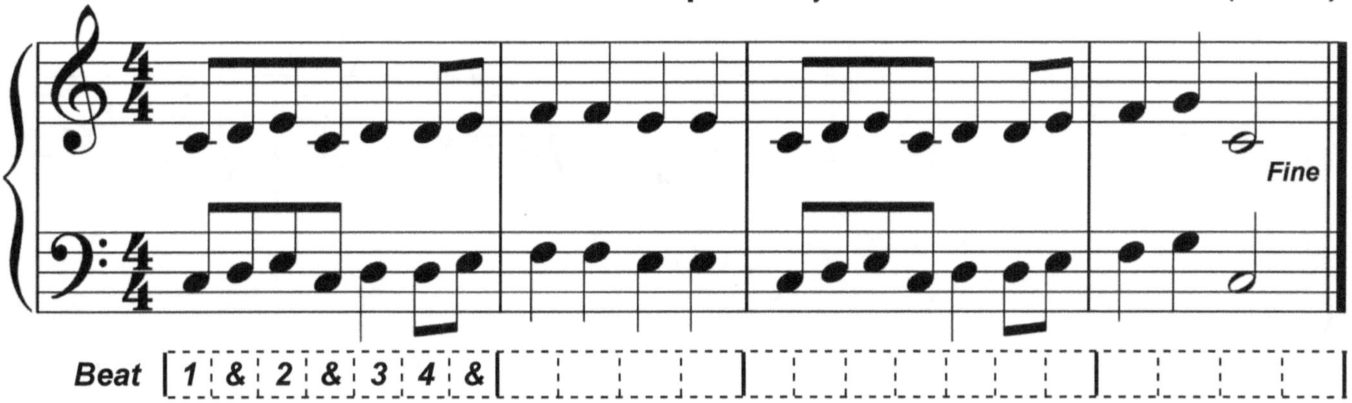

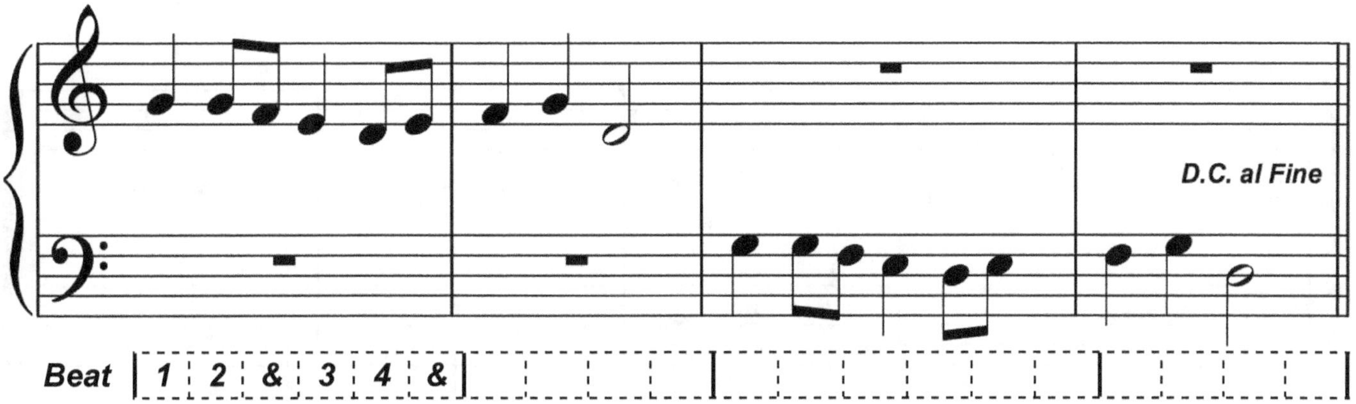

♫ 1: Ode to Joy

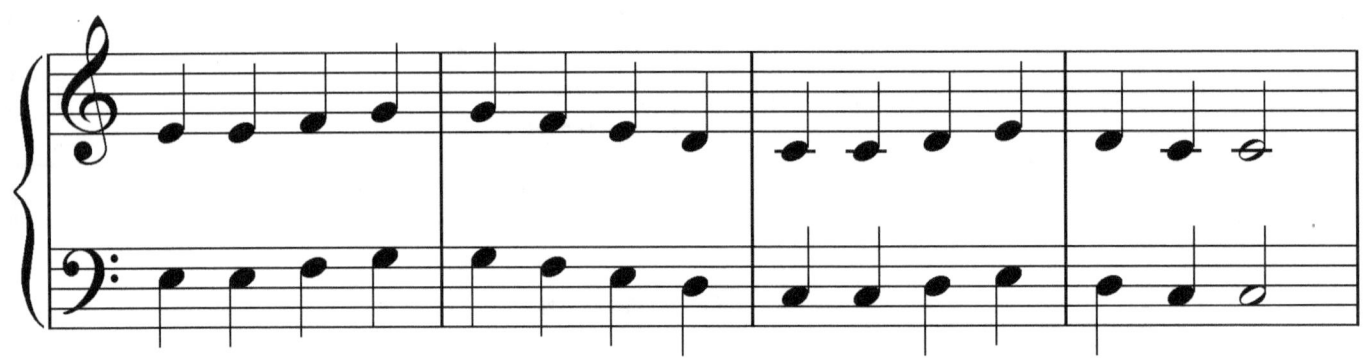

COMPOSITION THREE

♪ **2: Compose a rhythm** for **Measure 1** using only **half and/or quarter notes.** **Repeat** these notes in Measure 2 and 4. Measure 3 is filled in with quarter notes.

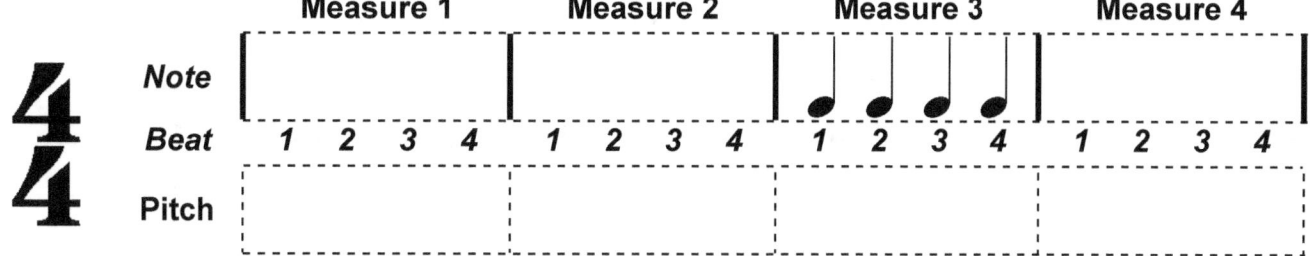

♪ **3: Select** only **C, D, or E** for each note in **Measure 1,** and fill in the Measure 1 pitch box **above** and repeat these pitches in the Measure 2 and 4 pitch boxes.

♪ **4: Select** a pitch using only **C, D or E** for each quarter note in **Measure 3** that **contrasts** with the melodic pattern in Measures 1, 2, and 4, and fill in the pitch box for Measure 3 above.

♪ **5: Notate** these pitches on both the **treble and bass clefs** below.

Draw oval heads on the correct line or space,
next add stems to the half and quarter notes,
then fill in the quarter note heads.

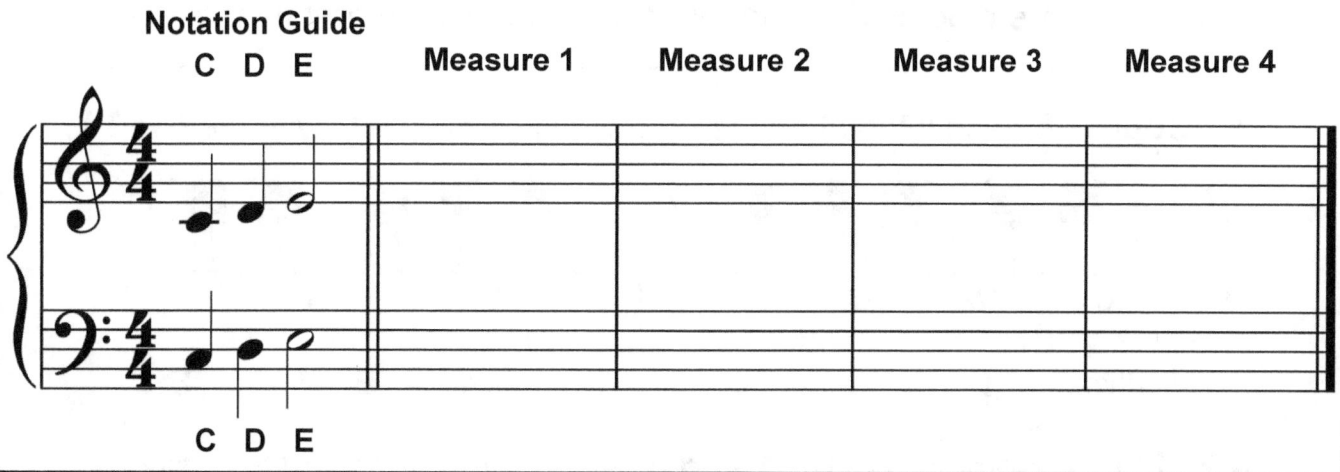

♪ **6: Improvise** changes in the pitch and/or rhythm patterns.

CHORDS ~ 7 a

> Whenever a pitch is created by the **vibrations of a string** or the air in a tube, other soft musical pitches called **overtones happen naturally**.
>
> When the **whole length** of a string vibrates, and creates a pitch such as **C**, the length of the string also vibrates in **2, 3, 4, 5, 6 parts at the same time** and quietly produces a **C** an octave higher, next a **G**, then **C, E, G** (the C chord).
>
>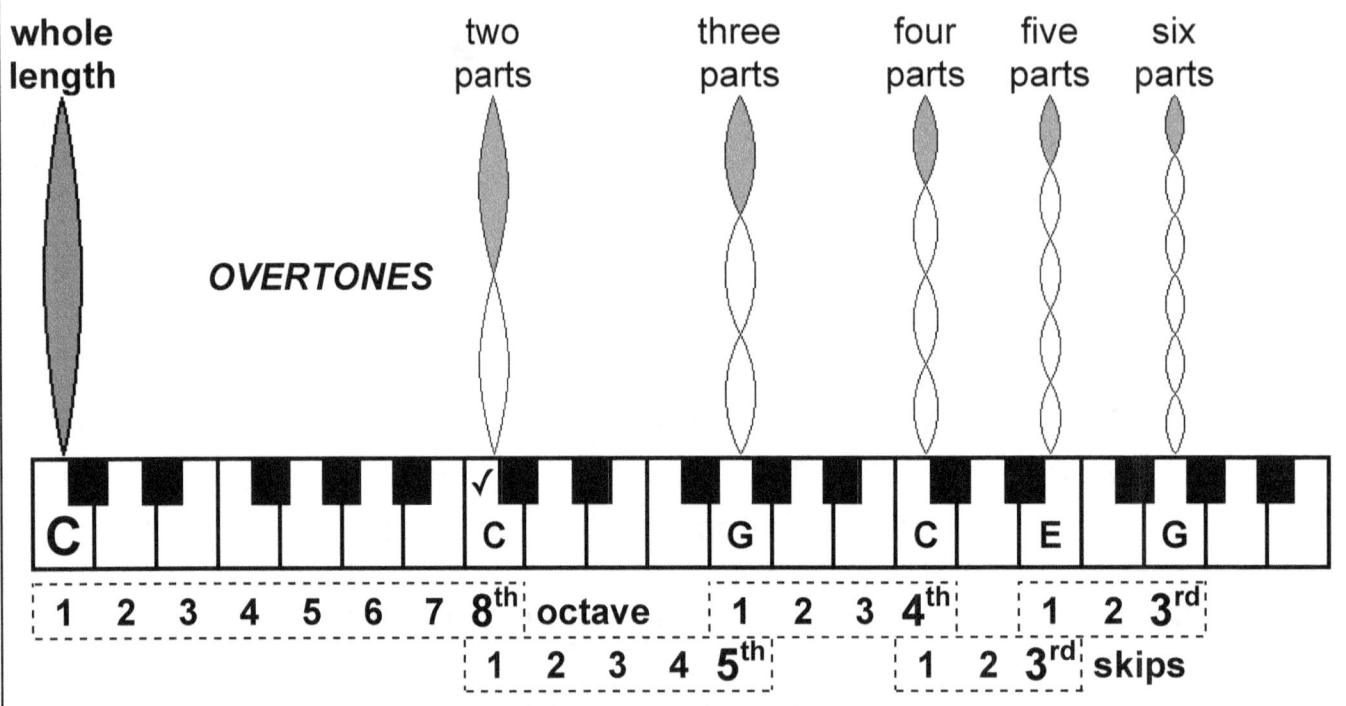
>
> **INTERVALS** are **the distances between two pitches**.
>
> **All pitches** within an interval count to name it, including the **first and last pitch**.
>
> The **intervals** produced by the **overtones** are very important in music.

♪ **1: Count off** each interval above from C below middle C with the **RH 2 ♭**.

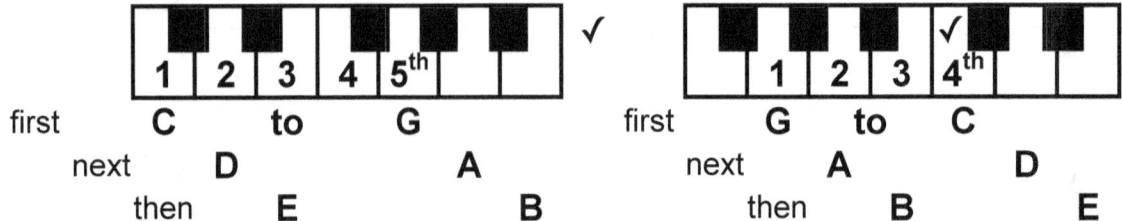

♪ **2: Improvise** 5ths with **RH 1 and 5** (slide up from position to position).

♪ **3: Improvise** 4ths with **RH 1 and 4** (the 5ths have turned upside down).

NOTATED INTERVALS

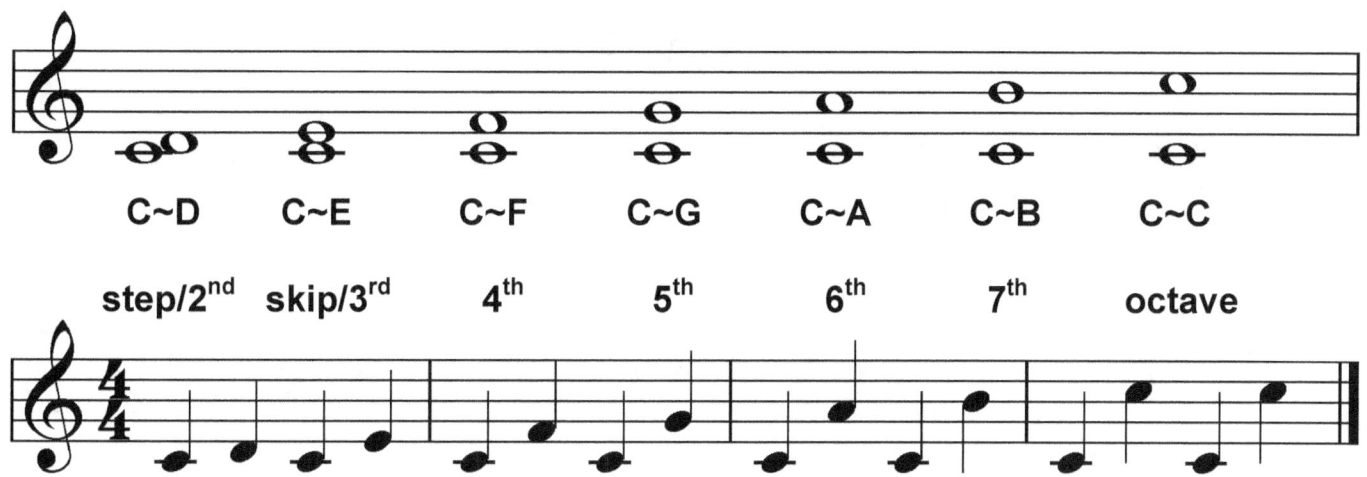

♪ 4: **Practice** the intervals above. **Count** each line and space.

♪ 5: **Improvise** these intervals.

♪ 6: **Aura Lee**

Circle the 4ths below in measures:
1 (C~F), 2 (G~D~G), 4 (F~C), 5 (C~F), and 6 (G~D~G)

♫ 1: **Circle** the 5ths and 4ths in these three melodies.

♫ 2: **Jingle Bells**

CHORDS ~ 8 a

CHORDS

Chords include **three or more pitches.** They add **harmony** to a melody.
Each chord is **built on** and **named after** a pitch called the **root note.**
The other pitches in these chords **skip by 3^{rds}** above the root note.

C chord = root C + skip a 3rd to E + skip a 3rd to G

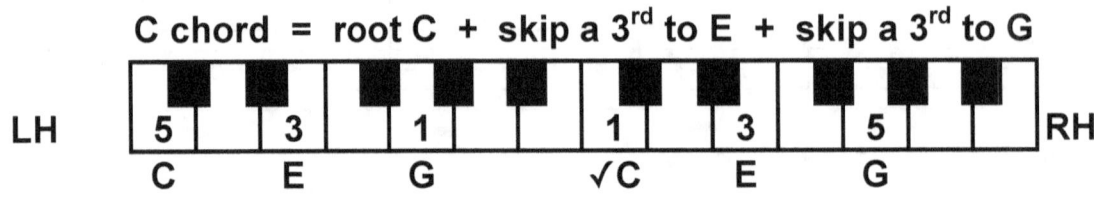

LH C E G √C E G RH (5 3 1 1 3 5)

♪ **1: Improvise** C chord with each hand alone in **block style,** playing the three keys **at the same time,** then **broken style** playing the three keys **in any order.**

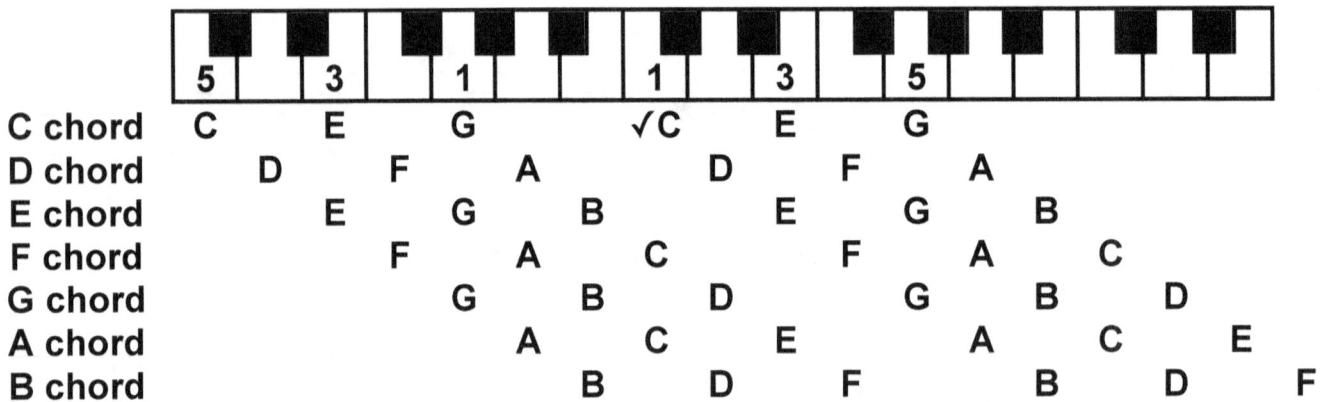

	5	3	1	1	3	5		
C chord	C	E	G	√C	E	G		
D chord		D	F	A	D	F	A	
E chord		E	G	B	E	G	B	
F chord			F	A	C	F	A	C
G chord			G	B	D	G	B	D
A chord				A	C	E	A	C	E
B chord				B	D	F	B	D	F

♪ **2: Say** the name and **play** each chord above, **LH 5 3 1,** followed by **RH 1 3 5,** then shift the hands up the keyboard by one key for the next chord.

NOTATED CHORDS
The heads of the notes in block chords are stacked on the same stem.

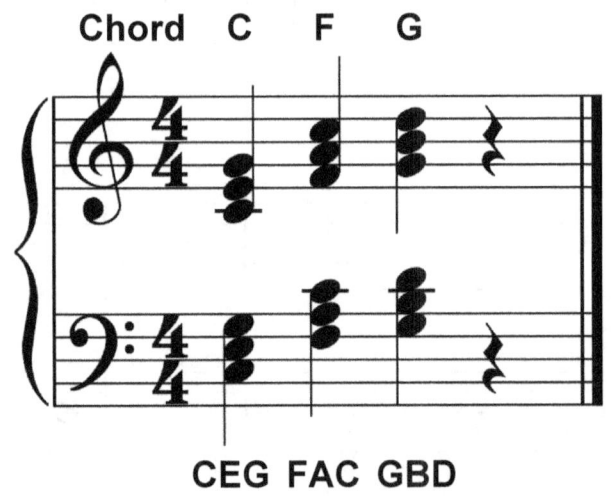

Chord C F G

♪ **3: Play** these chords three notes at a time: first right hand, next left hand, then hands together.

CEG FAC GBD

CHORD PROGRESSIONS

A chord progression is a **particular sequence** of chords.

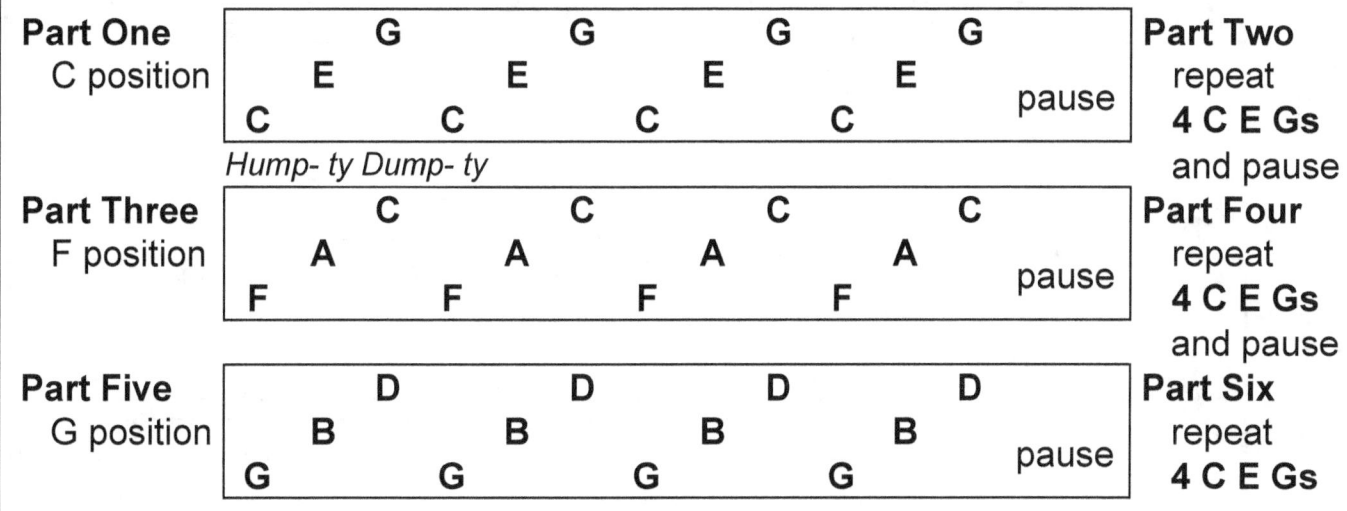

C chord   C   E   G
F chord   F   A   C
G chord   G   B   D

♪ **4: Practice** shifting each hand position from **C to F to C to G to C;** RH 135, then LH 531, in broken and block styles.

Common progression used for "In the Mood," 1938.

♪ **5: Swingin' Skips Progression C~C~F~C~G~C**

Play the six parts that repeat C, F, and G chords in broken style.

Play each set of skips four times, pause, then go on.

Play slowly and smoothly. Say "C skip up to E skip up to G, etc."

First right hand (135), next left hand (531), then hands together.

Part One C position	G E C *Hump- ty Dump- ty*	G E C	G E C	G E C	pause

Part Two repeat 4 C E Gs and pause

Part Three F position	C A F	C A F	C A F	C A F	pause

Part Four repeat 4 C E Gs and pause

Part Five G position	D B G	D B G	D B G	D B G	pause

Part Six repeat 4 C E Gs

♪ **6: Try** playing with a

"swing style" Hump-ty Dump-ty rhythm (long~short~long~short)

first with the right hand, next the left hand, then hands together.

♪ **7: Improvise** a chord progression with two or three chords beginning and ending on the same chord.

Example: C chord (CEG) to D chord (DFA), then back to C chord (CEG).

Keep the root notes within the same C to C octave.

The naturally **accented beats** in a 4/4 measure are the **1st or 1st and 3rd beats.**

The **root notes C or G** are played with the LH on the 1st, or 1st and 3rd beat.
These whole and half notes provide a contrast to the quarter notes
in the melodies. This allows the melodies to be clearly heard.

Move the LH to G position, 10 keys below middle C, for these four melodies.

♫ 1: Ode to Joy

From 9th Symphony by German L. v. Beethoven (1770–1827) for "brotherhood ode" by F. Schiller, 1785.

♫ 2: Old Ark's a-Moverin'

Adapted from spiritual "Old Ark's a-Moverin'."

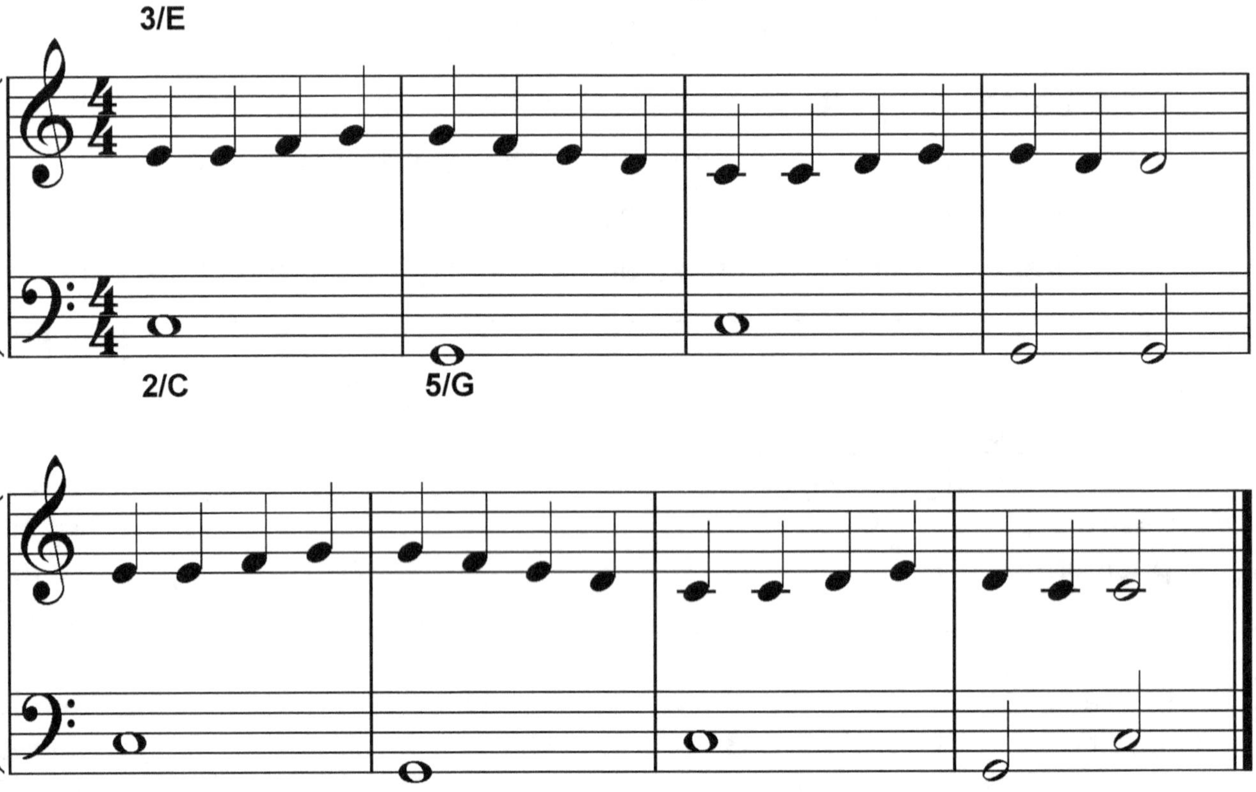

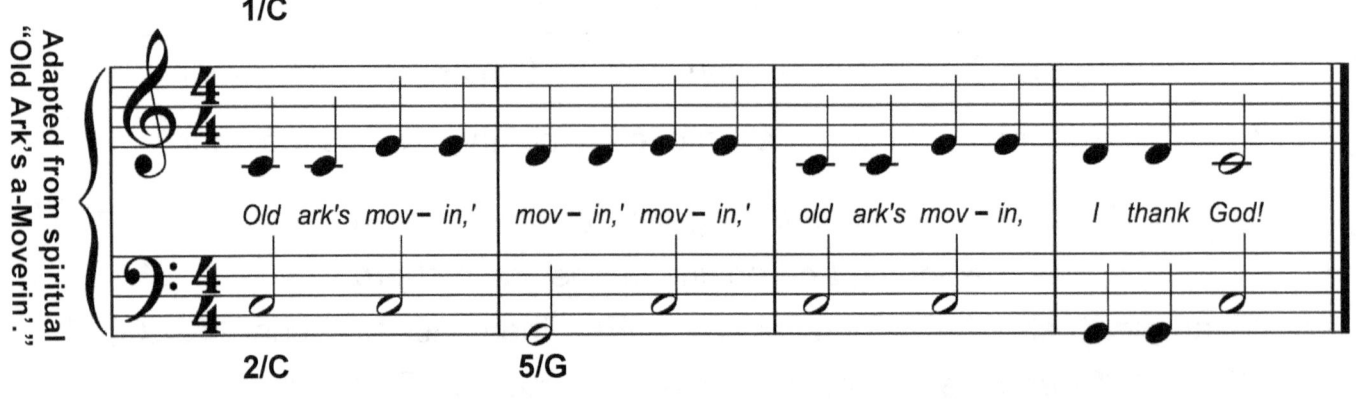

♪ 3: Mary Had a Little Lamb

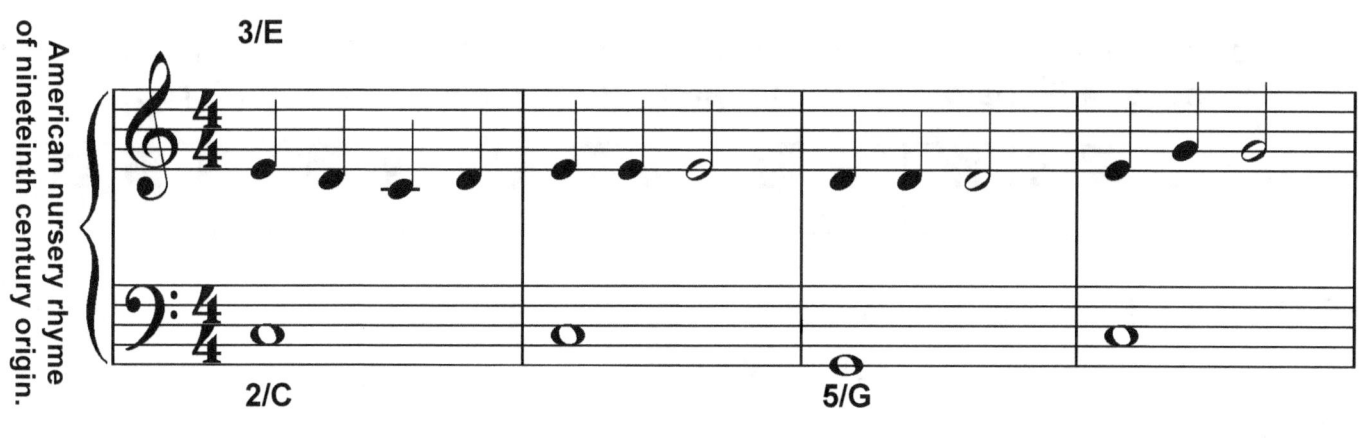

American nursery rhyme of nineteenth century origin.

♪ 4: French Shop

(see 5a)

An old folk song called "J'ai du bon tabac."

1/G move LH up to C position

CHORDS ~ 9 a

CHORD STRUCTURE

The structure of chords can also be described as **root + 3rd + 5th + optional 7th**.
F root is a 5th below the C root and G root is a 5th above the C root.

RH

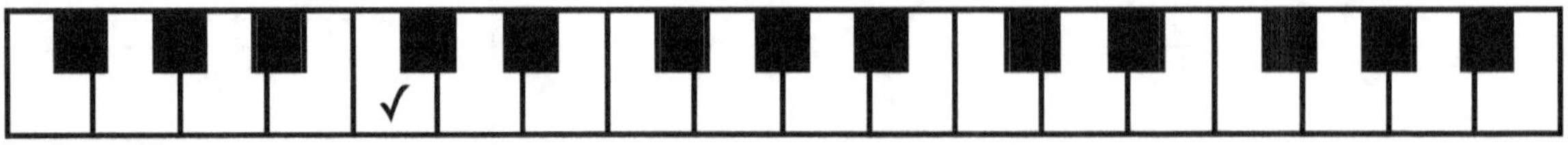

5th below C

F chord	**F**	A	C	
C chord		**C**	E	G
G chord			**G**	B	D
G7 chord	G chord + 7th above G	**G**	B	(D)	F
	"7" shows it's a 7th chord	5th above C		D is often omitted

CHORD INVERSION

Chords can be **inverted** (turned upside down) by **moving the octave of pitches**.

RH

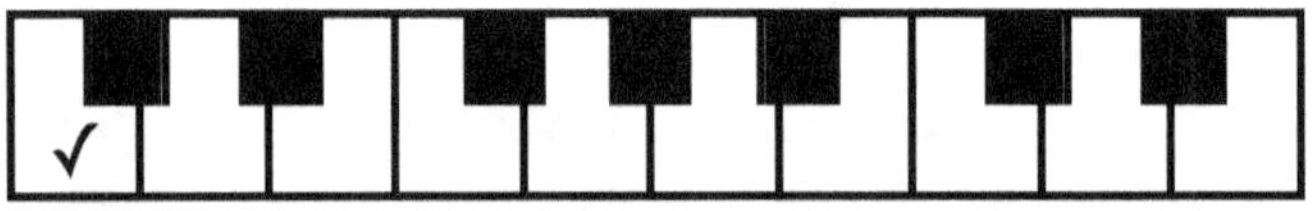

				Structure:
root on bottom	C	E	G	3rd + 5th above root
root on top		E	G	C	6th + 4th below root
root in middle			G	C	E	4th below/3rd above

♪ **1: Play** each RH chord above: root on bottom and in middle 135, on top 125;
say the intervals in the chord structures above and below the root.

5 FINGERS, 7 PITCHES

LH   B C   G A

All seven pitches can be reached from a single hand position by extending the **pinkie finger** and **thumb** back and forth.

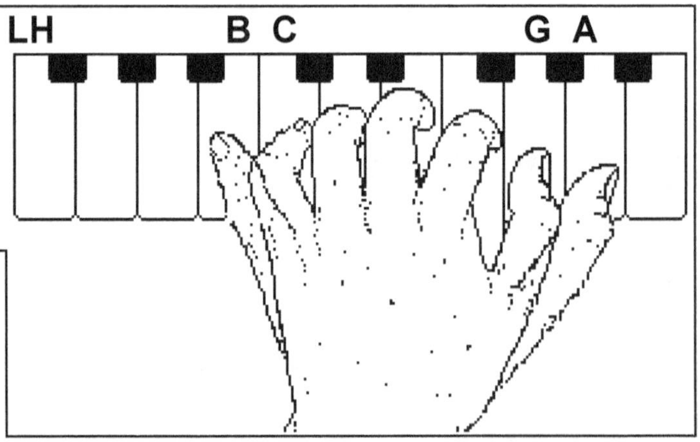

♪ **2: Practice** extending LH 5 and 1 between **B C and G A** an octave below middle C, then the **RH** from middle C.

> **Sliding the left hand** from root position to root position can be difficult.
> Instead, chords may be played
> **from one hand position** using **inversions of the chords**.

Progression C~F~C~G7~C

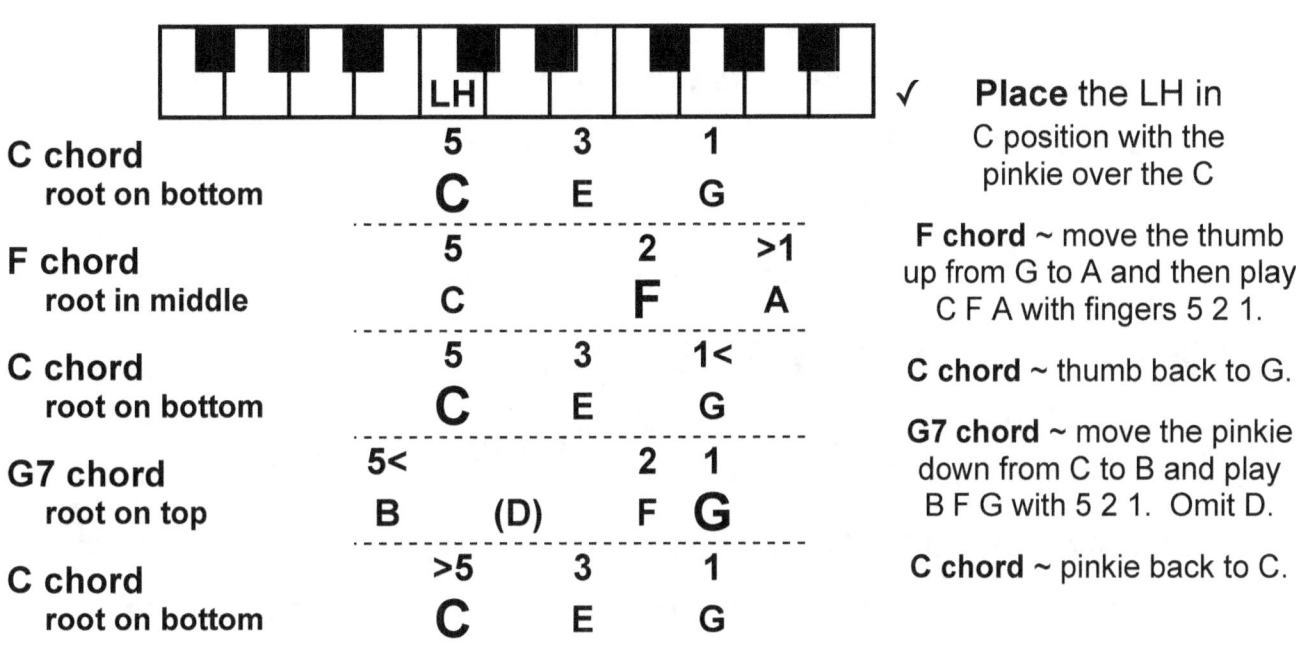

✓ **Place** the LH in C position with the pinkie over the C

F chord ~ move the thumb up from G to A and then play C F A with fingers 5 2 1.

C chord ~ thumb back to G.

G7 chord ~ move the pinkie down from C to B and play B F G with 5 2 1. Omit D.

C chord ~ pinkie back to C.

♪ **3: Practice** the left-hand C position chord progression **C~F~C~G7~C** above.
Prepare each chord before playing **without looking at the hands.**
Play the progression in block style, next broken style, then repeat both styles.

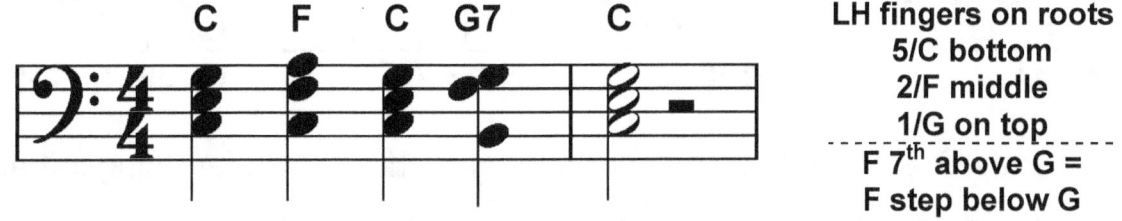

LH fingers on roots
5/C bottom
2/F middle
1/G on top
F 7th above G =
F step below G

♪ **4: Learn** to recognize these shapes and where the root notes are located.

♪ **5: Improvise** each chord with hands together in block and broken styles an octave apart.
The RH fingering for the C and F chords is 135, and for the G7 is 145.

IMPROVISED ENDINGS

Block Chord with Roots

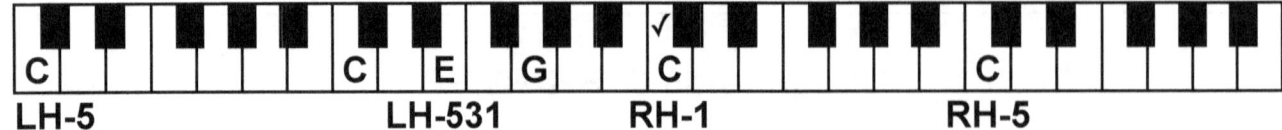

♫ **1: Play C chord block style** with the left fingers 531 below middle C holding the pedal. Then play Cs both **below and above** in any order.

Broken Chords with Roots

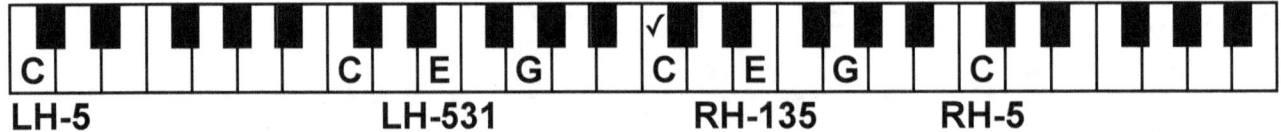

♫ **2: Play C chord broken style** C to E to G, one note at a time, with the left fingers 531, followed with the right fingers 135 an octave higher holding the pedal. Then play Cs both **below and above** in any order.

Arpeggio (crossing hands)

♫ **3: Play C arpeggio,** an extended broken chord, by alternating left and right hands an octave apart with **C broken chord** C to E to G, one note at a time, from a low C position on the keyboard holding the pedal.

Cross the left hand **over** the right hand **and** then right hand **under** the left to repeat the same broken C chord in the higher octaves.
End with a high and/or low C in any order.

COMPOSITION FOUR

Chord progressions often inspire melodies.

♪ **4: Play** the patterns below. The LH holds a C chord as the RH plays a melodic pattern of single notes within each measure that emphasize pitches from that chord on the 1st beat, or 1st and 3rd beat, the accented beats.

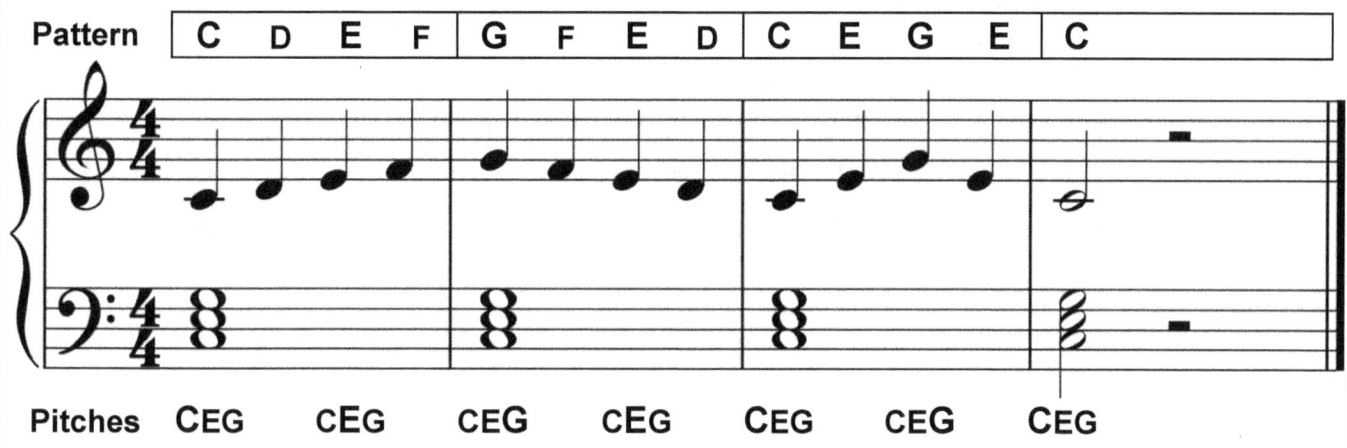

♪ **5: Compose** and fill in RH **melodic patterns** on the 1st beat, or 1st and 3rd beat that emphasize the pitches from the chords below, then **play.**

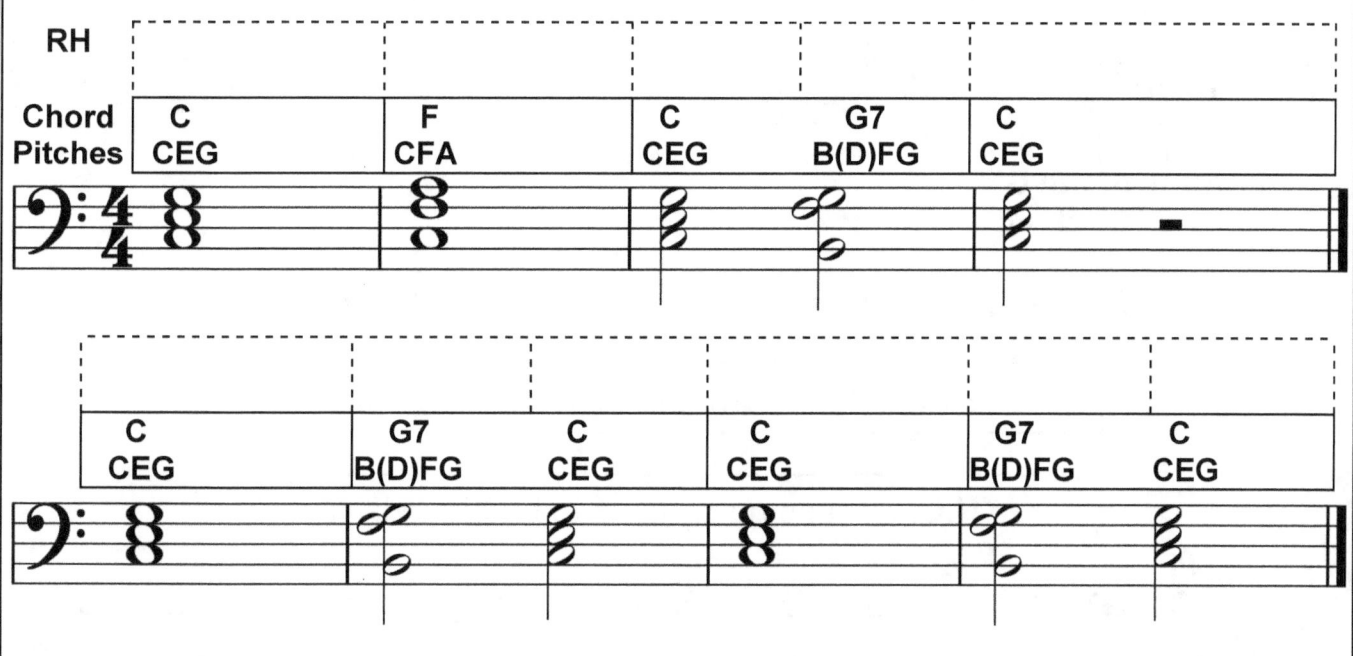

♪ **6: Improvise** a LH **progression** with chords C, F, and G7.
Compose RH **melodic patterns** that emphasize the pitches in each chord.

CHORDS ~ 10 a

> ## LEAD SHEETS
>
> Chords bring out the **rhythm and pitch patterns** in melodies,
> and they help create the fuller sound called **harmony**.
> The chords added to melodies are called **accompaniments**.
>
> A melody with **chord symbol** names above the **treble staff**
> is called a **"lead sheet"** (and is also called a "chart").
> "Fake books" are collections of lead sheets.
>
> **Lead sheets show the chords to be played (without notation).**
> Chords are played on **beat 1, often beat 3,** and sometimes the **other beats.**
> Once written, a chord symbol **stays in effect** until a new chord symbol is written.

♫ **1: Hot Cross Buns** ~ practice with notated chords.

531/CEG 521/BFG
C chord G7 chord

♫ **2: Hot Cross Buns** ~ play LH chords from the lead sheet.

" * " The C chord **remains in effect** on beat 1.

"N.C." means no chord is to be played.

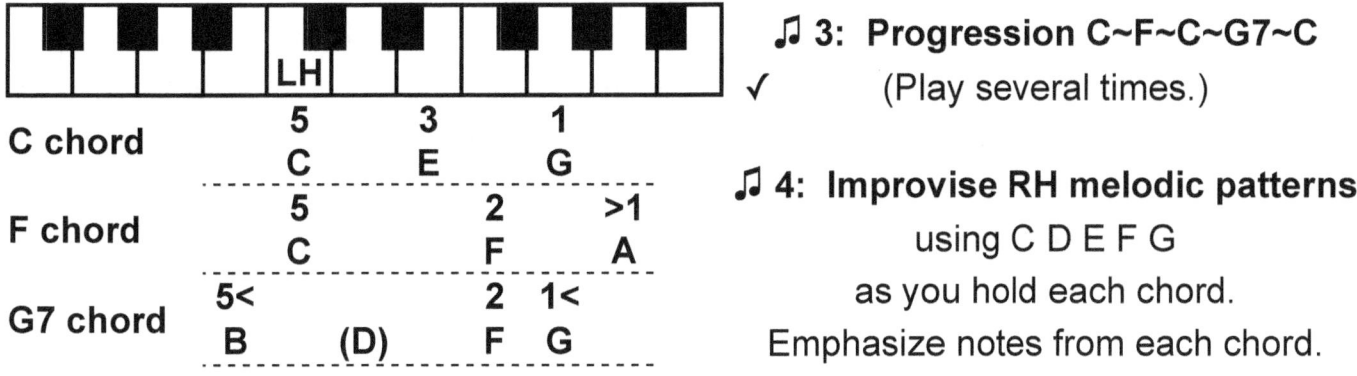

C chord	5 C	3 E	1 G
F chord	5 C	2 F	>1 A
G7 chord	5< B (D)	2 F	1< G

♪ 3: **Progression C~F~C~G7~C**
✓ (Play several times.)

♪ 4: **Improvise RH melodic patterns**
using C D E F G
as you hold each chord.
Emphasize notes from each chord.

Think about the fingers that play the chord pitches, NOT the pitch names.

After the hands are placed in C position, **watch the music, NOT the hands.**

Practice **each hand alone,** then **hands together** by preparing

first the chord, **next** the melody notes, **then** playing hands together.

♪ 5: Old Ark's a-Moverin' (lead sheet)

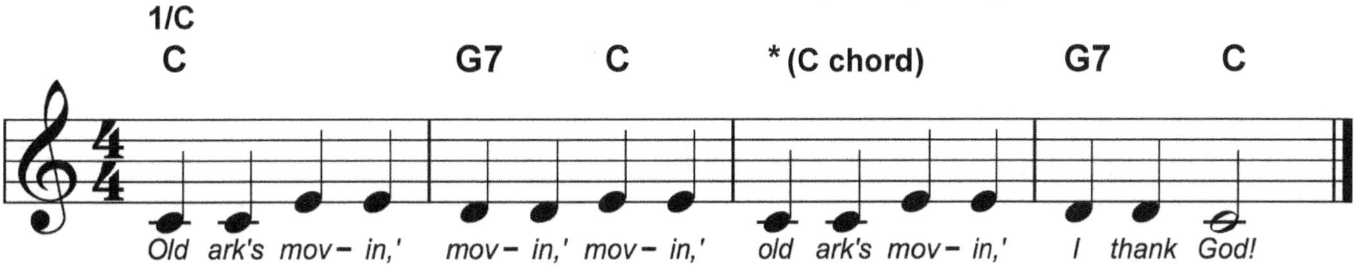

1/C
C — G7 — C — *(C chord) — G7 — C

Old ark's mov-in,' mov-in,' mov-in,' old ark's mov-in,' I thank God!

♪ 6: Ode to Joy (lead sheet)

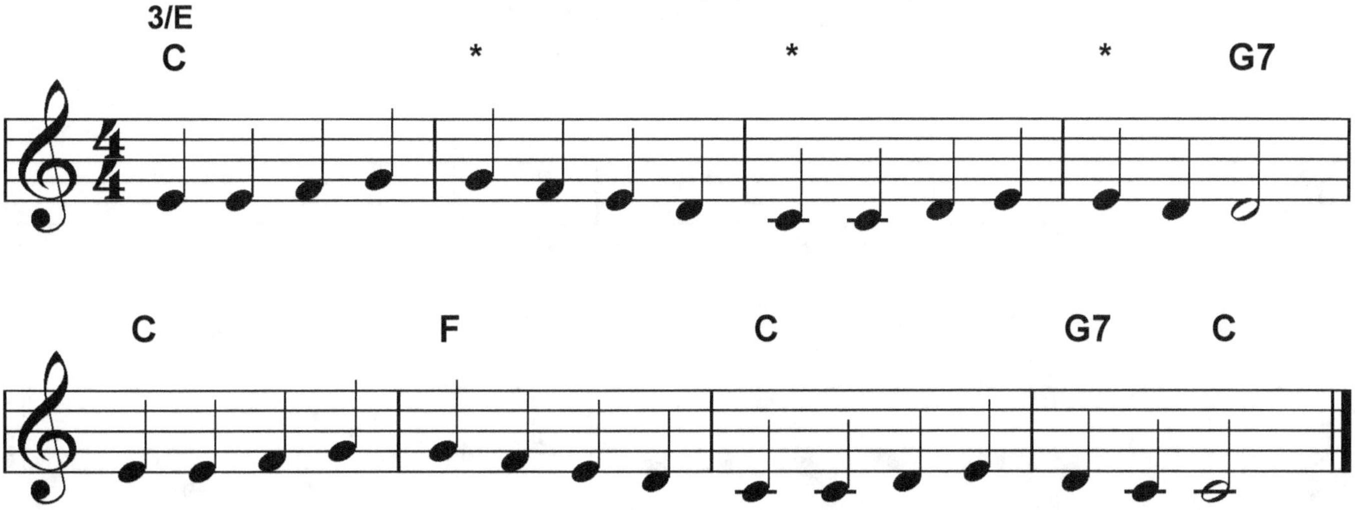

3/E
C — * — * — * — G7

C — F — C — G7 — C

♪ **1:** When a keyboard is played, the sound can fade quickly.
Improvise chords C or G7 with the melodies on these two pages
with the whole and tied notes to keep the rhythm and sound continuous.

♪ **2: Add an ending** to these melodies by improvising their last chord.

♫ 5: **When the Saints Go Marching In** (lead sheet)

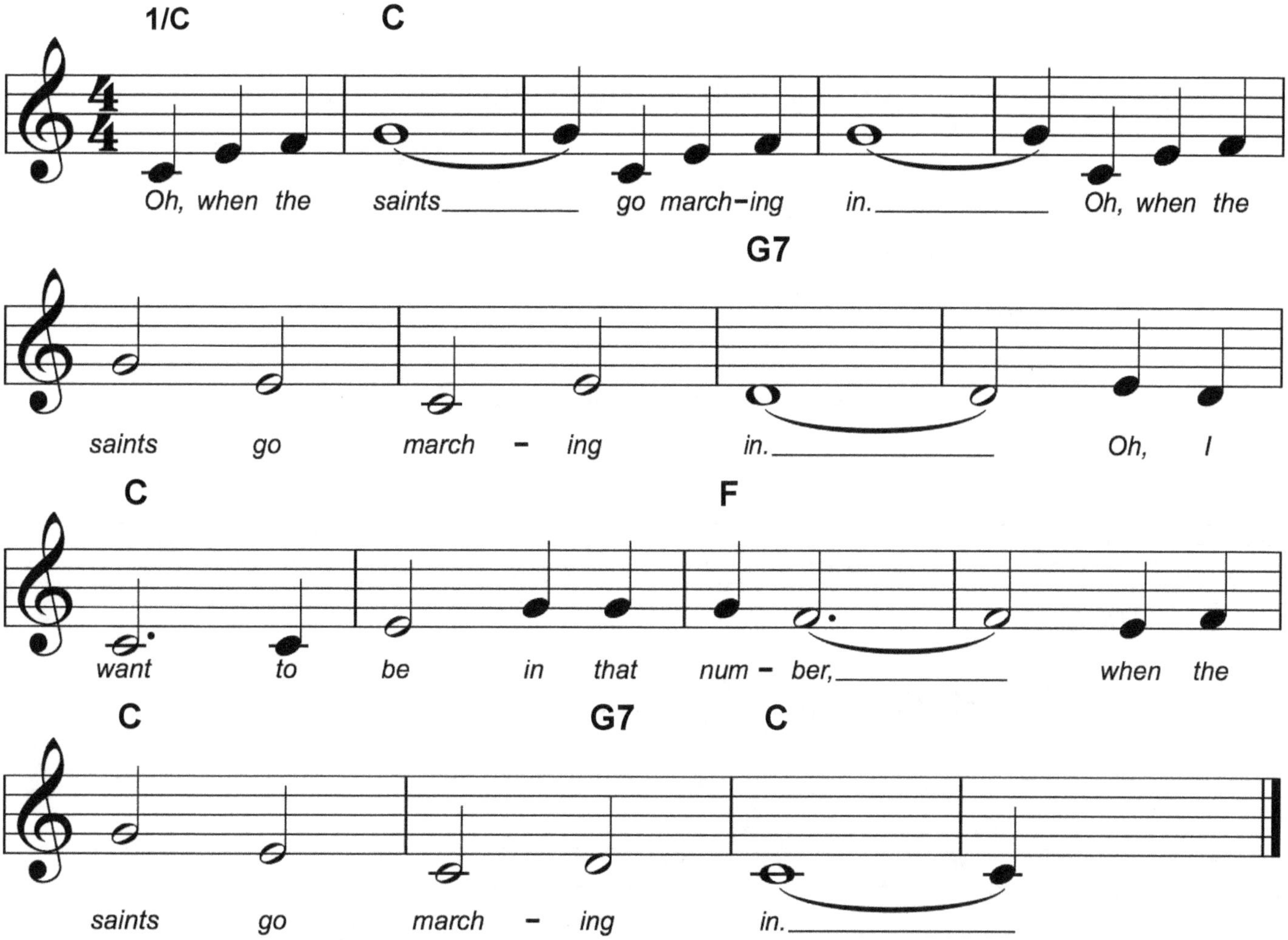

COMPOSITION FIVE

♫ 6: **Choose** a C or G7 chord for each measure that fits the melody, then **play.**

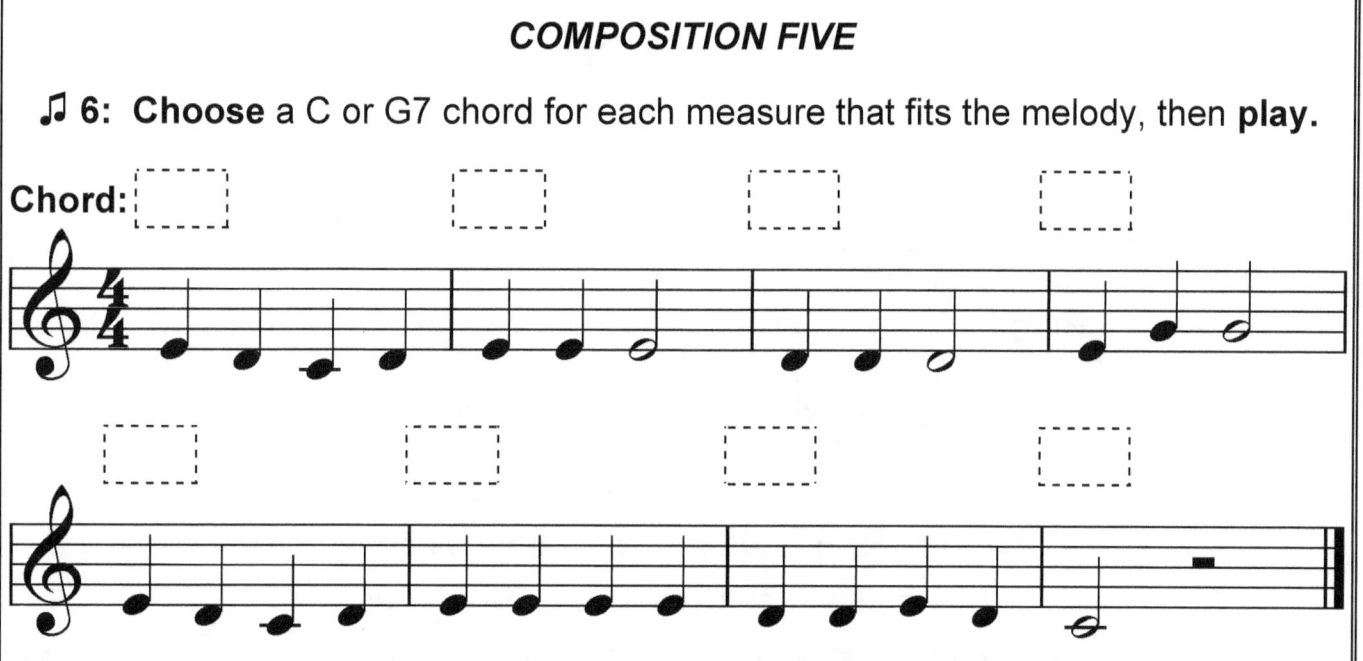

CHORDS ~ 11 a

CHORDING STYLES

Improvise different left-hand chording styles.

5/C   1/G

♪ **1: Play** single roots of chords C and G.

51/CG

♪ **2: Play** the "open 5th" (C and G together) of the C chord.

5/C 3/E 1/G   5/B 2/F 1/G

♪ **3: Play** broken chords C and G7 (single notes).

5/C 31/EG   5/B 21/FG

♪ **4: Play** broken chords C and G7 (single and double notes).

The "**French Lullaby**" on the next page
uses broken and block C and G7 chords
to contrast with a slower, softer melody.

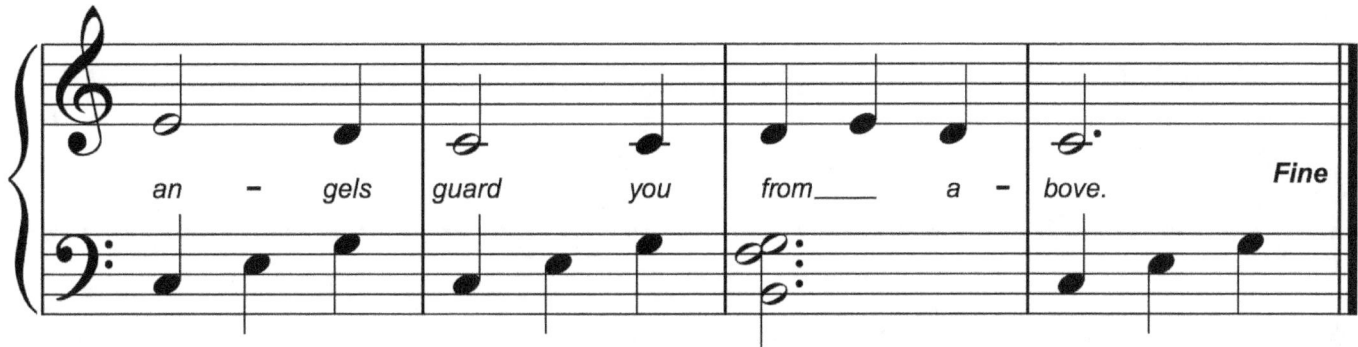
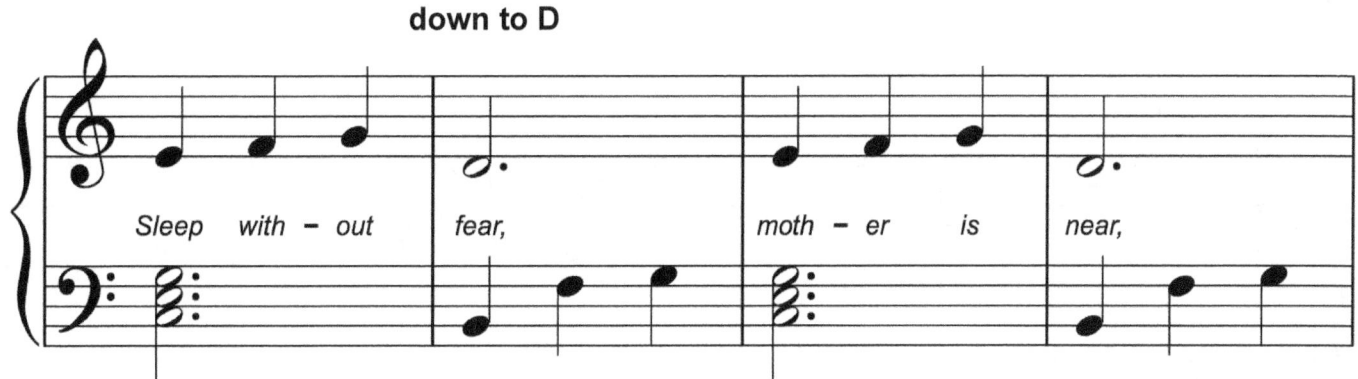
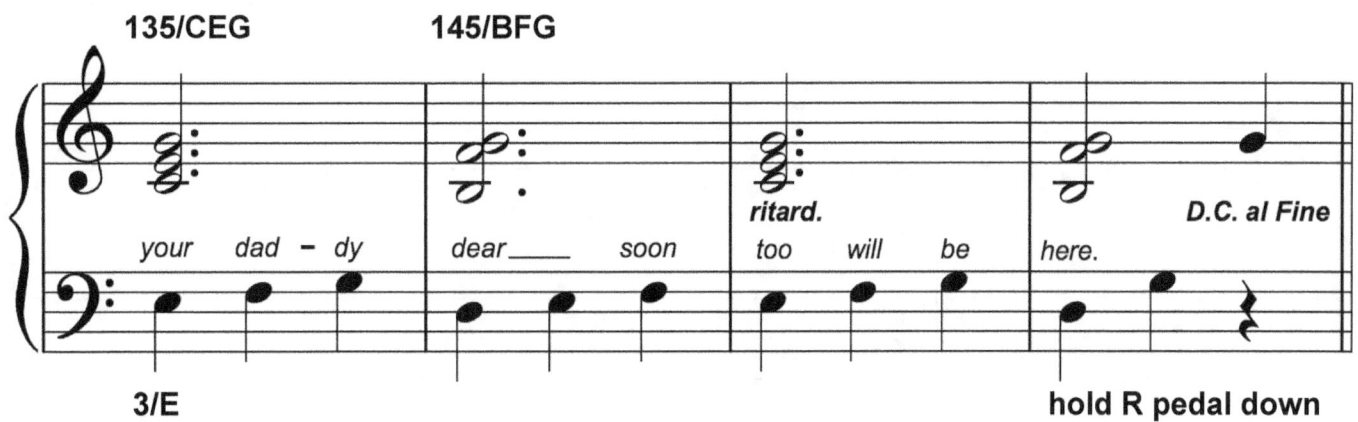

♫ 1: Ode to Joy

This melody uses whole note block chords
that allow the quarter note melody to be heard clearly.
Contrast is shown when the melody is played without chords in measures 9 to 12.

♫ 2: French Shop

This is a melody with low and sustained open 5th accompaniment
for rhythmic contrast, a melody alternating between the RH and LH for
contrast in a higher and lower octave, and an ending emphasizing the 5th repetition.

The left-hand Cs and Gs are two octaves below middle C
except in measures 7 and 8 where the hand is one octave below middle C.

♪ 1: Progression C~G7~C~G7
(Play several times.)

SONG ACCOMPANIMENT
Sing the lyrics to these melodies and
play RH chords and LH root notes.

LH option, double the root notes by adding the octave below the root note.

Double-bars with dots means to **repeat the notation** between these bars.

♪ 2: Frère Jacques

♪ 3: He's Got the Whole World in His Hands

♫ 4: Row, Row, Row Your Boat

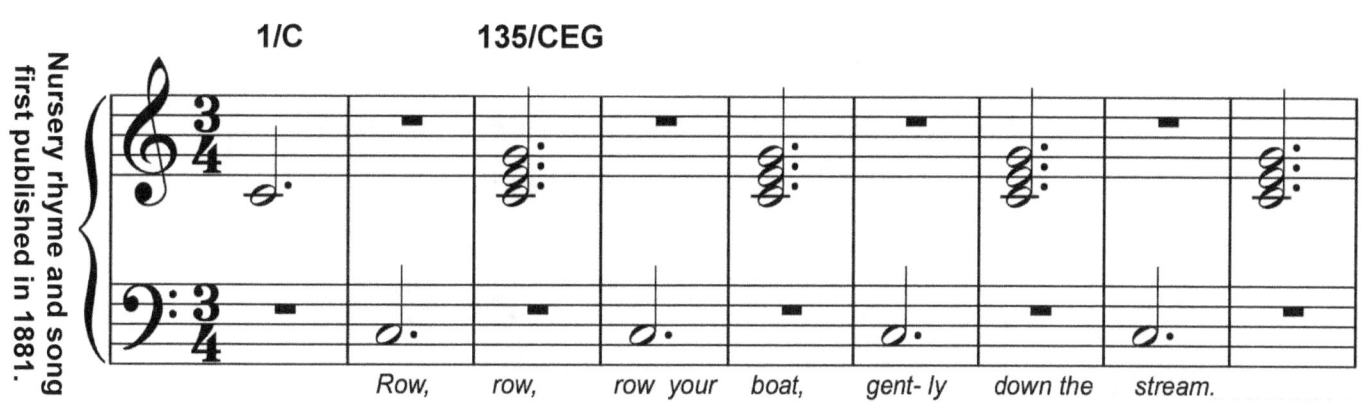

Nursery rhyme and song first published in 1881.

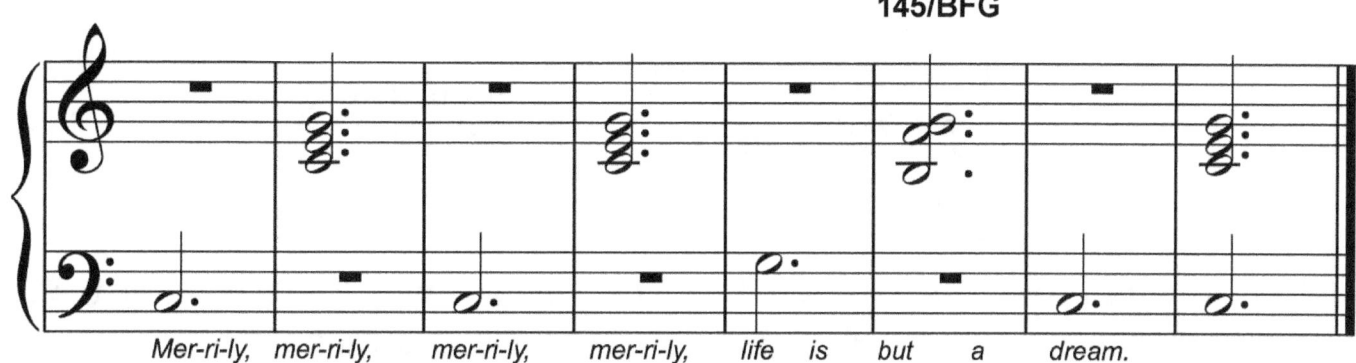

Triplets. The number 3 over a group of three notes means this group is the same length as a quarter or two eighths.

ROCK STYLES

F MAJOR ~ 12 a   51

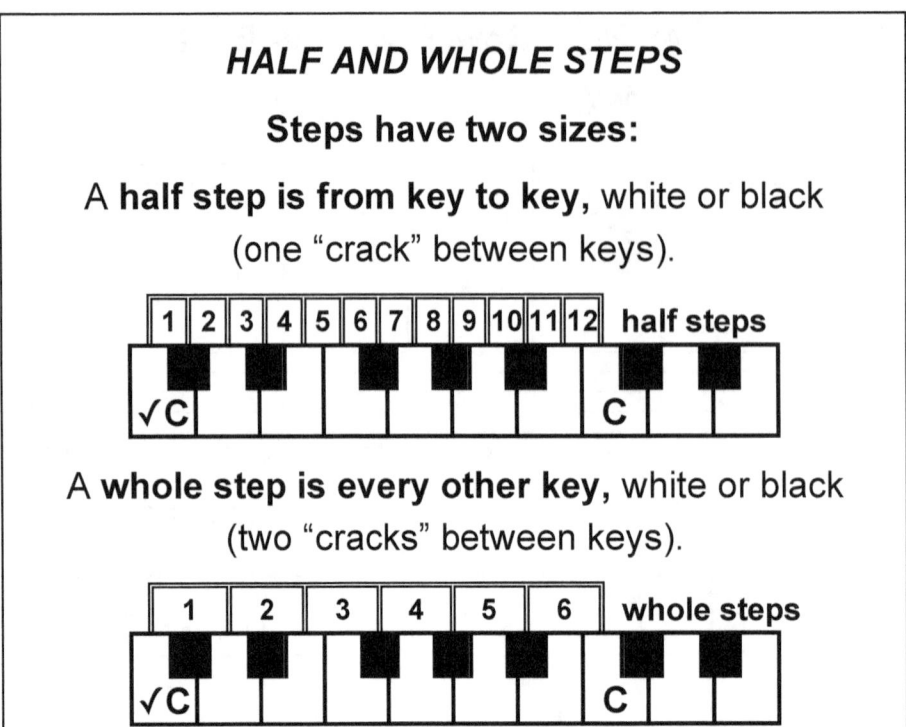

♪ **1:** Play the **12 half steps** (use RH 2 ♭): **C** to **black key** to **D** to **black key** to **E**, then **F** to **black key,** etc.; and **count** each half-step "**1 2 3 4 5 6 7 8 9 10 11 12.**"

♪ **2:** Play the **6 whole steps** (use RH 2 ♭): **C** to **white key** to **white key** to **black key** to **black key** to **black key** to **C**; and **count** each whole-step "**1 2 3 4 5 6.**"

C MAJOR SCALE

The term "major" will be explained later.

Scales are the basis of chords and melodies.
The step structure for the C to C white key scale is:
whole whole half whole whole whole half
W~W~H~W~W~W~H

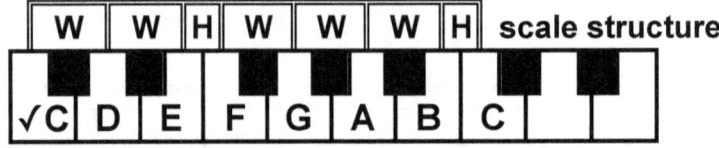

♪ **3: Play** (RH 2 ♭) **and say:** "**C, whole step** D, **whole step** E, **half step** F, **whole step** G, **whole step** A, **whole step** B, **half step** C."

♪ **4: Improvise** whole and half steps between any white and black keys.

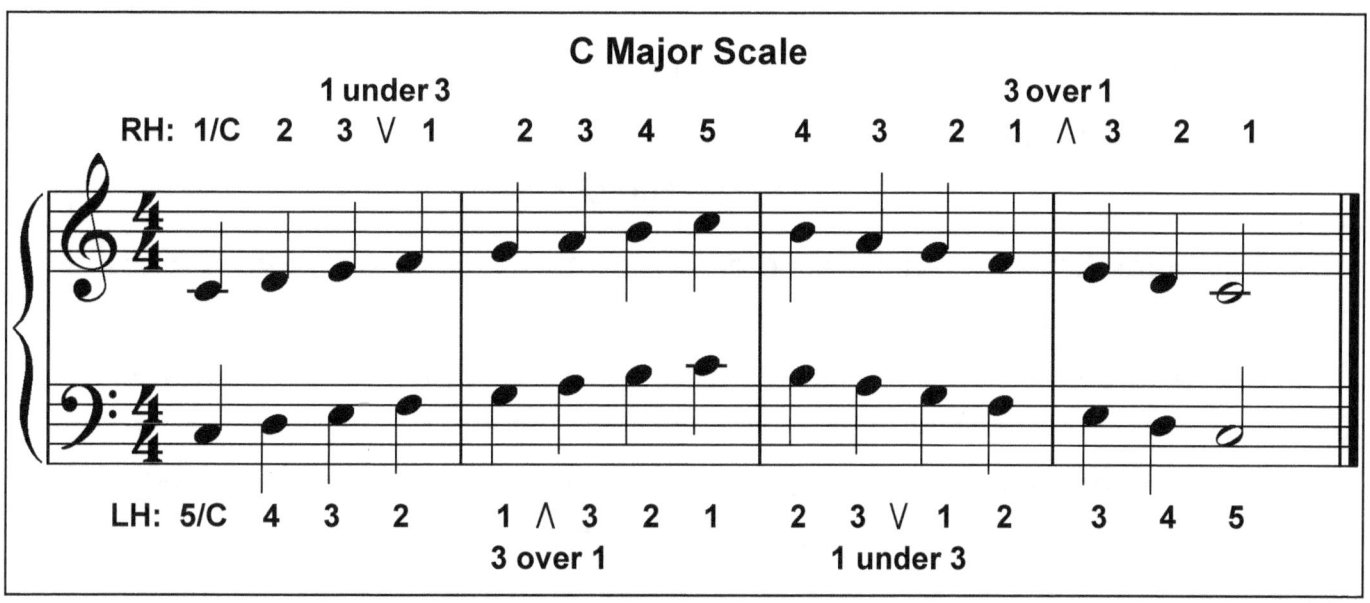

♪ **5: Practice the C major scale,** first RH, next LH, then hands together.

BLACK KEY NAMES

A **sharp "♯"** is a sign that a pitch has been **raised by a half step.**
A **flat "♭"** is a sign that a pitch has been **lowered by a half step.**

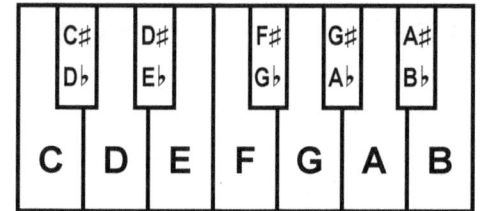

Sharps/flats use the **letter name** of their raised/lowered pitch. Each black key therefore has **two names,** such as **C♯ and D♭.**

♪ **6: Play** (RH 2 ♭) and **say:** "C C♯ D♭ D D♯ E♭ E F F♯ G♭ G G♯ A♭ A A♯ B♭ B"

NOTATED ACCIDENTALS

If a **sharp "♯"** or **flat "♭"** sign is placed in front of a note head, it stays in effect for that **line or space in that measure only**
unless cancelled by a **natural "♮"** sign that returns the note to its original pitch.

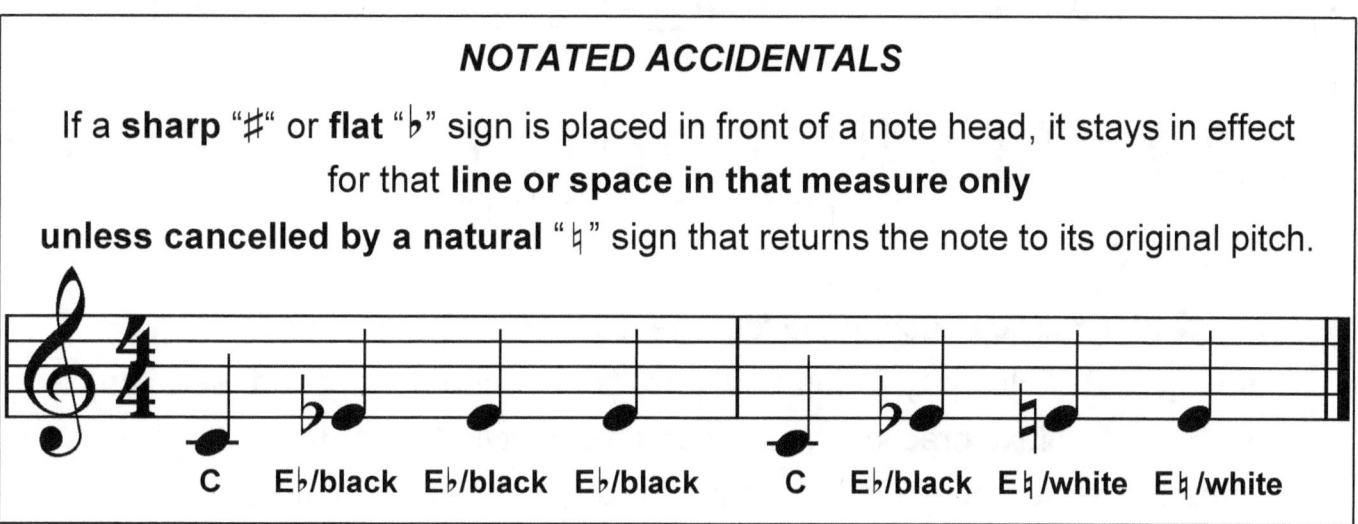

♪ **7: Play** (RH 2 ♭) and **say** the note names above.

SCALES

Various scales have been developed through time,
across cultures, and for different styles of music.

The **black keys** are an example of a **pentatonic scale with five pitches**
that has been used for many melodies such as
"Amazing Grace," "This Little Light of Mine," and "Old MacDonald."

♪ **1: Improvise** on the **black keys** with RH or LH fingers extended
in any octave while holding the pedal down.

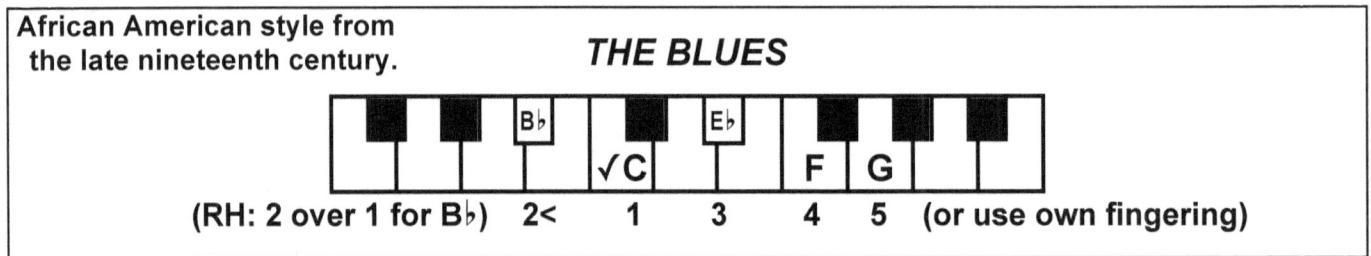

African American style from the late nineteenth century.
THE BLUES
(RH: 2 over 1 for B♭) 2< 1 3 4 5 (or use own fingering)

♪ **2: Practice** this pentatonic blues scale using C F G (chord roots) B♭ and E♭.

Melodic Blues Patterns

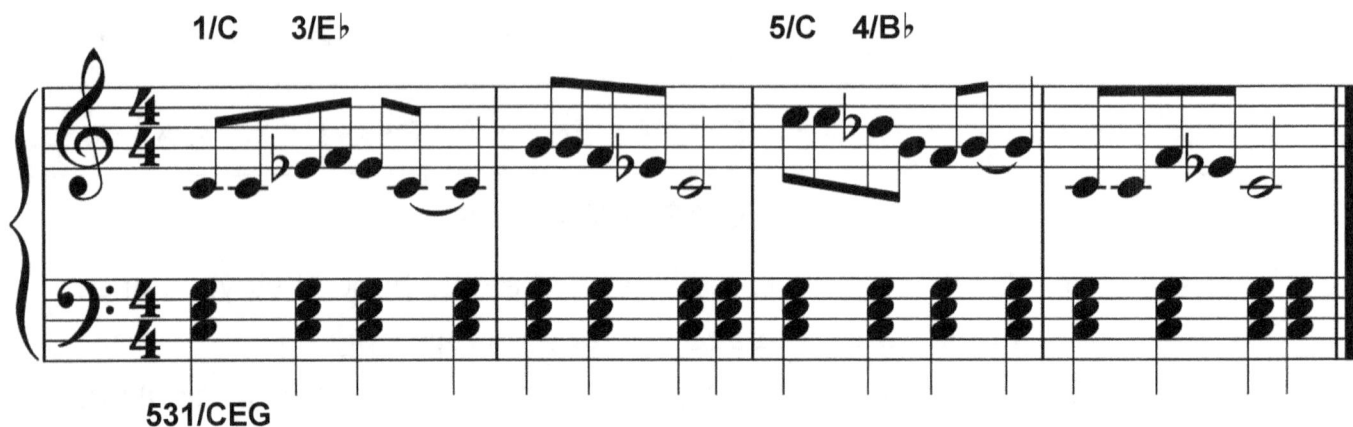

♪ **3: Practice** each of the four measures for the right hand with a
"swing style" Hump-ty Dump-ty rhythm (long~short~long~short: see 8aa).
Next, practice the left-hand block style C chords,
then play the treble and bass parts for each measure hands together.

♪ **4: Improvise RH melodic patterns** using this blues scale.

♫ **5: Twelve-Bar Blues (12 measures) ~ Improvise** RH melodic patterns.

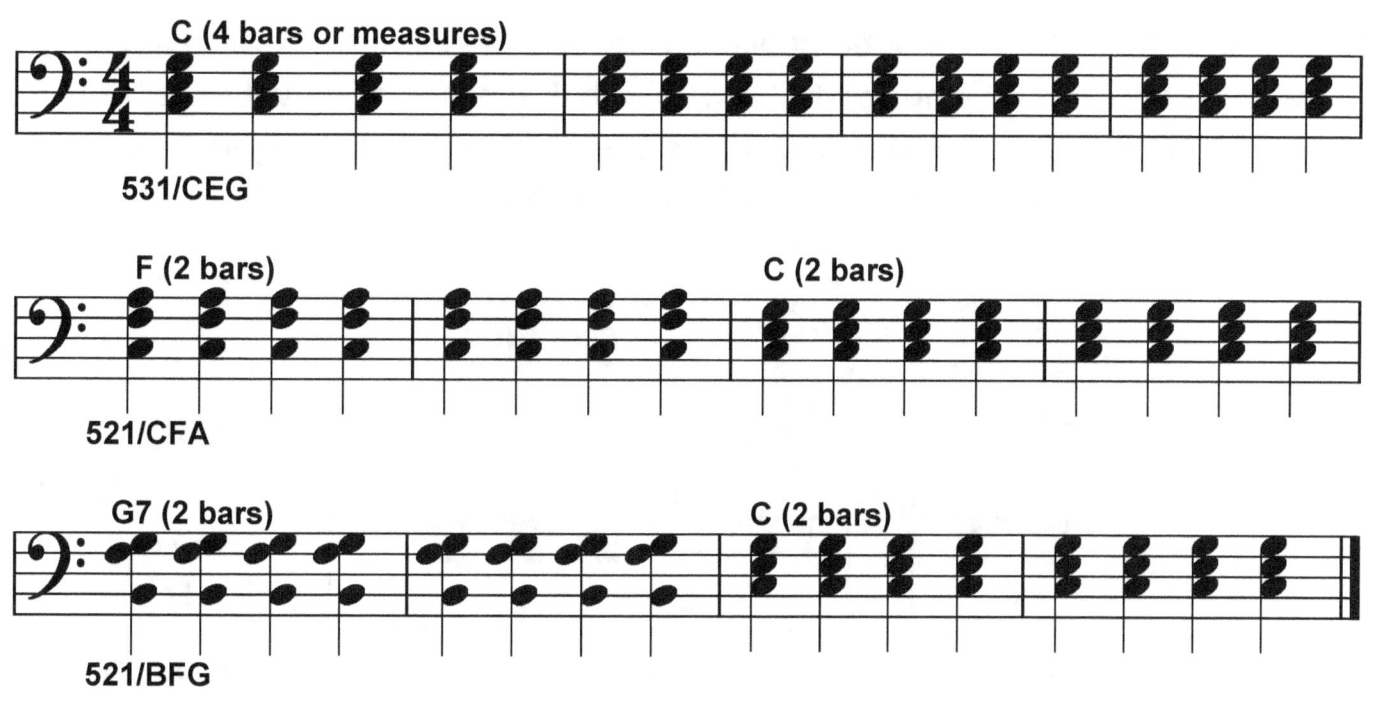

♫ **6: Broken Chord Blues ~ Improvise** RH melodic patterns.

These are broken C F G chords with a **6th interval above the root note**.
Extend both the LH 2 and 1 fingers to play the 5th and 6th intervals.

F MAJOR ~ 13 a

TRANSPOSITION

Any one of the white or black pitches can be the **keynote** on which the **whole~whole~half~whole~whole~whole~half** major scale structure is built. **The keynote**, also called **the key,** can be **transposed** (moved) higher or lower. The other keys also change, **but the whole and half step scale pattern remains.**

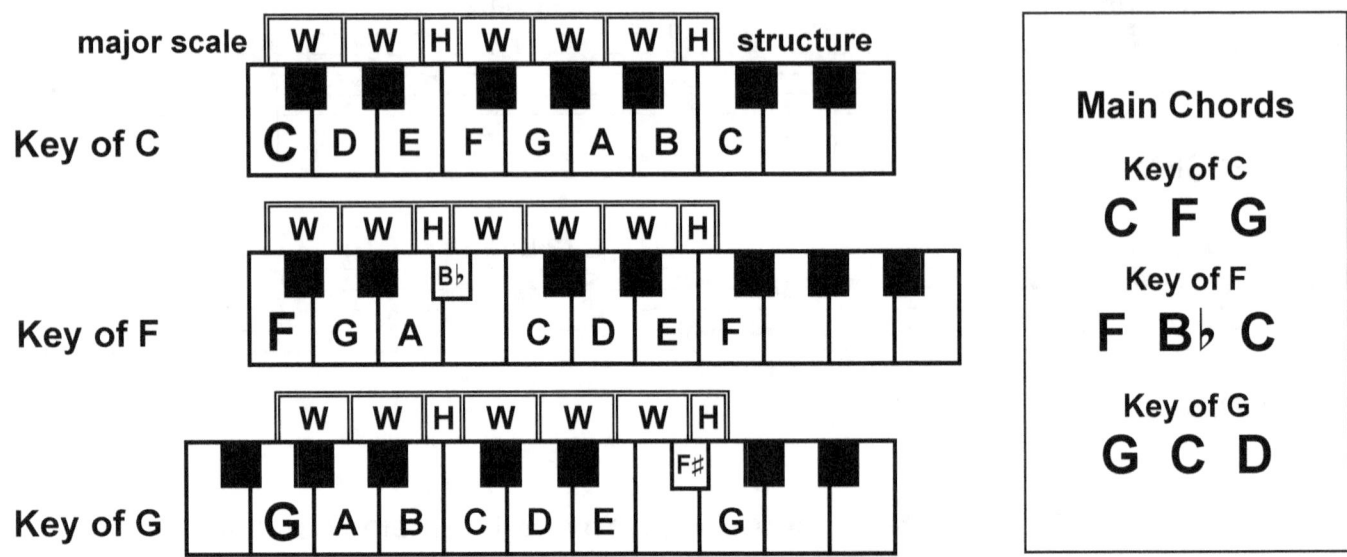

♫ **1: Play** the C, F, and G major scales with the RH 2 ♭ starting on the keynote and **say** the major scale structure. For example, **Key of F:** "F, whole step G, whole step A, half step B♭, whole step C, whole step D, whole step E, half step F."

KEY SIGNATURES

Key signatures are placed between the **clef sign** and the **time signature.** The key signature shows the notes that are to be **sharped or flatted in all octaves and measures.**

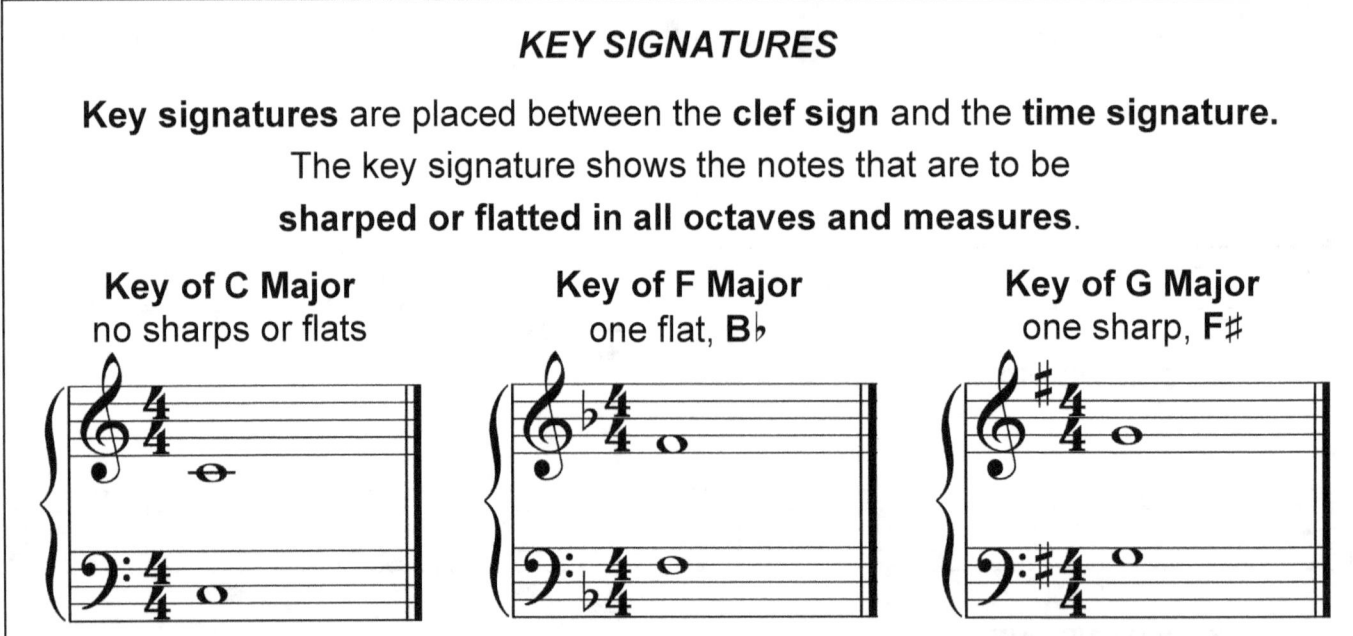

Key of F ~ Hand Positions

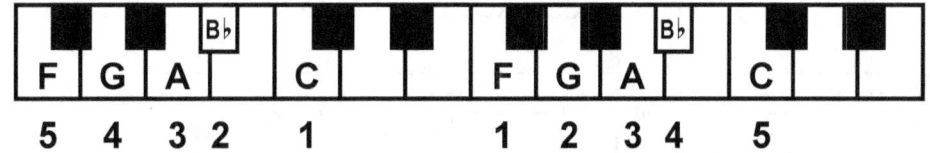

♪ **2: Practice** each hand alone, then hands together.

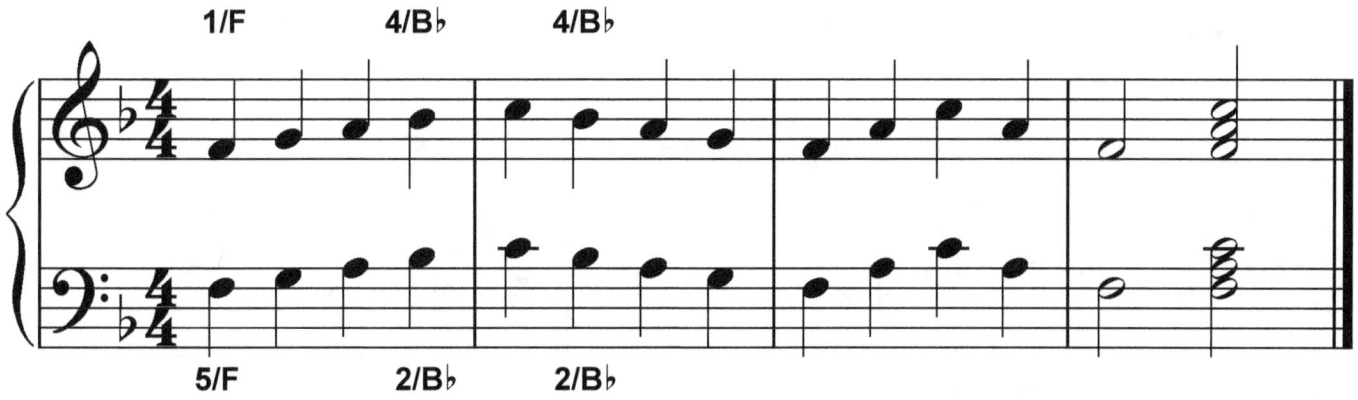

♪ **3: Practice** stepping and skipping in F position above with a **B♭**.

♪ 4: Ode to Joy

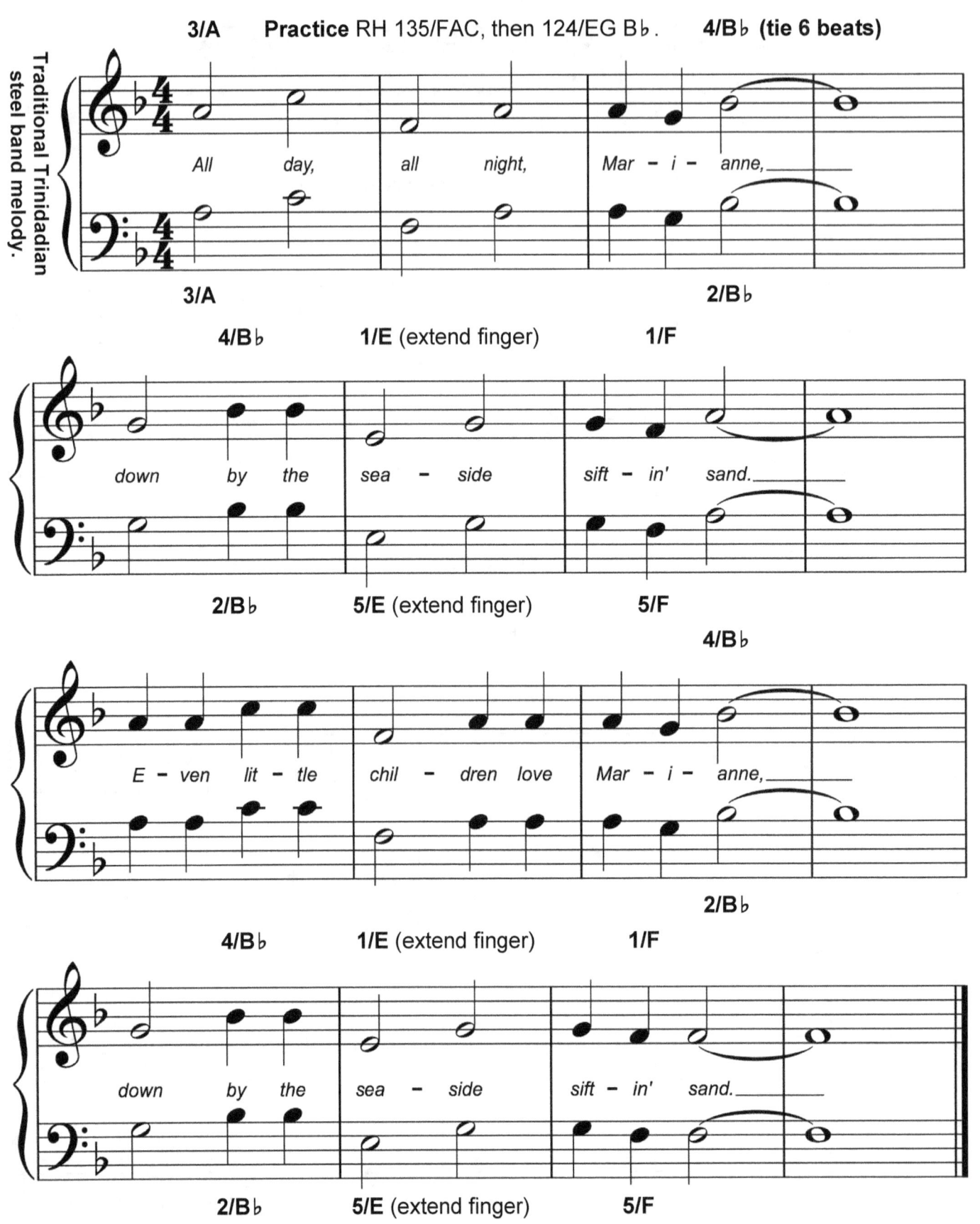

♫ 2: **French Lullaby**

(see 5a)

F MAJOR ~ 14 a

SCALE DEGREES

Each **degree** (step) in a scale is identified by the same **Roman numeral** in all keys.

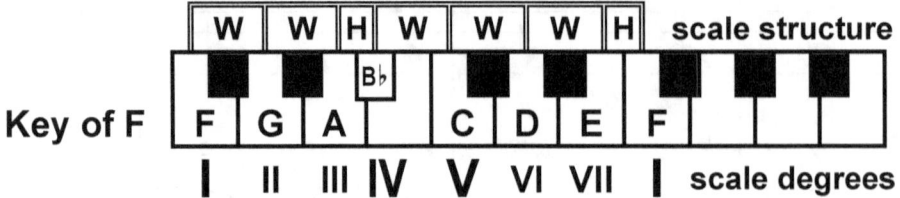

The **major chords** are built on the **I** (tonic), **IV** (subdominant), and **V** (dominant).

CHORD STRUCTURE

The structure of chords includes the **root** + a **3rd** + a **5th** + an **optional 7th**.

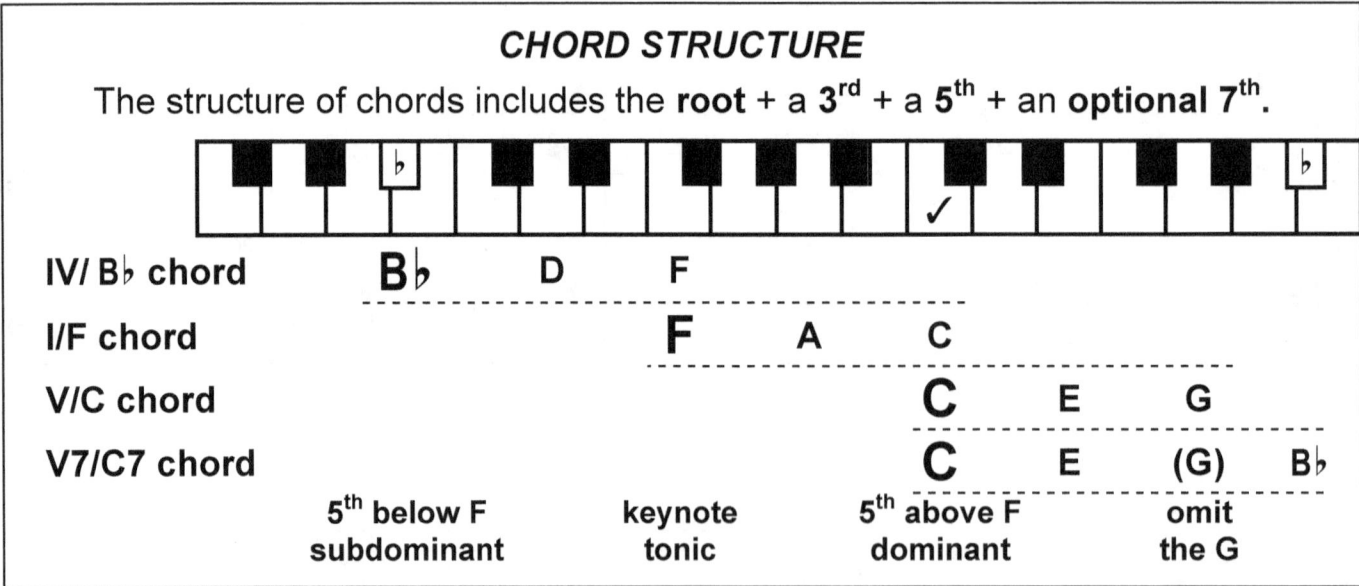

IV/ B♭ chord	B♭	D	F	
I/F chord		F	A	C
V/C chord			C	E	G
V7/C7 chord			C	E	(G)	B♭
	5th below F subdominant	keynote tonic	5th above F dominant	omit the G

♪ **1: Play and say** the chord numeral and name: "IV and B♭," etc.

CHORD INVERSION

Chords are **inverted** (turned upside down) by **moving the octave of pitches**.

				structure
root on bottom	F	A	C	3rd + 5th above root
root on top		A	C	F	6th + 4th below root
root in middle			C	F	A	4th below/3rd above

♪ **2: Play** each RH chord above: root on bottom and in middle 135, on top 125;
say the intervals in the chord structures above and below the root.

Progression F~B♭~F~C7~F

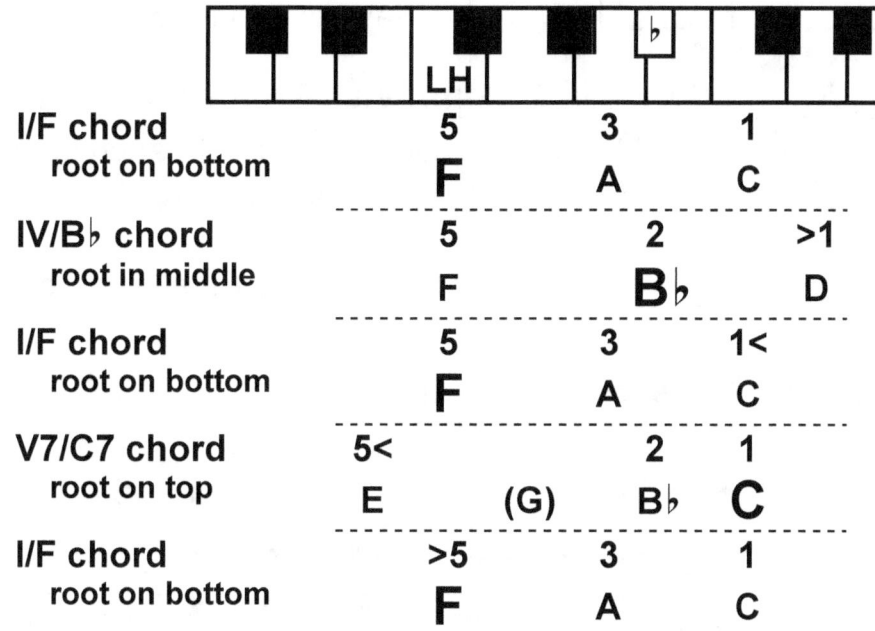

Place the LH in F position with the 2 over the black key B♭.

B♭ chord ~ move the thumb up from C to D and then play F B♭ D with fingers 5 2 1.

F chord ~ thumb back to C.

C7 chord ~ move the pinkie down from F to E and play E B♭ C with 5 2 1. Omit G.

F chord ~ pinkie back to F.

♪ **3: Practice** the left-hand F position chord progression **F~B♭~F~C7~F** above.
Prepare each chord before playing **without looking at the hands.**
Play the progression in **block** style, next **broken** style, and then repeat.

LH fingers on roots
5/F bottom
2/B♭ middle
1/C on top
B♭ 7th above C =
whole step below C

♪ **4: Learn** to recognize these shapes and where the root notes are located.

♪ **5: Improvise** each chord with hands together in block and broken styles an octave apart.
The RH fingering for the F and B♭ chords is 135, and for C7 is 145.

KEY CHANGE

SCALE ~ The whole/half-step structure stays the same in all keys. Black keys (sharps or flats) replace white keys while keeping the alphabetical name order.
MELODY ~ Pitch motion (direction and distance) stays the same in all keys.
HARMONY ~ Chord structure (I, IV, V, V7, etc.) stays the same in all keys.

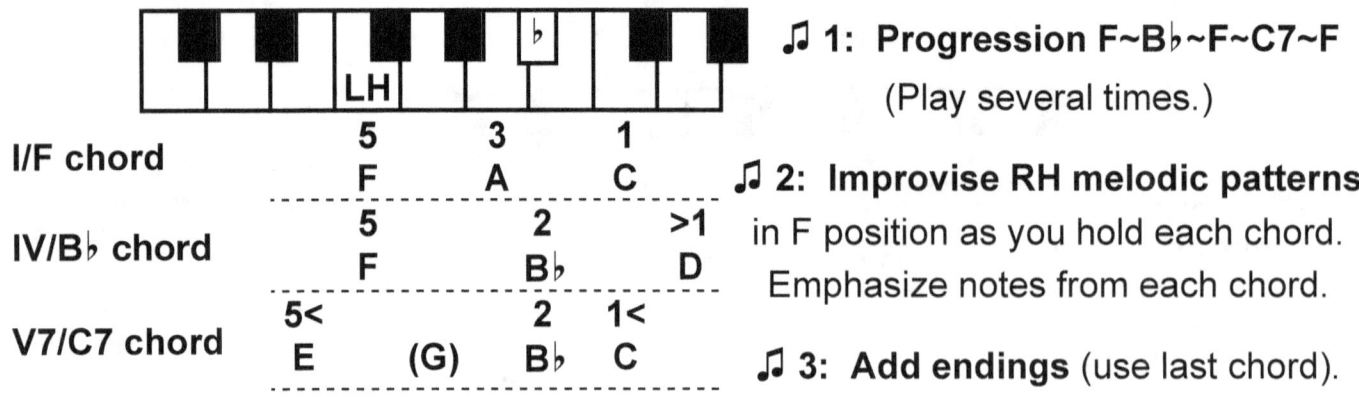

♪ 1: **Progression F~B♭~F~C7~F** (Play several times.)

♪ 2: **Improvise RH melodic patterns** in F position as you hold each chord. Emphasize notes from each chord.

♪ 3: **Add endings** (use last chord).

♪ 4: **Hot Cross Buns** (lead sheet)

♪ 5: **Old Ark's a-Moverin'** (lead sheet)

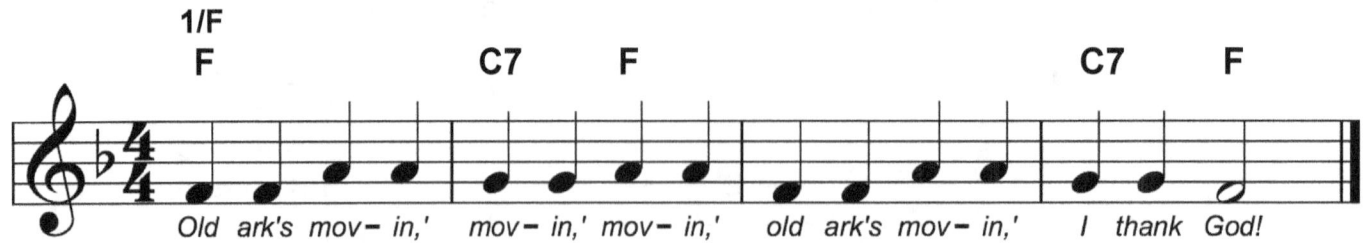

♪ 6: **Ode to Joy** (lead sheet)

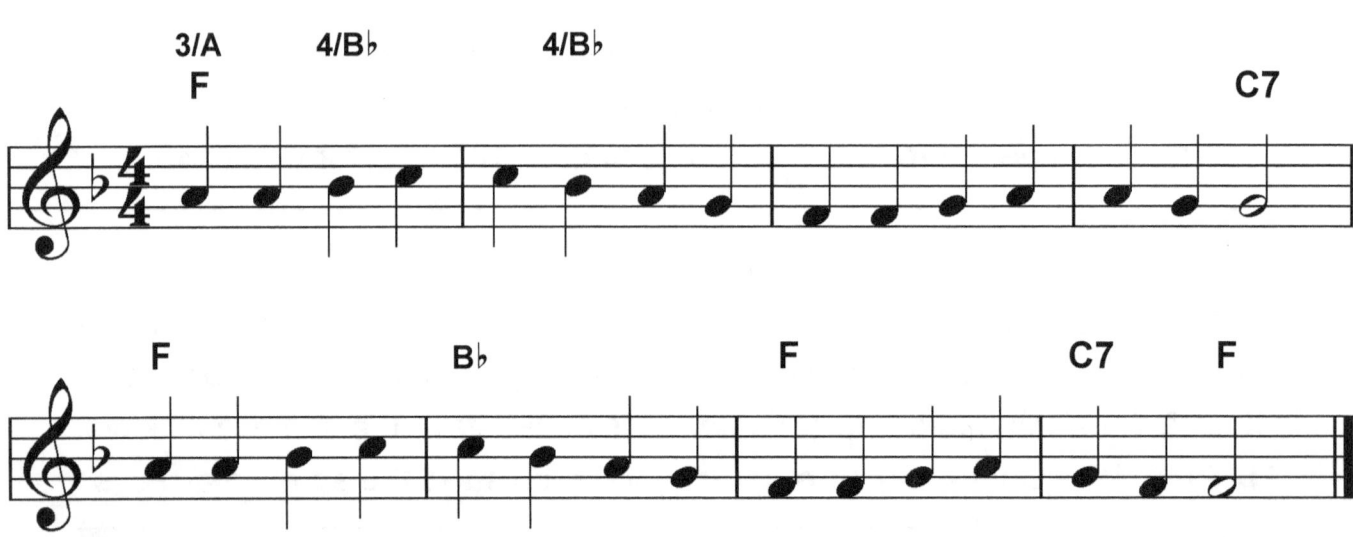

3/A ♫ 7: **Theme from the New World** (lead sheet)

3/A ♫ 8: **Skip to My Lou** (lead sheet)

Early American song and partner stealing dance.

COMPOSITION SIX

♫ 9: **Choose** an F or C7 chord for each measure that fits the melody, then **play.**

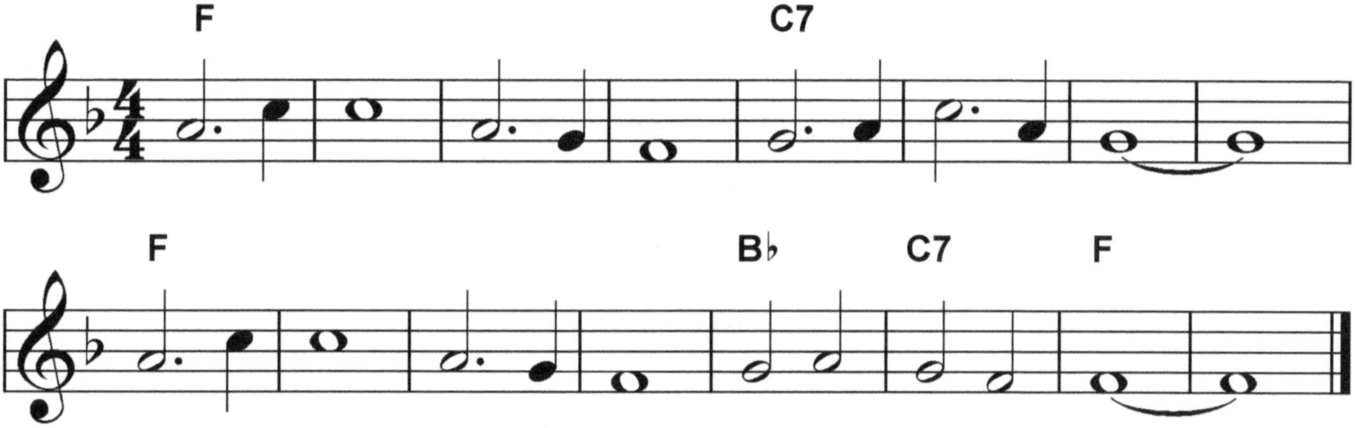

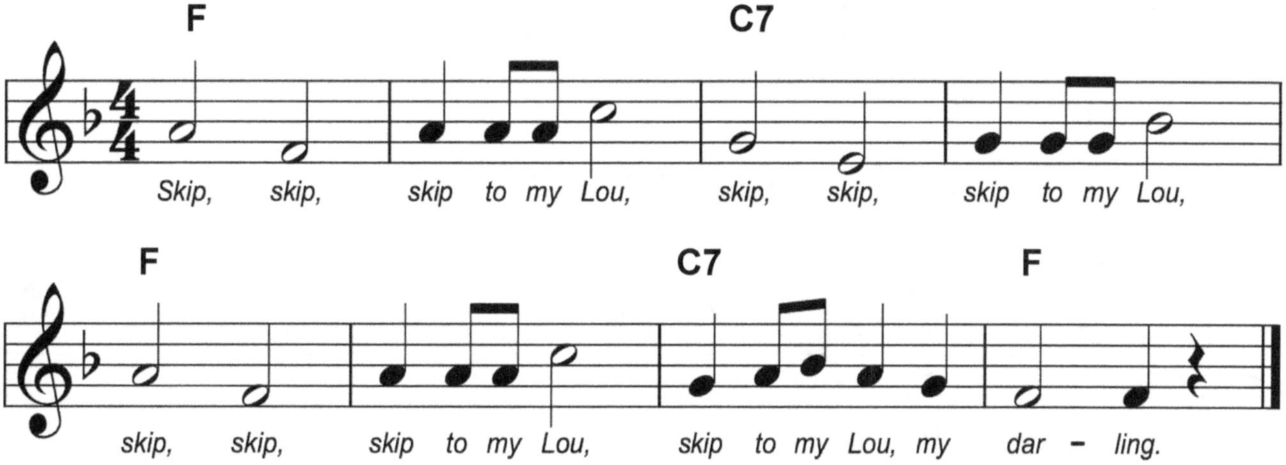

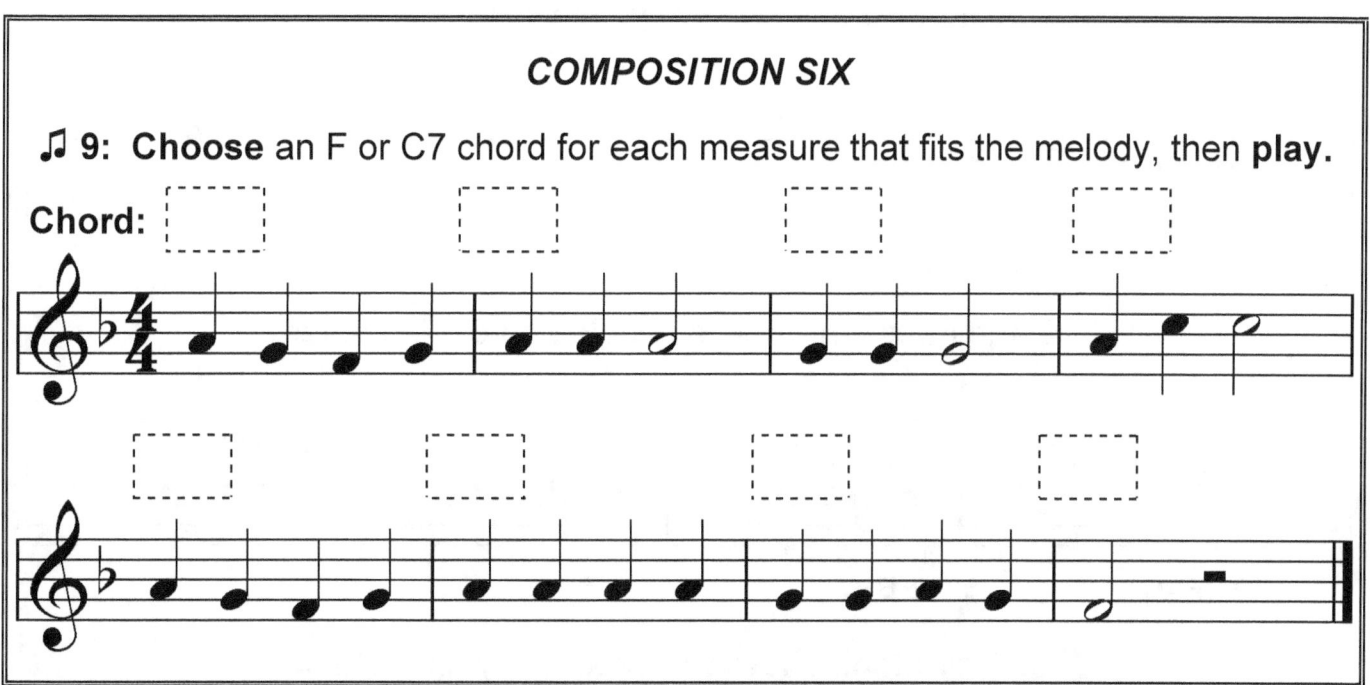

F MAJOR ~ 15 a

CHORDING STYLES

Left hand in F position below middle C.

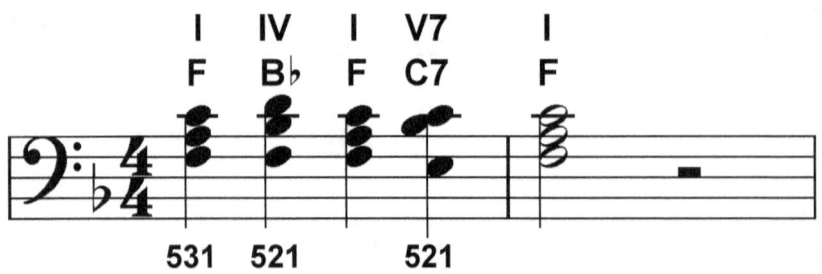

♪ 1: **Play block chords.**

♪ 2: **Play root notes** (single notes).

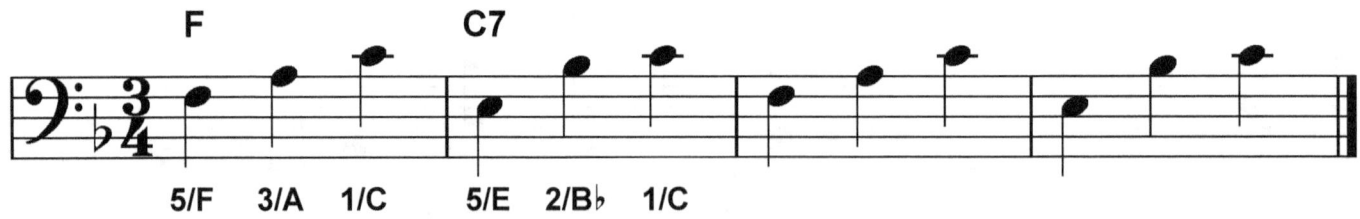

♪ 3: **Play broken chords** (single notes).

♪ 4: **Play broken chords** (single and double notes).

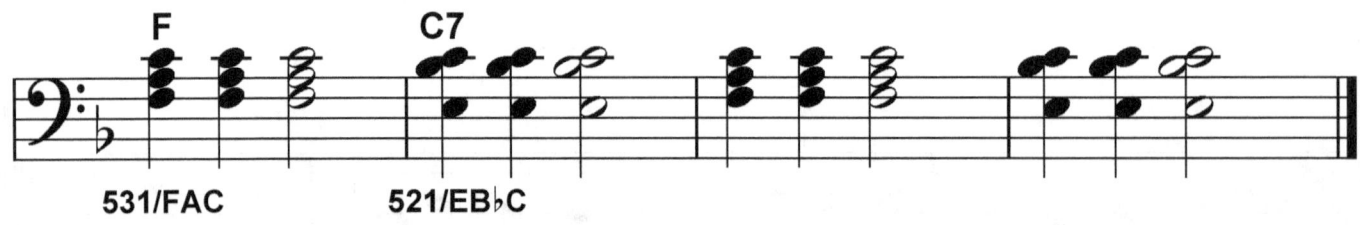

♪ 5: **Play block chords** (repeated rhythm pattern).

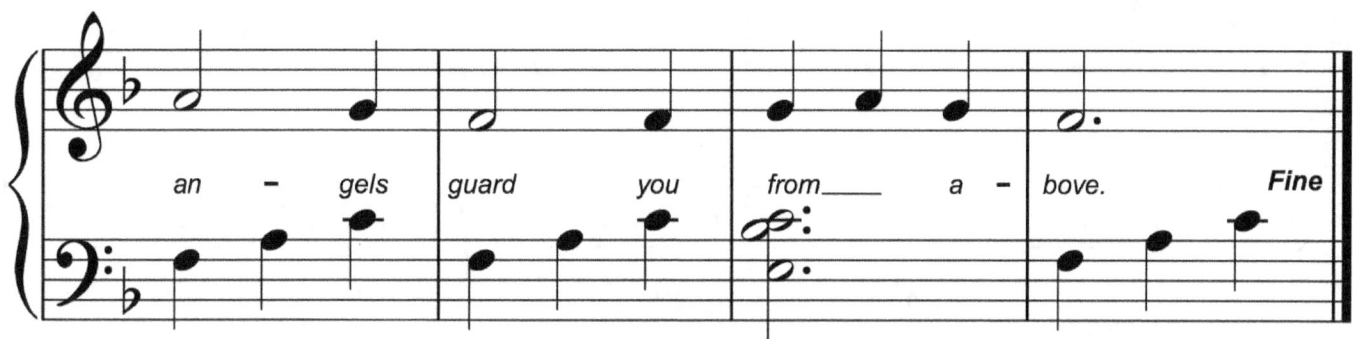
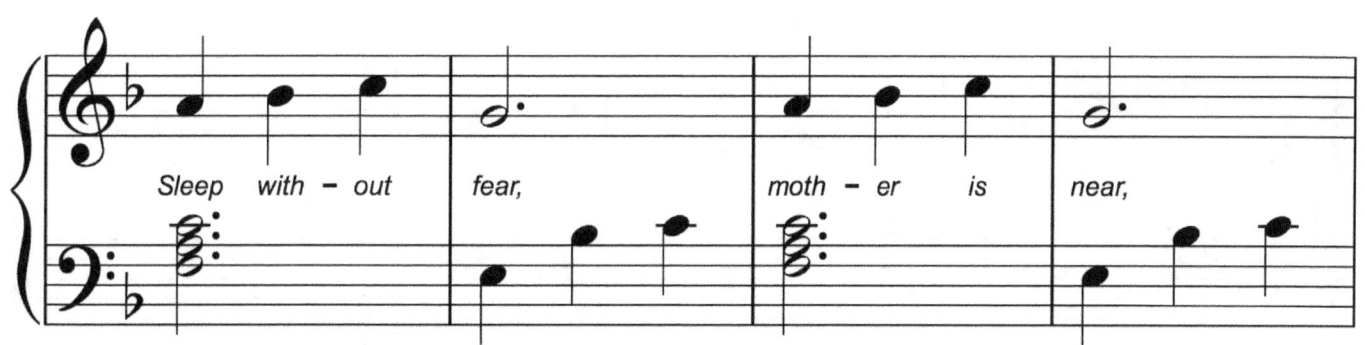
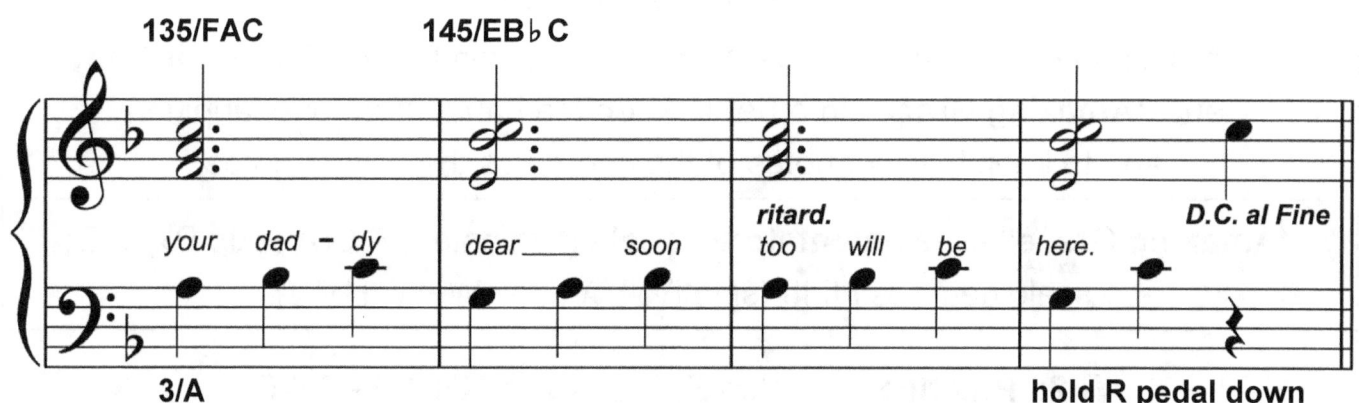

HAND CHANGES

Music that was not originally written for a keyboard, such as **"Happy Birthday,"** often requires awkward fingering and/or hand position changes. The least movement possible should be used. Prepare each new hand change or finger extension **before playing notes in that position.**

A **fermata** "𝄐" sign means to **pause or hold momentarily** on that note.

Melody from song "Good Morning to All" in 1893.

♫ 1: Happy Birthday

PARTIAL CHORDS

The partial chords F B♭ and C7 are arranged to accompany **"Happy Birthday"** and **"Amazing Grace"** in order to keep the hands from overlapping, and to keep the root notes of the chords as the lowest notes.

"Amazing Grace" uses a **pentatonic scale** (five notes) F G A (skip B♭) C D; scale degrees I II III (skip IV) V VI (W~W~W+H~W).

♫ 2: **Practice** C D (skip E) F G A with RH 1 2 - 3 4 5.

♫ 3: Amazing Grace

In 1847, *Southern Harmony*, W. Walker added John Newton's words to the traditional "New Britain."

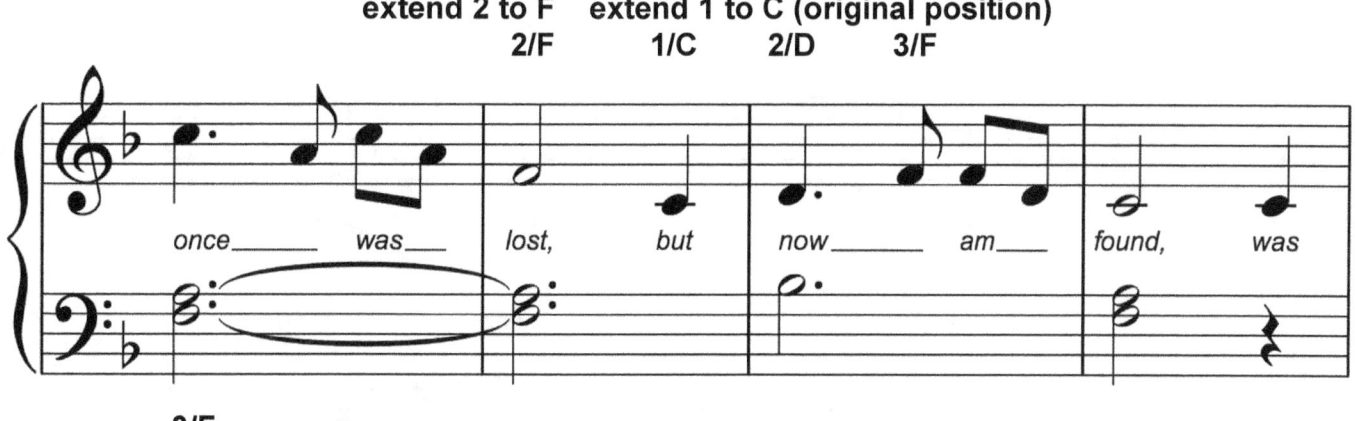

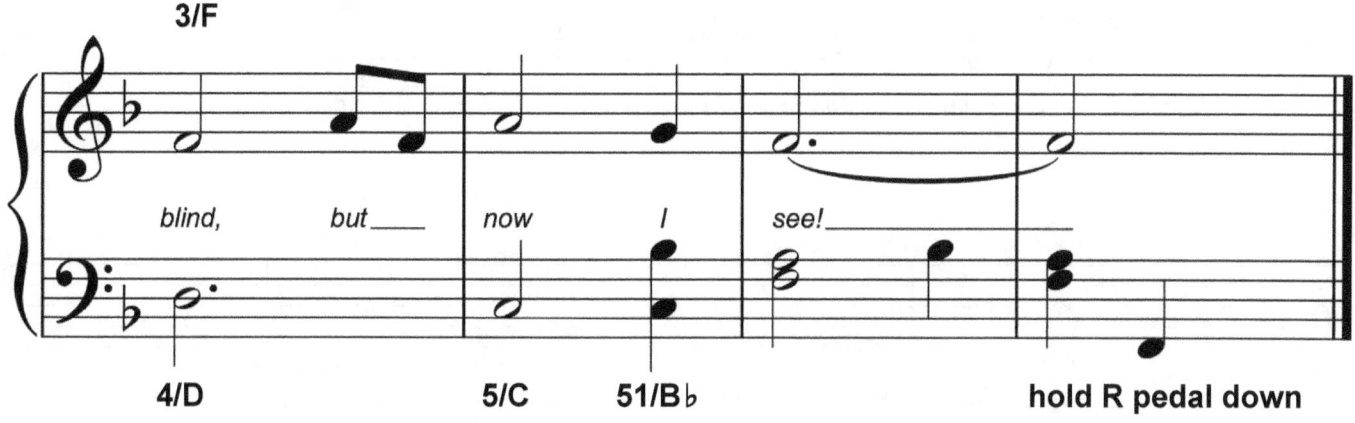

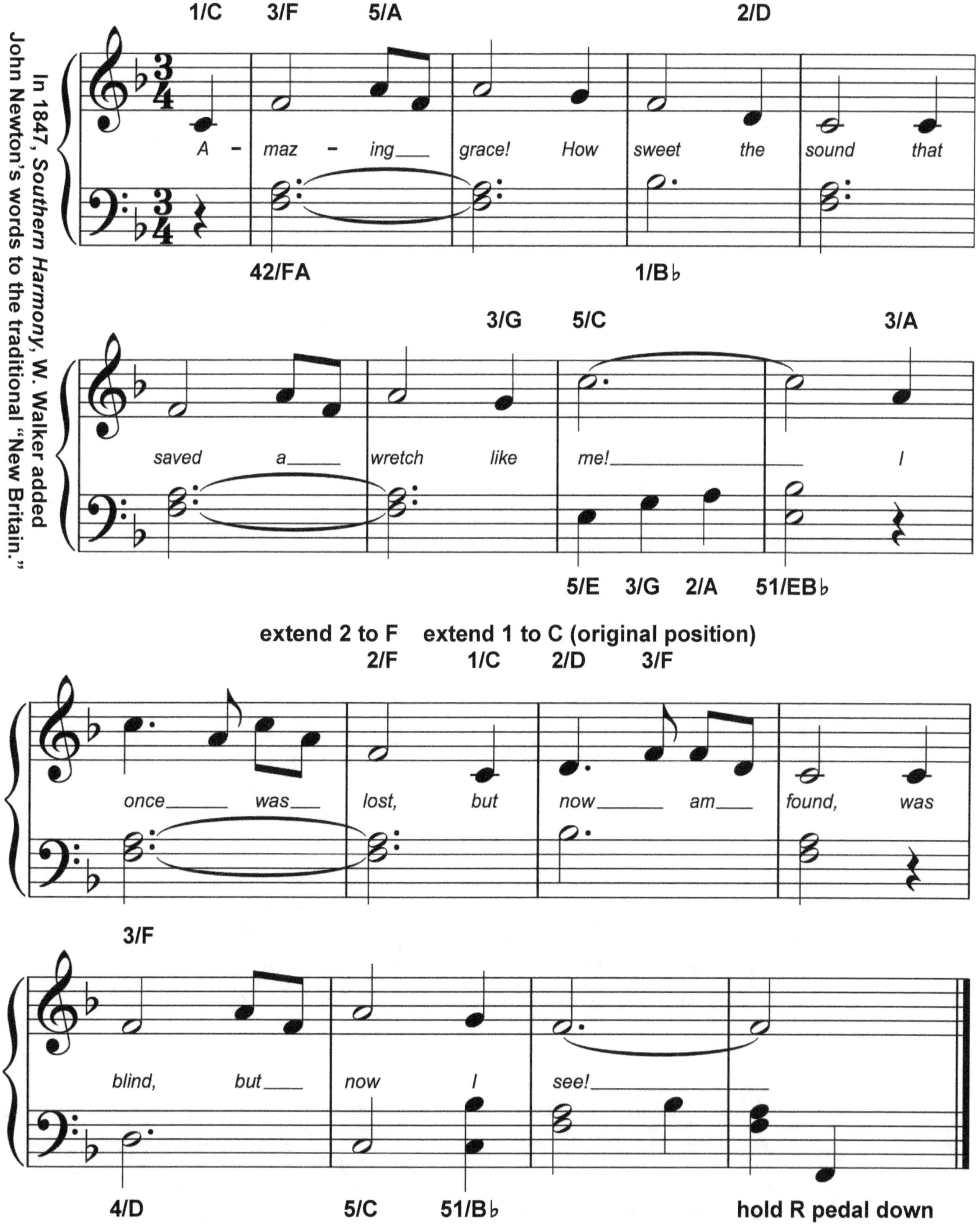

F MAJOR ~ 16 a

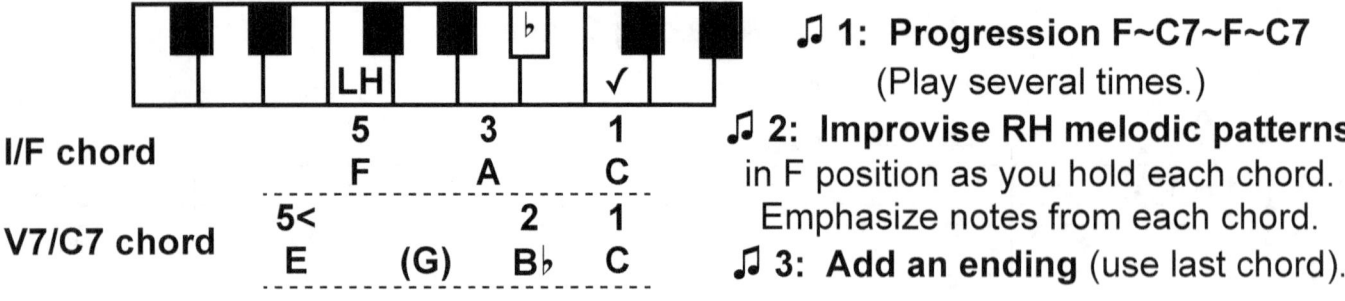

I/F chord — 5 3 1 / F A C
V7/C7 chord — 5< 2 1 / E (G) B♭ C

♫ 1: **Progression F~C7~F~C7**
(Play several times.)
♫ 2: **Improvise RH melodic patterns**
in F position as you hold each chord.
Emphasize notes from each chord.
♫ 3: **Add an ending** (use last chord).

♫ 4: **Marianne** (lead sheet)

Improvise LH chords for measures 4, 8, 12, and 16 for the RH whole notes
to keep the rhythm and sound of the music continuous.

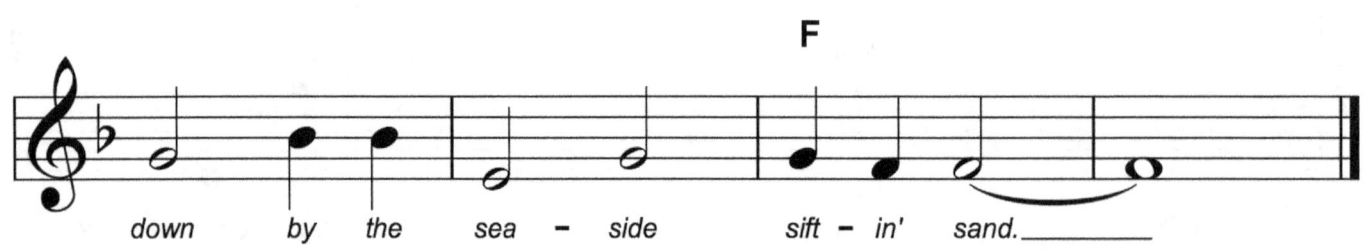

♪ 5: Ode to Joy

1: Progression F~B♭~F~C7~F
(Play several times.)

SONG ACCOMPANIMENT
Sing the lyrics to these melodies.

Play RH chords and **LH roots**
alternating ♫2 ♫4; together ♫3 ♫6.
LH option, double the root notes.

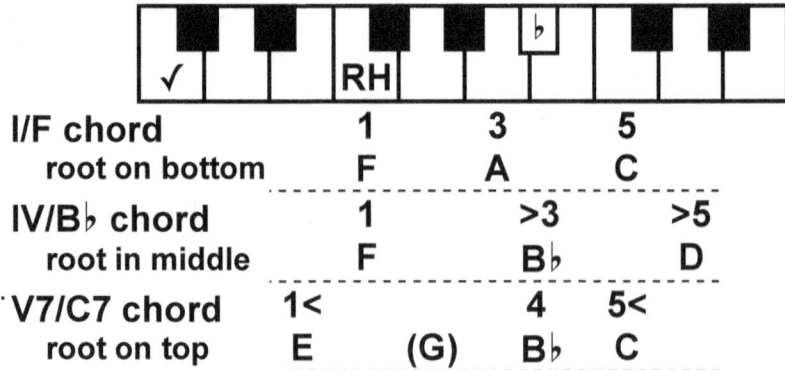

		1	3	5
I/F chord root on bottom		F	A	C
IV/B♭ chord root in middle	1	>3	>5	
	F	B♭	D	
V7/C7 chord root on top	1<		4	5<
	E	(G)	B♭	C

♫ 2: Frère Jacques

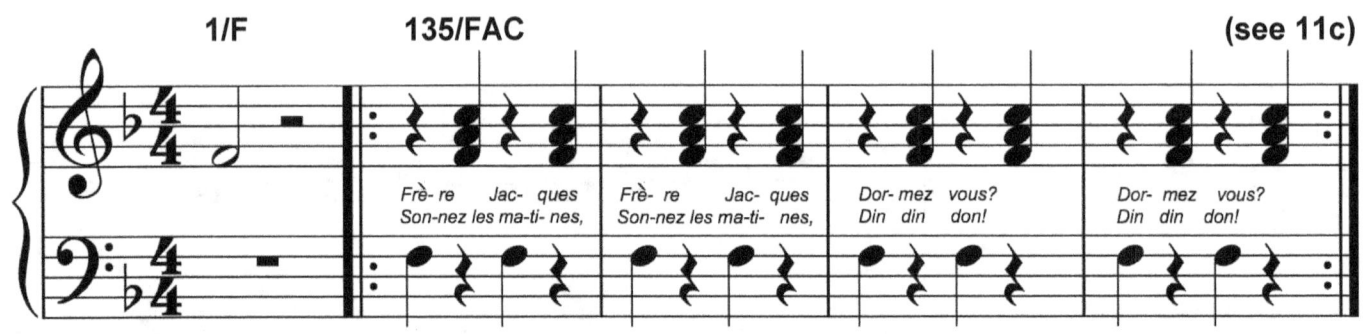

♫ 3: Happy Birthday

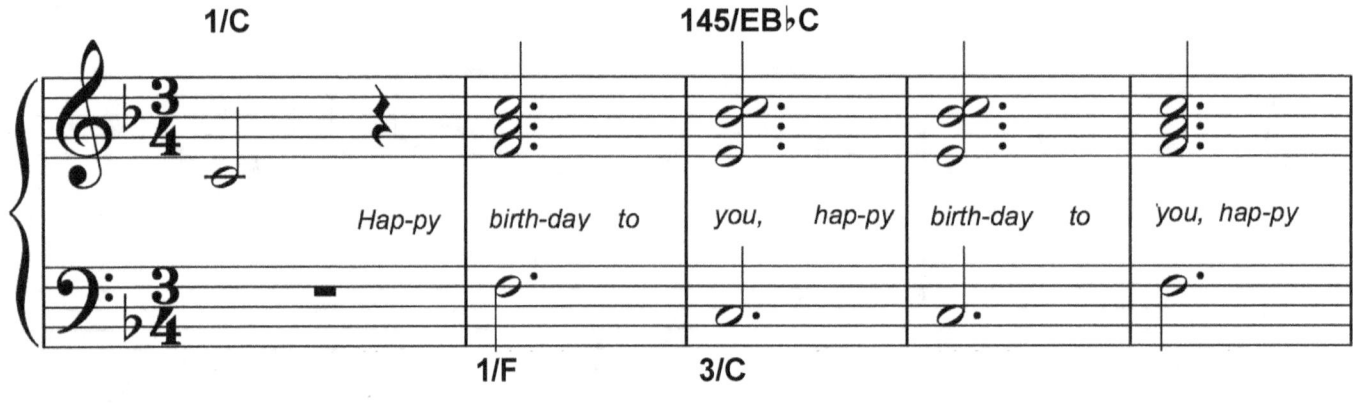

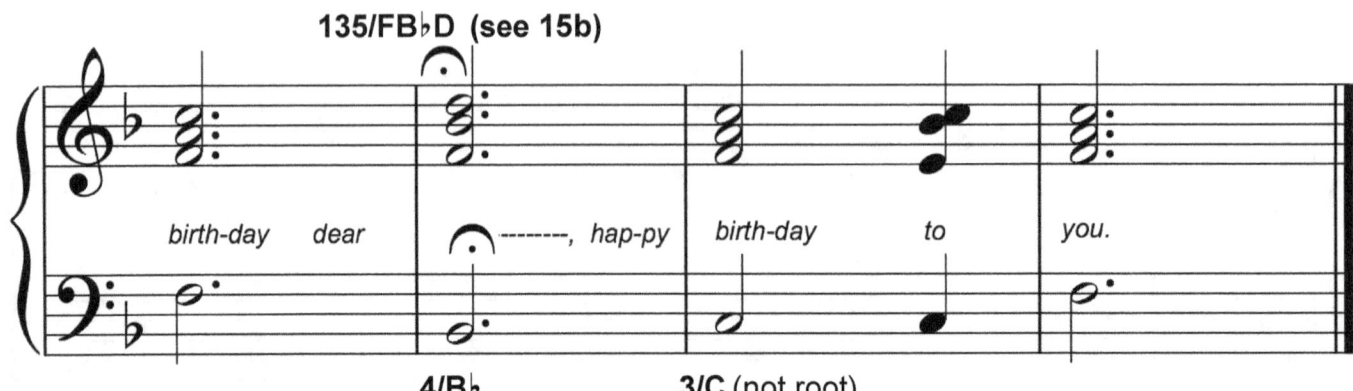

♫ 4: Mary Had a Little Lamb

♫ 5: Progression F~B♭~F~C7~F lowered position
(Play several times.)

Accompany the song lyrics with **RH chords** in extended C position and **LH roots** for a fuller sound.

LH option, double root notes.

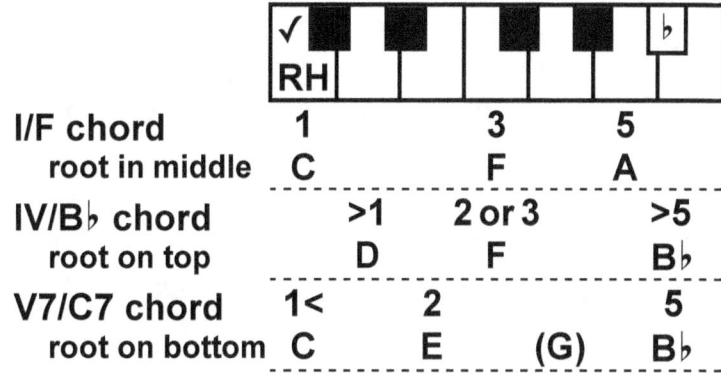

♫ 6: Happy Birthday

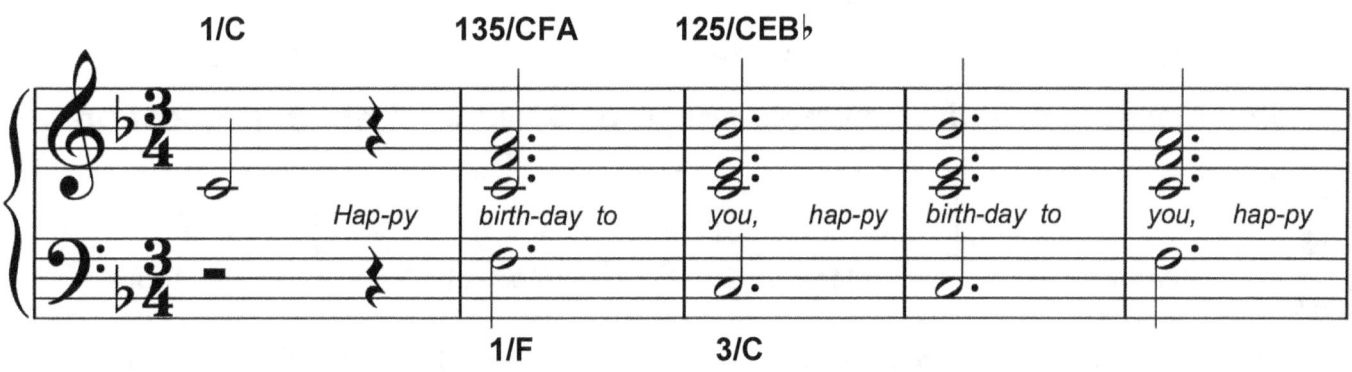

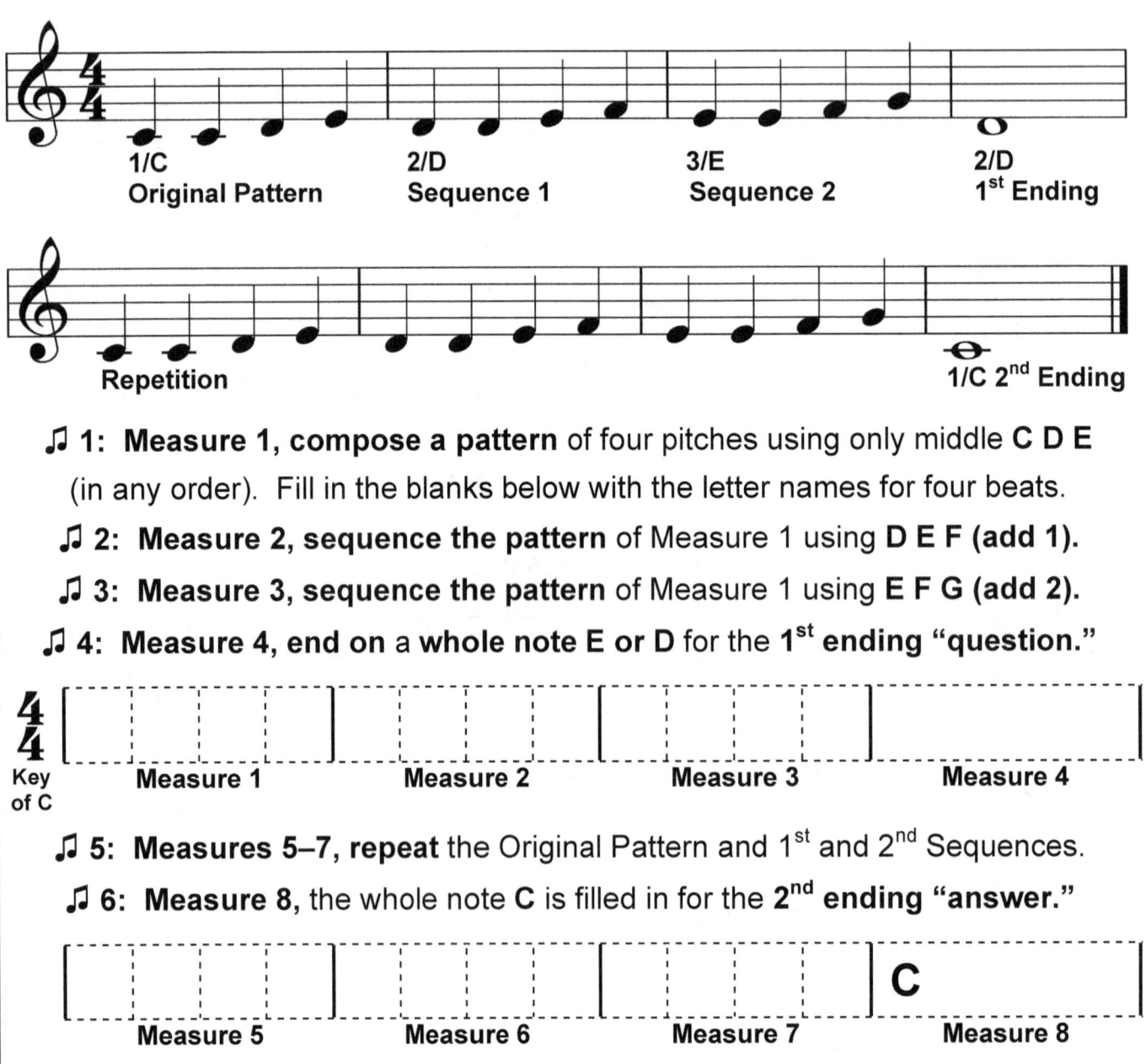

COMPOSITION SEVEN

♪ **8: Notate the melody** (treble staff). **Choose and notate** a whole note chord, C, F, or G7, in each (bass staff) measure that shares notes with the melody.

Notation Guide ~ Key of C

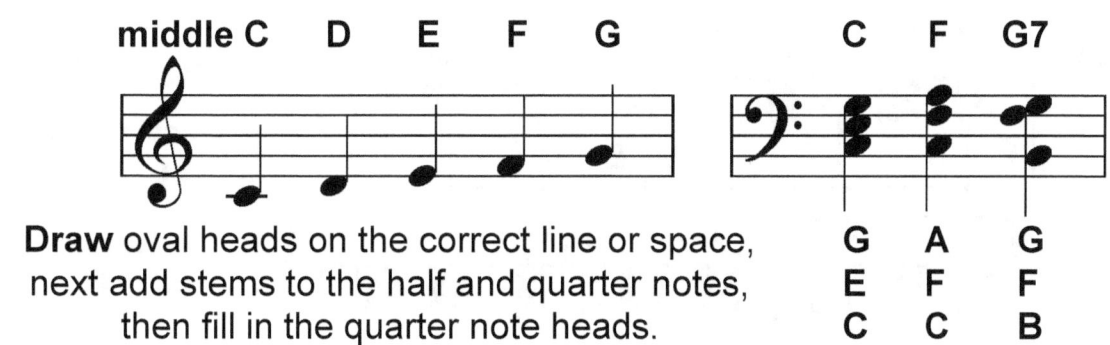

Draw oval heads on the correct line or space,
next add stems to the half and quarter notes,
then fill in the quarter note heads.

```
        G   A   G
        E   F   F
        C   C   B
```

♪ **9: Play and improvise C chord** at the end of the melody, **hold R pedal down**.

♪ **10: Draw a staff;** renotate the melody with chords in the key of F Major.

G MAJOR ~ 17 a

TRANSPOSITION

Any one of the white or black pitches may be the **keynote** on which the **whole~whole~half~whole~whole~whole~half** major scale structure is built. **The keynote,** also called **the key,** can be **transposed** (moved) higher or lower. The pitches in the scale change, **but the whole/half step pattern remains.**

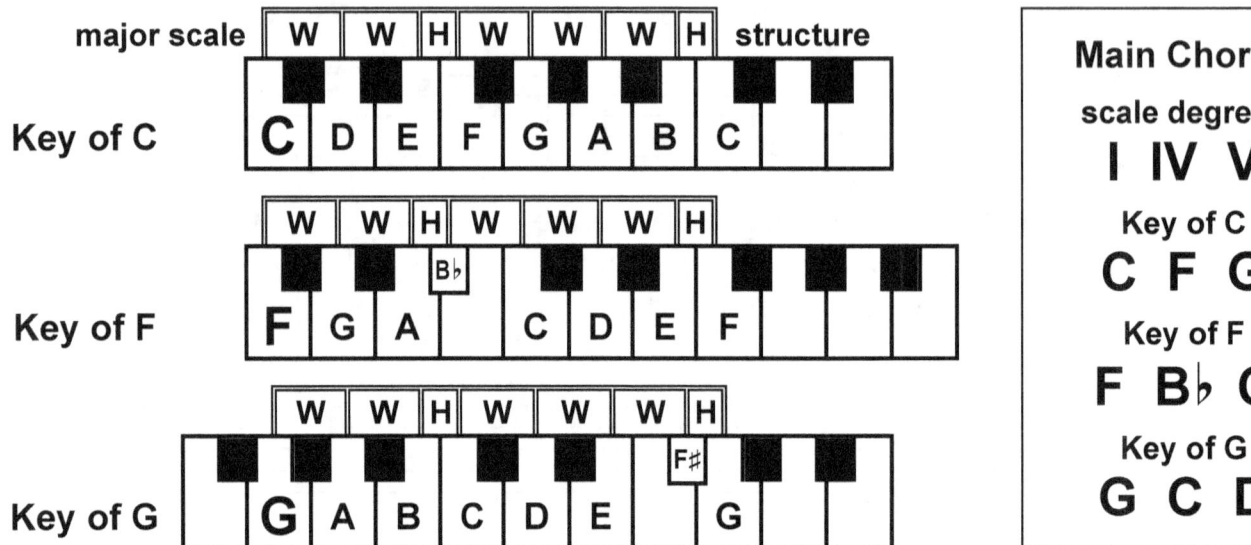

♪ **1: Play** the C, F, and G major scales with the RH 2 ♭ starting on the keynote and **say** the major scale structure. For example, **Key of G:** "G, **whole step** A, **whole step** B, **half step** C, **whole step** D, **whole step** E, **whole step** F♯, **half step** G."

KEY SIGNATURES

Key signatures are placed between the **clef sign** and the **time signature.** The key signature shows the notes that are to be **sharped or flatted in all octaves and measures.**

Key of C Major
no sharps or flats

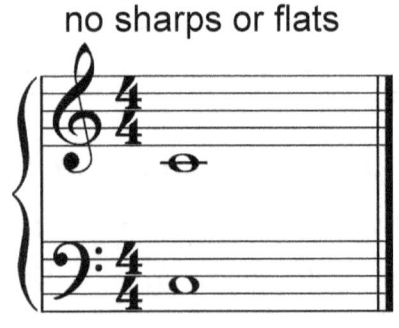

Key of F Major
one flat, **B♭**

Key of G Major
one sharp, **F♯**

Key of G ~ Hand Positions

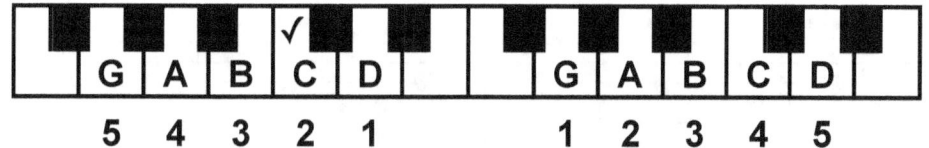

♫ **2: Practice** each hand alone, then hands together.

♫ **3:** Practice **stepping and skipping** in G position.

♫ **4: Ode to Joy**

♫ 1: **French Shop** ~ fill in the beats

♫ 2: Chorale

German J.S. Bach "Jesu, Joy of Man's Desiring."

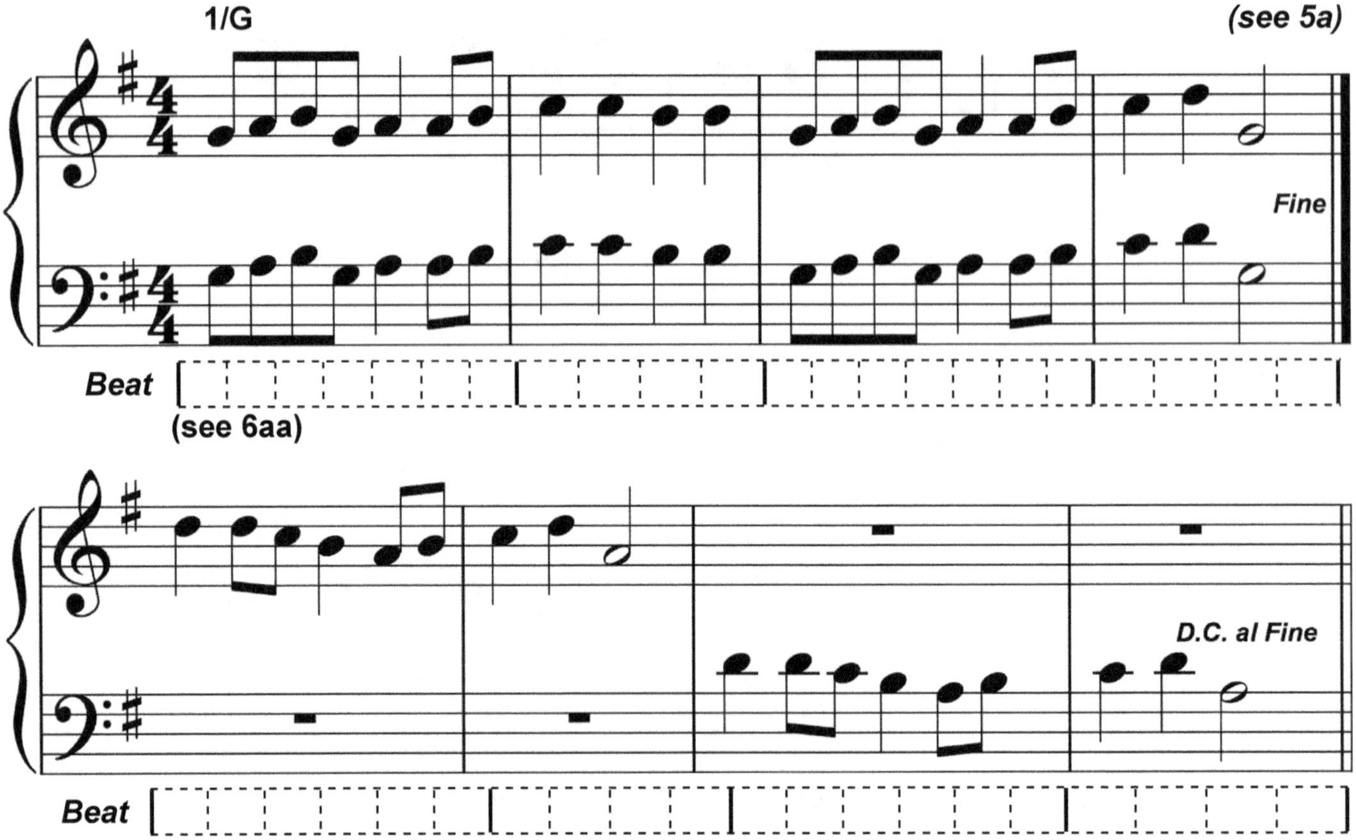

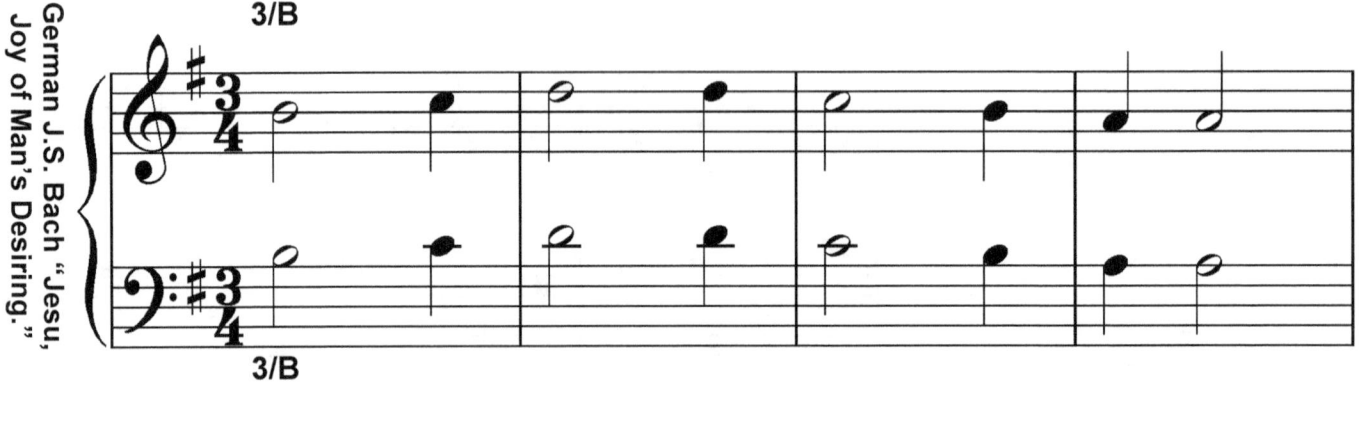

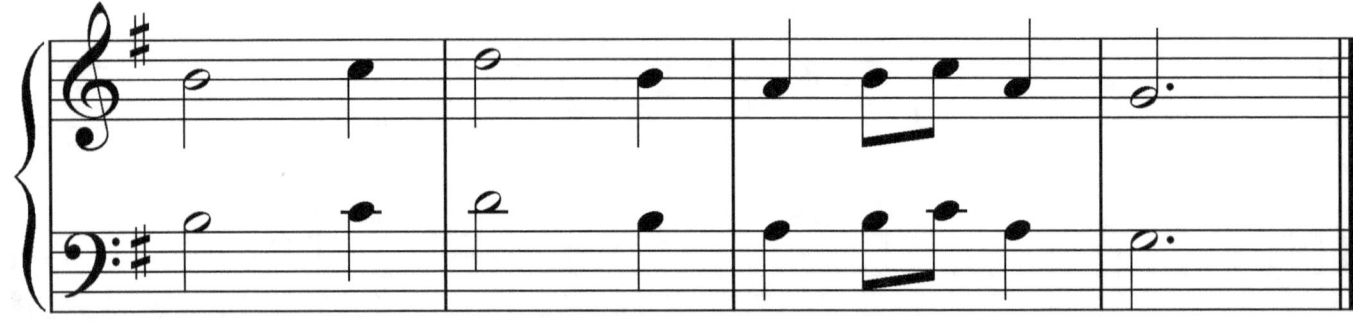

♫ 3: Skip to My Lou

♫ 4: Morning (pentatonic I II III — V VI of major scale)

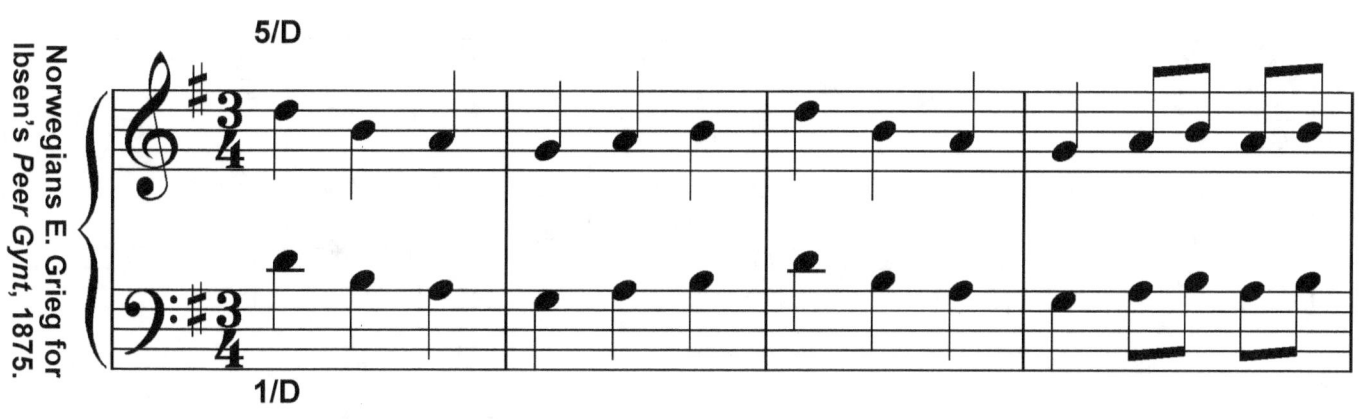

Norwegians E. Grieg for Ibsen's *Peer Gynt*, 1875.

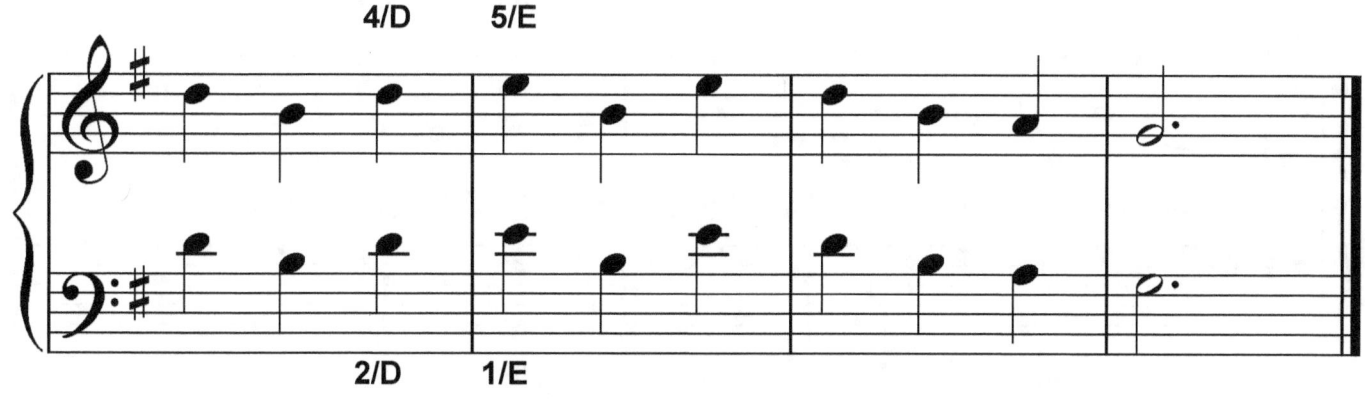

Key of G ~ D Hand Positions

F♯
D
E
G
A
√
D
E
F♯
G
A
5 4 3 2 1
1 2 3 4 5

1/D
3/F♯
3/F♯
step/2nd
skip/3rd
4th
5th
2nd
3rd
4th
5th
5/D
3/F♯
3/F♯

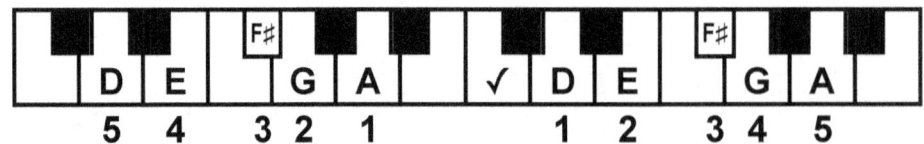

♫1: Play intervals

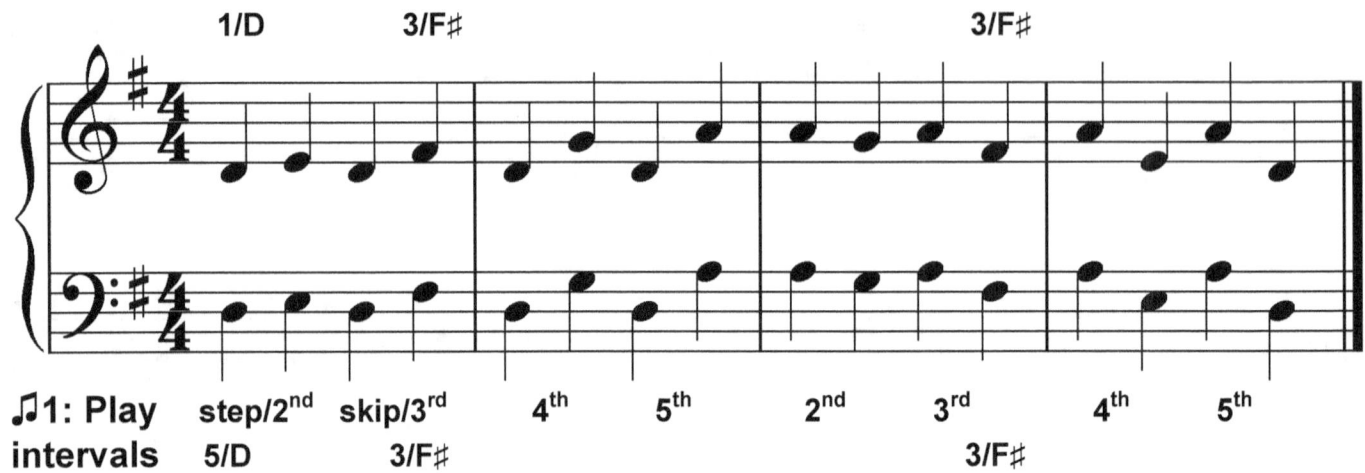

♫ 2: Aura Lee

Circle the 4ths in measures 1, 2, 4, 5, and 6.

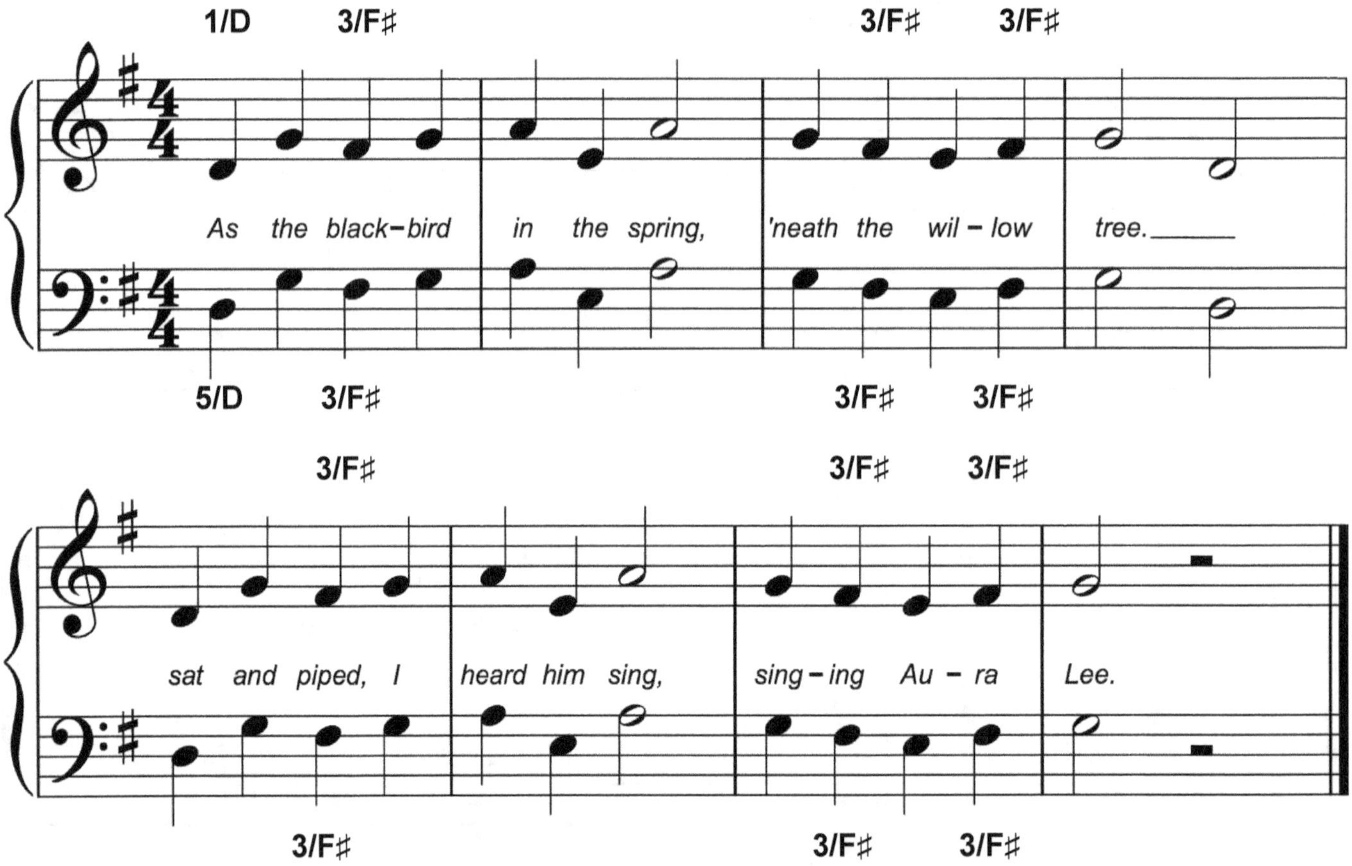

1/D
3/F♯
3/F♯
3/F♯
As the black–bird in the spring, 'neath the wil – low tree.
5/D
3/F♯
3/F♯
3/F♯
3/F♯
3/F♯
3/F♯
sat and piped, I heard him sing, sing – ing Au – ra Lee.
3/F♯
3/F♯
3/F♯

♫ 3: Alleluia

♫ 4: Southern Roses Waltz

G MAJOR ~ 18 a

SCALE DEGREES

Each **degree** (step) in a scale is identified by the same **Roman numeral** in all keys.

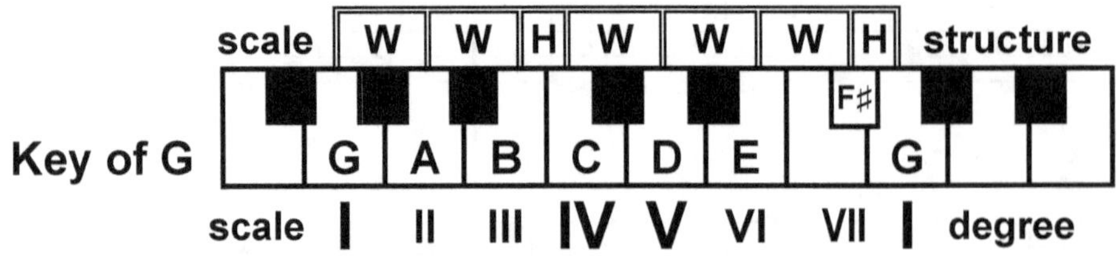

scale structure	W	W	H	W	W	W	H
Key of G	G	A	B	C	D	E	F#	G
scale degree	I	II	III	**IV**	**V**	VI	VII	I

The **major chords** are built on the **I** (tonic), **IV** (subdominant), and **V** (dominant).

CHORD STRUCTURE

The structure of chords includes the **root** + a **3rd** + a **5th** + an optional **7th**.

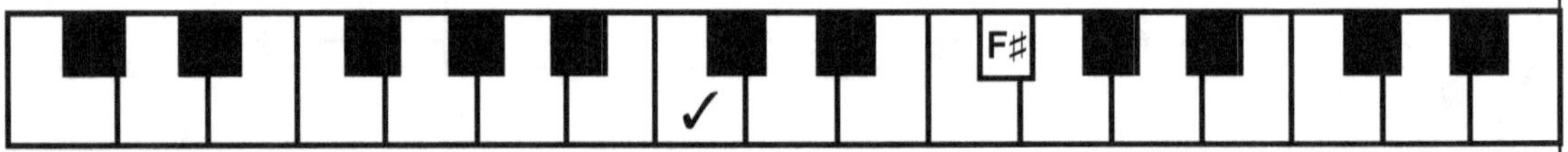

IV/C chord	C	E	G		
I/G chord			G	B	D
V/D chord				D	F#	A
V7/D7 chord				D	F#	(A)	C
	5th below G subdominant	keynote tonic	5th above G dominant	omit the A

♪ **1: Play and say** the chord numeral and name: "IV and C," etc.

CHORD INVERSION

Chords are **inverted** (turned upside down) by **moving the octave of pitches**.

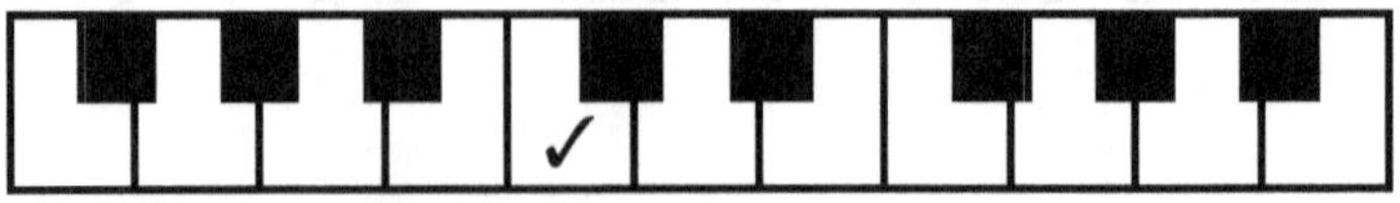

					structure
root on bottom	G	B	D		3rd + 5th above root
root on top		B	D	G	6th + 4th below root
root in middle			D	G	B	4th below/3rd above

♪ **2: Play** each RH chord above: root on bottom and in middle 135, on top 125; **say** the intervals in the chord structures above and below the root.

Progression G~C~G~D7~G

I/G chord root on bottom	5 **G**	3 B	1 D	**Place** the LH in G position with the 5 near the black key F♯.
IV/C chord root in middle	5 G	2 **C**	>1 E	**C chord** ~ move the thumb up from D to E and then play G C E with fingers 5 2 1.
I/G chord root on bottom	5 **G**	3 B	1< D	**G chord** ~ thumb back to D.
V7/D7 chord root on top	5< F♯	(A)	2 C	1 **D**	**D7 chord** ~ move the pinkie down from G to F♯ and play F♯ C D with 5 2 1. Omit A.
I/G chord root on bottom	>5 **G**	3 B	1 D	**G chord** ~ pinkie back to G.

♪ **3: Practice** the left hand G position chord progression **G~C~G~D7~G** above.
Prepare each chord before playing without looking at the hands.
Play the progression in **block** style, next **broken** style, and then repeat.

LH fingers on roots
5/G bottom
2/C middle
1/D on top
C 7th above D =
whole step below D

♪ **4: Learn** to recognize these shapes and where the root notes are located.

♪ **5: Improvise** each chord with hands together in
block and broken styles an octave apart.
The RH fingering for the G and C chords is 135, and for the D7 is 145.

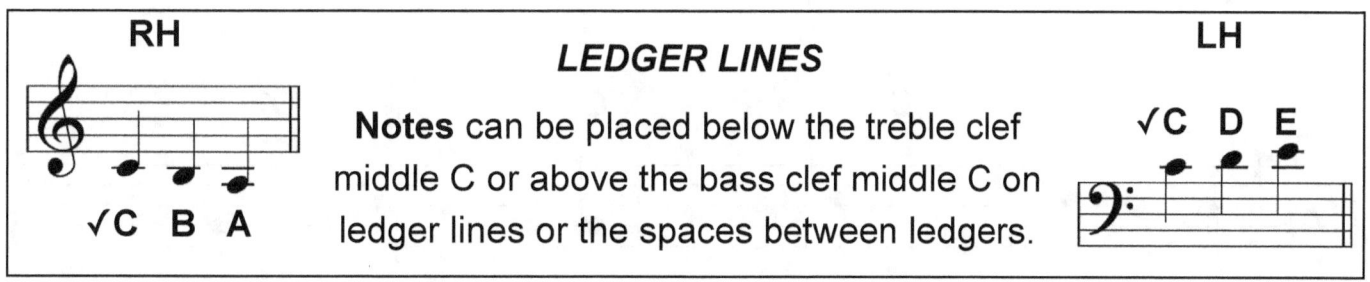

LEDGER LINES

Notes can be placed below the treble clef middle C or above the bass clef middle C on ledger lines or the spaces between ledgers.

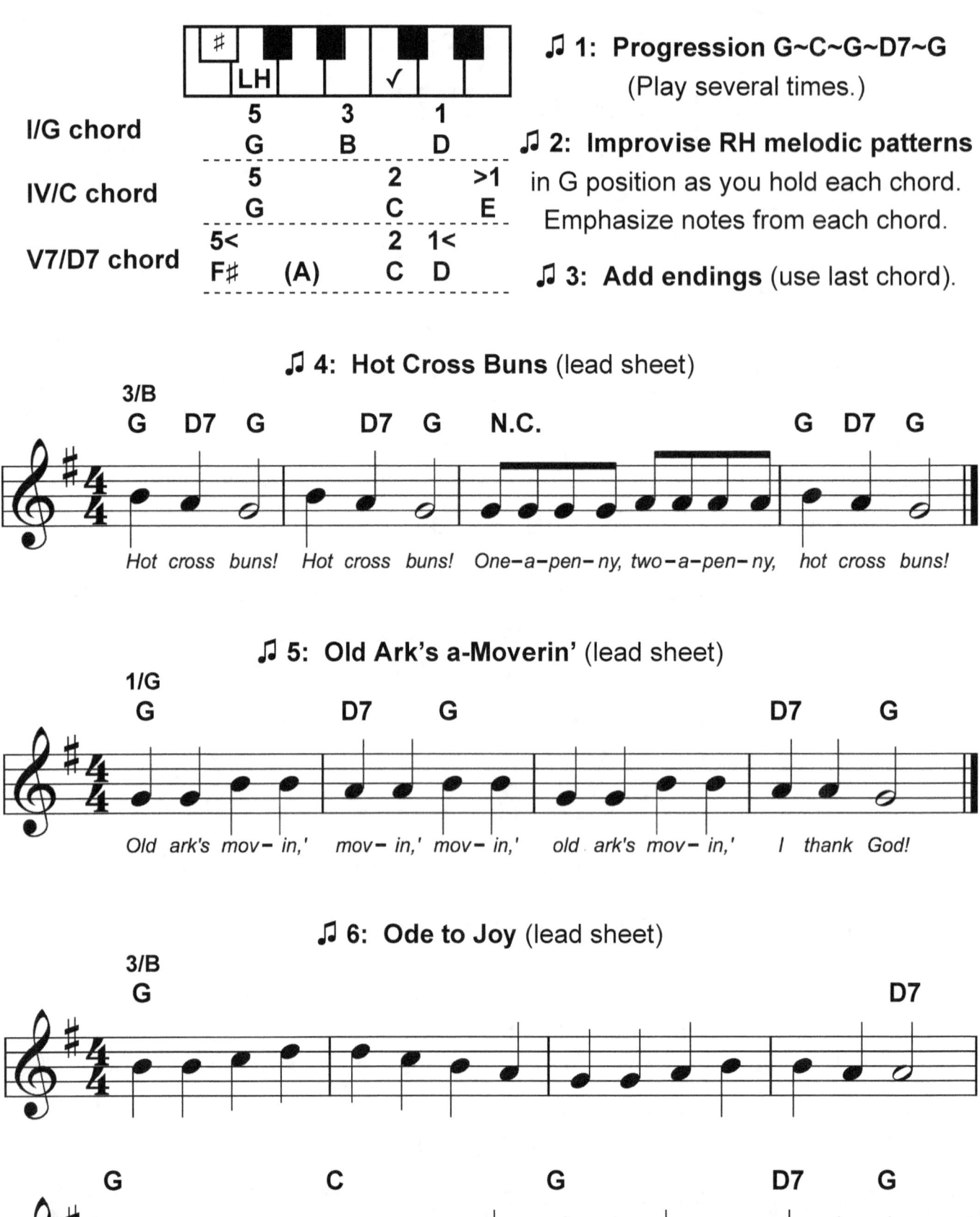

♪ 7: Mary Had a Little Lamb (lead sheet)

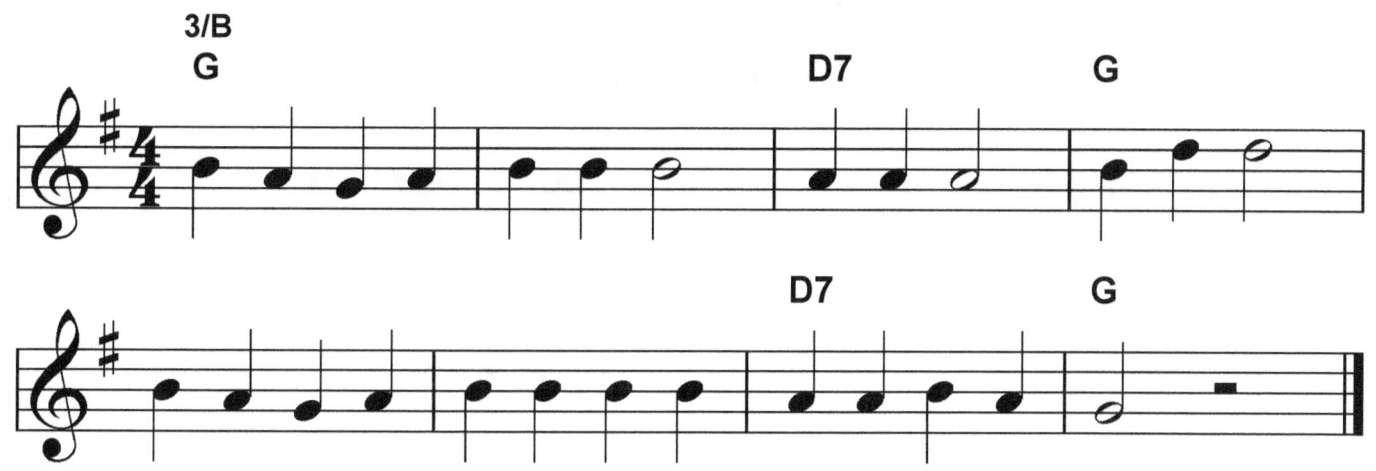

♪ 8: French Shop (lead sheet)

♪ 9: Skip to My Lou (lead sheet)

G MAJOR ~ 19 a 83

DOTTED QUARTER NOTES

A dot after a note increases its length by one-half.

| Half Note | Dotted Half Note |
| 𝅗𝅥 = 2 beats | 𝅗𝅥. = 3 beats |

| Quarter Note | Dotted Quarter Note |
| ♩ = 1 beat | ♩. = 1½ beats |

The **tie** in b) is replaced by the **dot** in c).

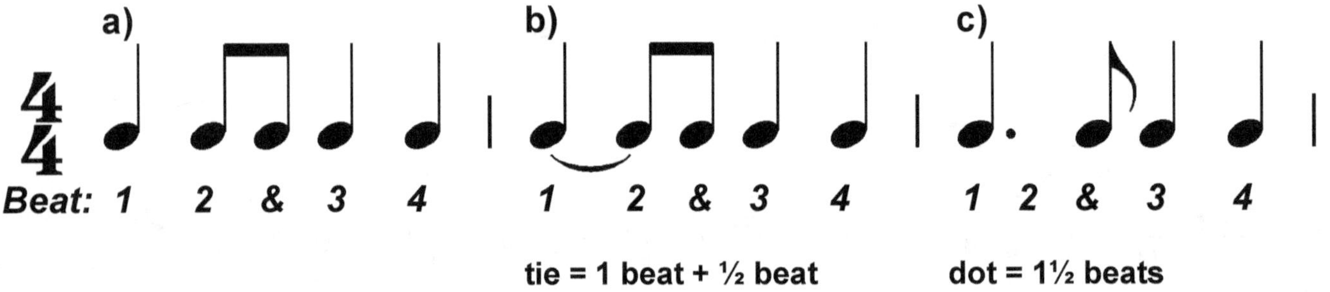

a)   b)   c)

4/4

Beat: 1 2 & 3 4 | 1 2 & 3 4 | 1 2 & 3 4

tie = 1 beat + ½ beat   dot = 1½ beats

♪ **1: Count** aloud as you **clap** examples a, b, and c above.

♪ **2: Ode to Joy**

Practice playing dotted quarter notes, count the beats below.

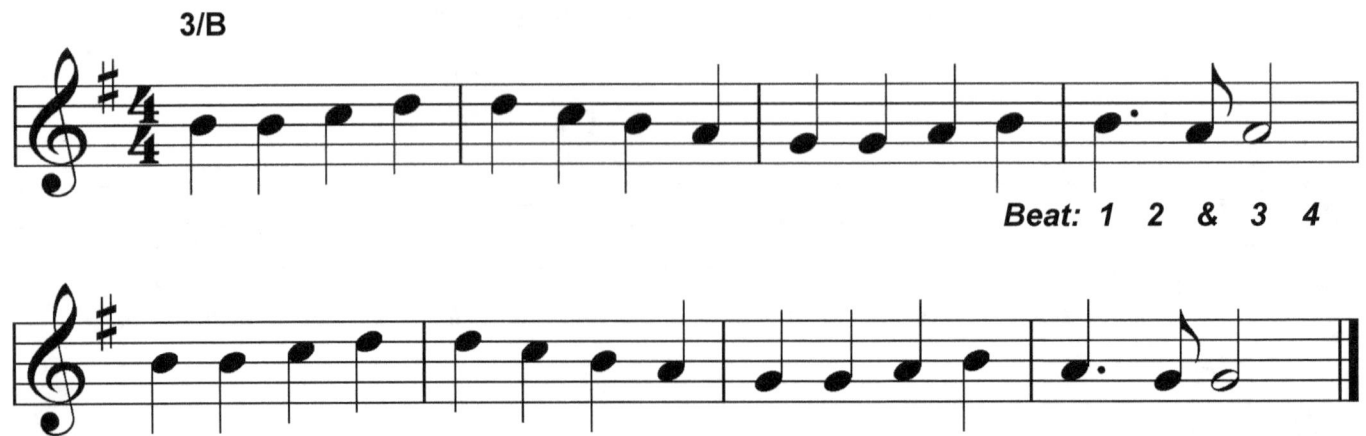

Beat: 1 2 & 3 4

"Mozart Melody" next page: RH in G position, LH in C position below middle C; LH uses single chord notes for the accompaniment.

♫ 3: Mozart Melody

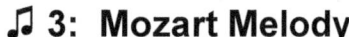

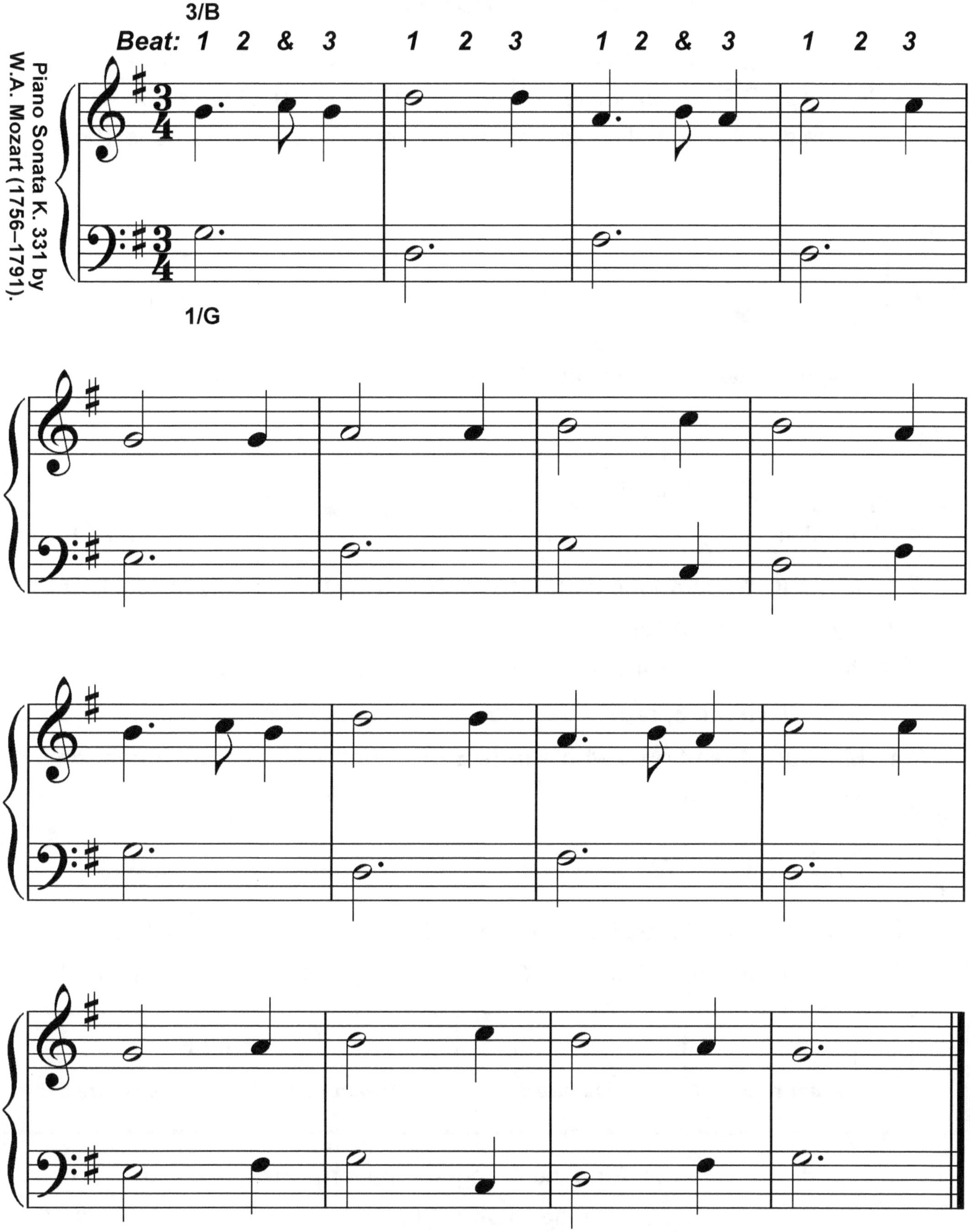
3/B
Beat: 1 2 & 3 1 2 3 1 2 & 3 1 2 3
Piano Sonata K. 331 by W.A. Mozart (1756–1791).
1/G

COMPOSITION EIGHT

A **retrograde** (reverse) turns a pitch motion pattern **backward** (CCDE to EDCC for example). (A sequence of an original pattern keeps the same direction and distance, but starts higher or lower; see page 16c.)

Example of four notes from **"Ode to Joy" (Key of C)**.

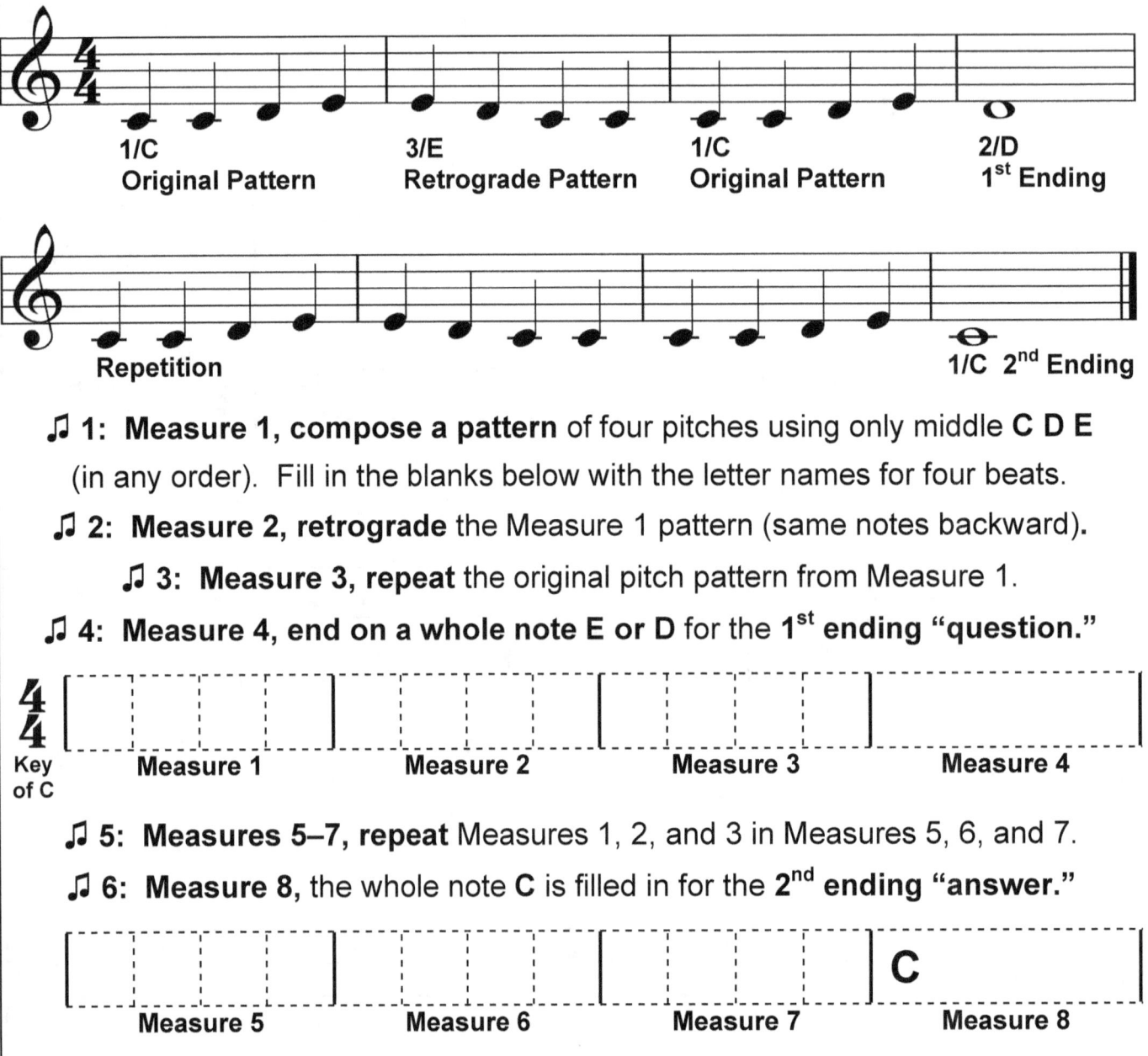

♪ 1: **Measure 1, compose a pattern** of four pitches using only middle **C D E** (in any order). Fill in the blanks below with the letter names for four beats.

♪ 2: **Measure 2, retrograde** the Measure 1 pattern (same notes backward).

♪ 3: **Measure 3, repeat** the original pitch pattern from Measure 1.

♪ 4: **Measure 4, end on a whole note E or D** for the **1ˢᵗ ending "question."**

♪ 5: **Measures 5–7, repeat** Measures 1, 2, and 3 in Measures 5, 6, and 7.

♪ 6: **Measure 8,** the whole note **C** is filled in for the **2ⁿᵈ ending "answer."**

♪ 7: **Find** the retrograde patterns in **"Ode to Joy" (19a).**

COMPOSITION EIGHT

♪ **8:** **Notate the melody** (treble staff). **Choose and notate** a whole note chord, C, F, or G7, in each (bass staff) measure that shares notes with the melody.

Notation Guide ~ Key of C

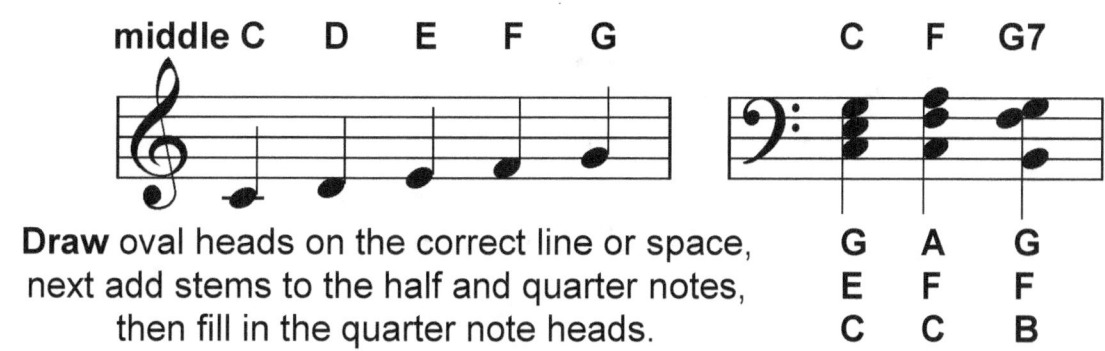

Draw oval heads on the correct line or space,
next add stems to the half and quarter notes,
then fill in the quarter note heads.

```
       C    F    G7
       G    A    G
       E    F    F
       C    C    B
```

♪ **9:** **Play and improvise C chord** at the end of the melody, **hold R pedal down.**

♪ **10:** **Draw a staff;** renotate the melody with chords in the key of G Major.

G MAJOR ~ 20 a

CHORDING STYLES

Left hand in G position below middle C.

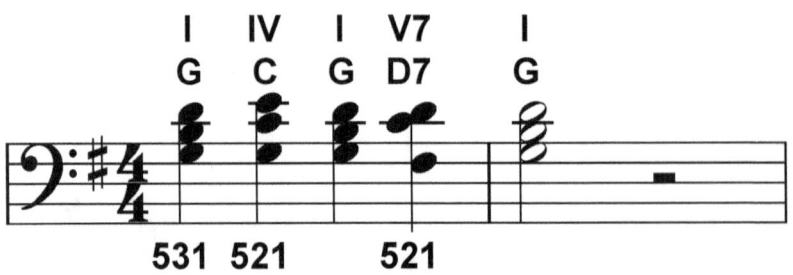

♩ **1: Play** block chords.

♩ **2: Play** broken chords G and D7 with single and double notes.

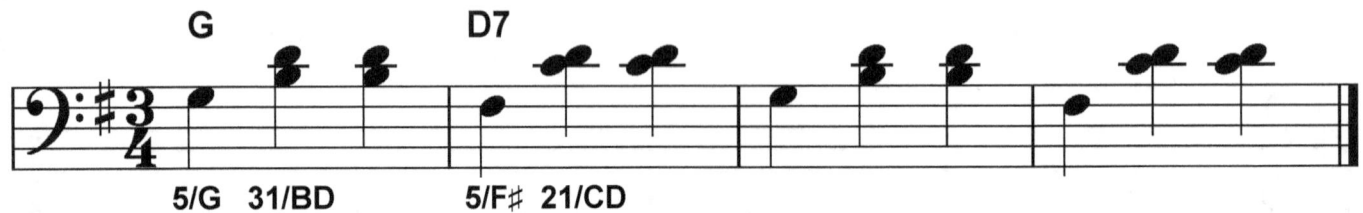

♩ **3: Play** broken chords with single and double "um-pah-pah" notes.

♩ **4: Play** partial chords in F position with extended LH 5.

♫ 5: Czerny Melody

Play in a faster tempo called **"allegretto"** in Italian.

The single and double chord notes in the arrangement
provide support for the melody's rhythmic drive and clarity;
block chords in measures 8 and 16 emphasize the endings of phrases.

♫ 1: Ode to Joy

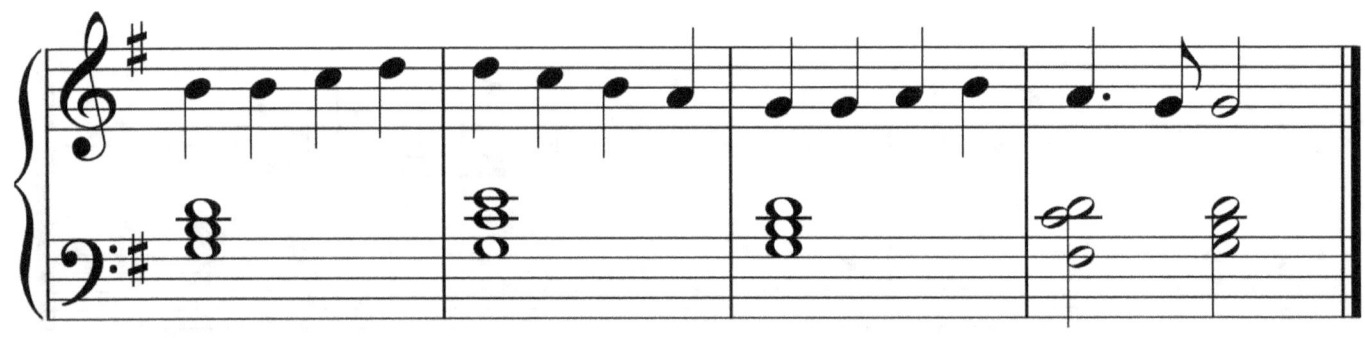

♫ 2: German Folk Song

The change to single note accompaniment in measure 8 brings out the end of a phrase. The held chord followed by silence in measures 13 and 14 gives clarity to the highest melody note and ending.

🎵 1: Progression G~C~G~D7~G
(Play several times.)

SONG ACCOMPANIMENT
Sing the lyrics to these melodies.

Play RH chords and **LH roots** alternating 🎵2 🎵4; together 🎵3 🎵6.

LH option, double the root notes.

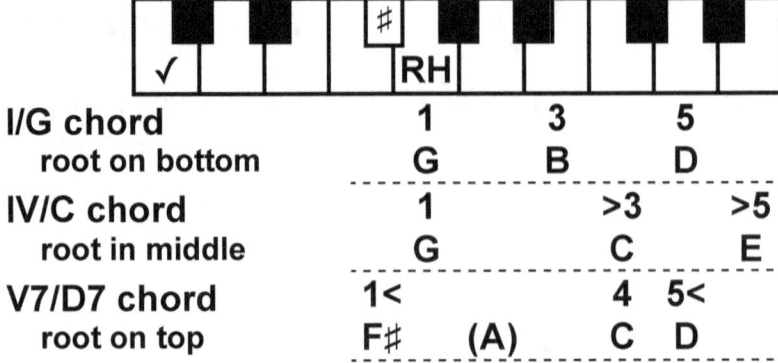

I/G chord root on bottom	1 G		3 B	5 D
IV/C chord root in middle	1 G		>3 C	>5 E
V7/D7 chord root on top	1< F♯	(A)	4 C	5< D

🎵 2: Frère Jacques

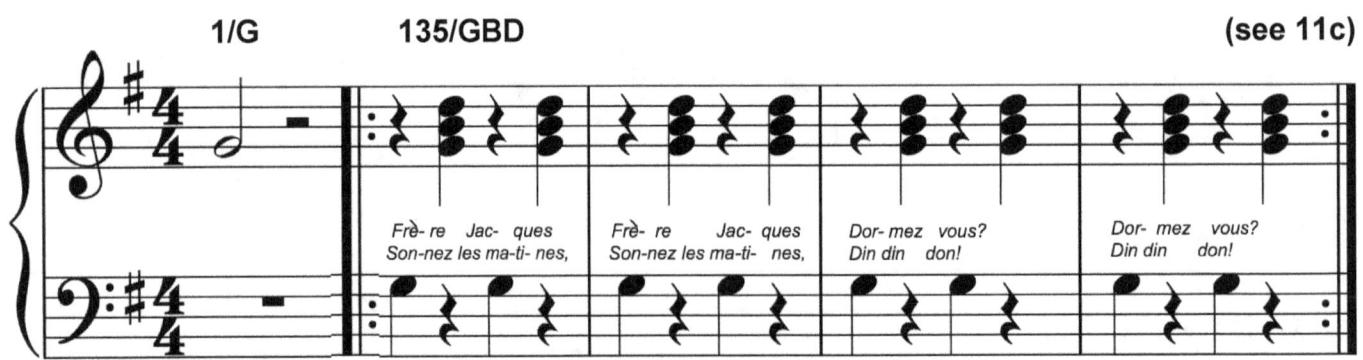

🎵 3: Happy Birthday

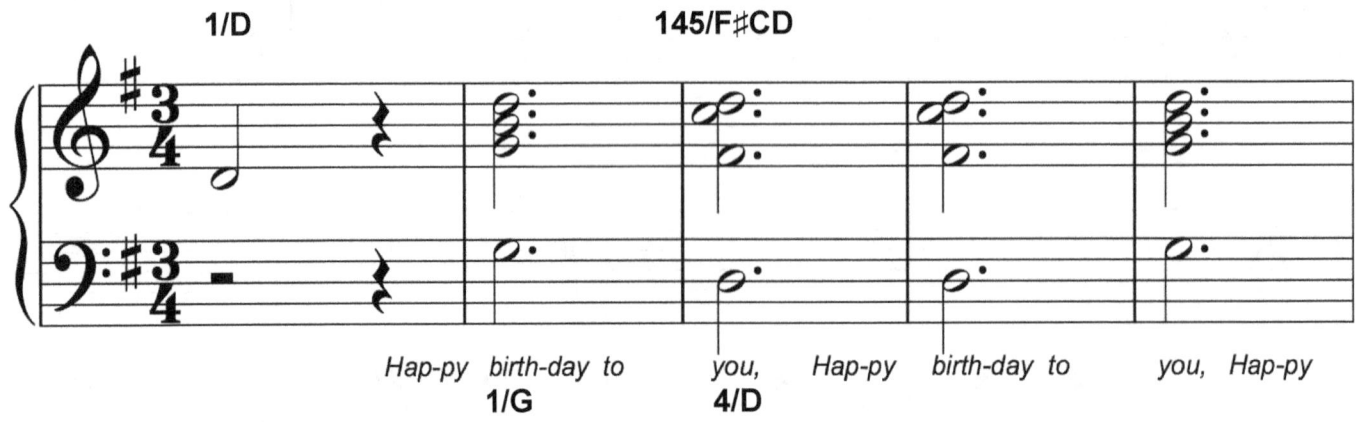

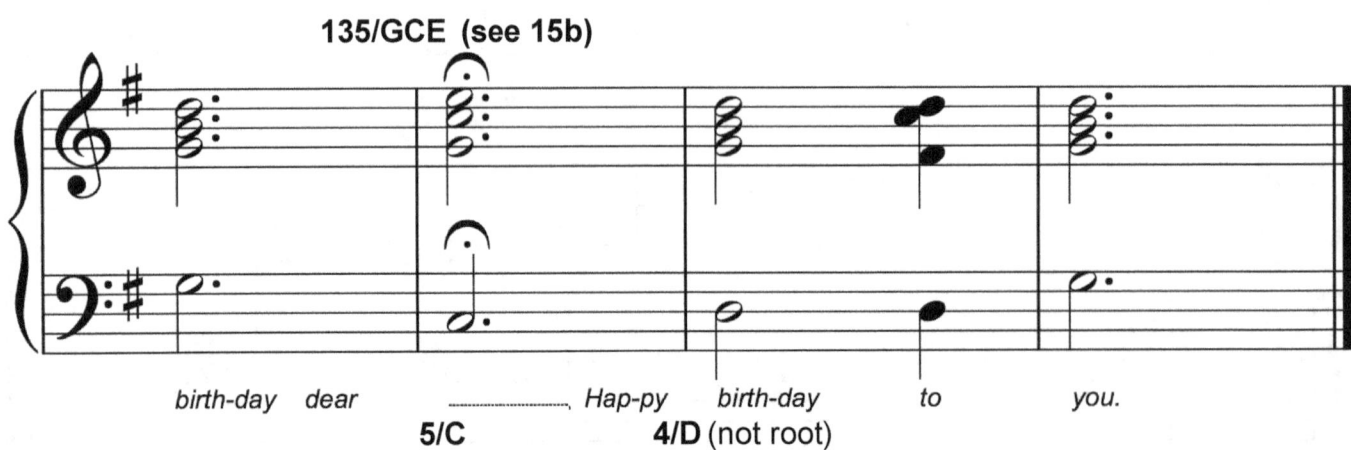

♫ 4: Mary Had a Little Lamb

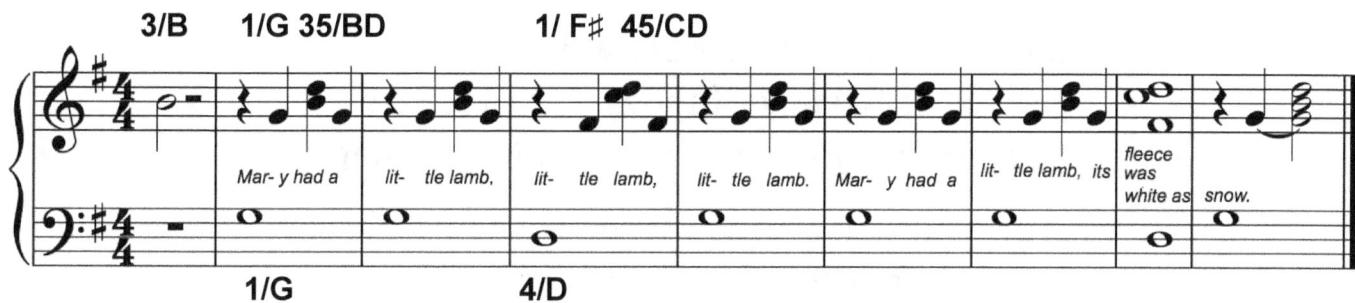

♫ 5: Progression G~C~G~D7~G
lowered position
(Play several times.)

Accompany the song lyrics with **RH chords** in extended D position with **LH roots** for a fuller sound.

LH option, double root notes.

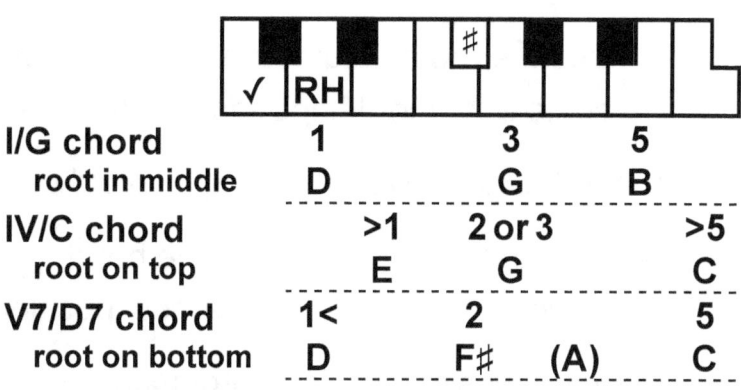

	✓	RH			
I/G chord root in middle		1 D		3 G	5 B
IV/C chord root on top		>1 E		2 or 3 G	>5 C
V7/D7 chord root on bottom		1< D	2 F♯	(A)	5 C

♫ 6: Happy Birthday

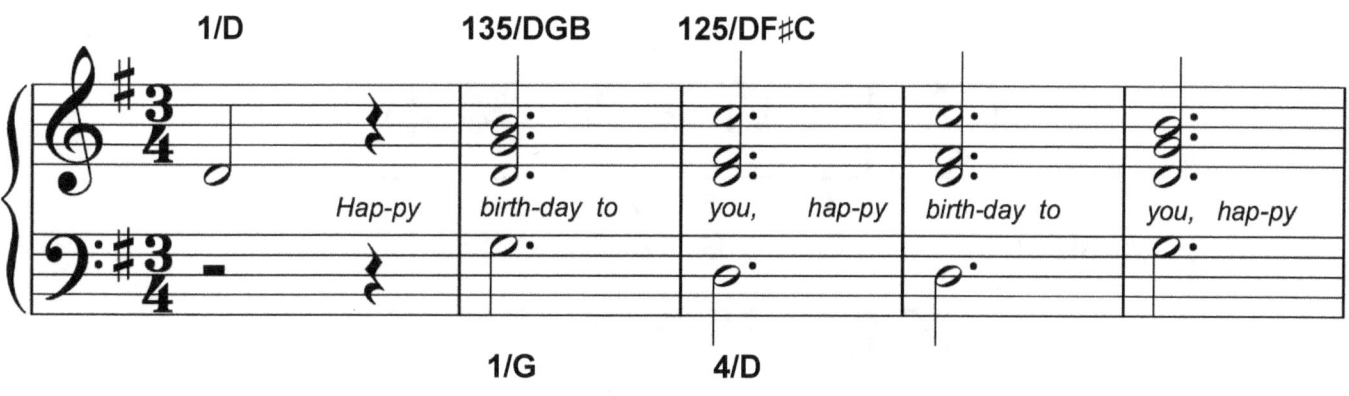

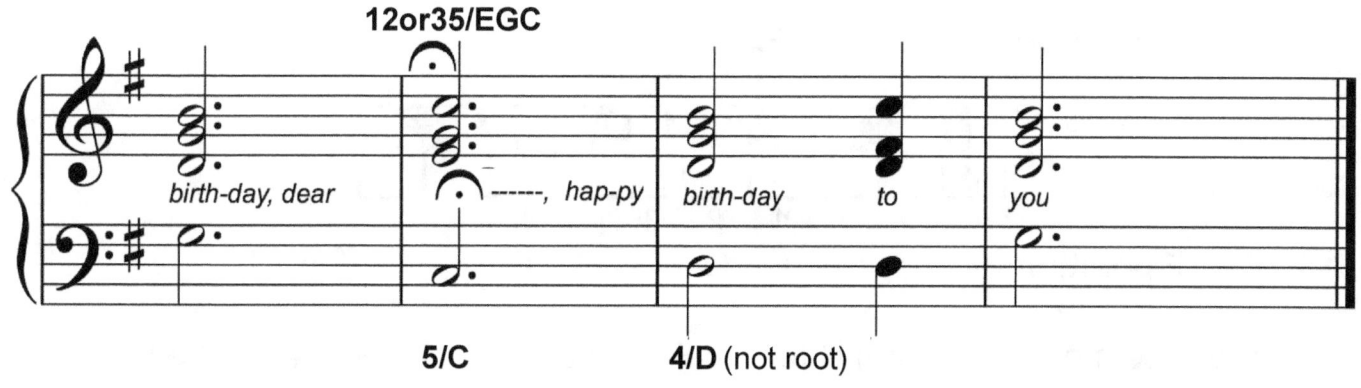

G MAJOR ~ 21 a

HAND CHANGES

Music that was not originally written for keyboard, such as **"Happy Birthday,"** often requires **awkward fingering** and **hand position changes.**

Prepare each new hand change or finger extension **before playing notes in that position so you can use the least amount of hand movement possible.**

Use the most natural positions such as white key five finger positions, scale and chord fingerings, or finger extensions from a hand position.

Extend fingers over black keys; avoid using the 1 or 5 fingers on black keys.

Avoid sliding by contracting the hand, using finger substitution on a held or repeated note, or moving to a new position at the end of a phrase if possible.

Changing position while coordinating pitch and rhythm requires extra practice: **First anticipate changing position, next prepare the position, then play.**

Pencil in finger changes; keep the same changes for repeated phrases.

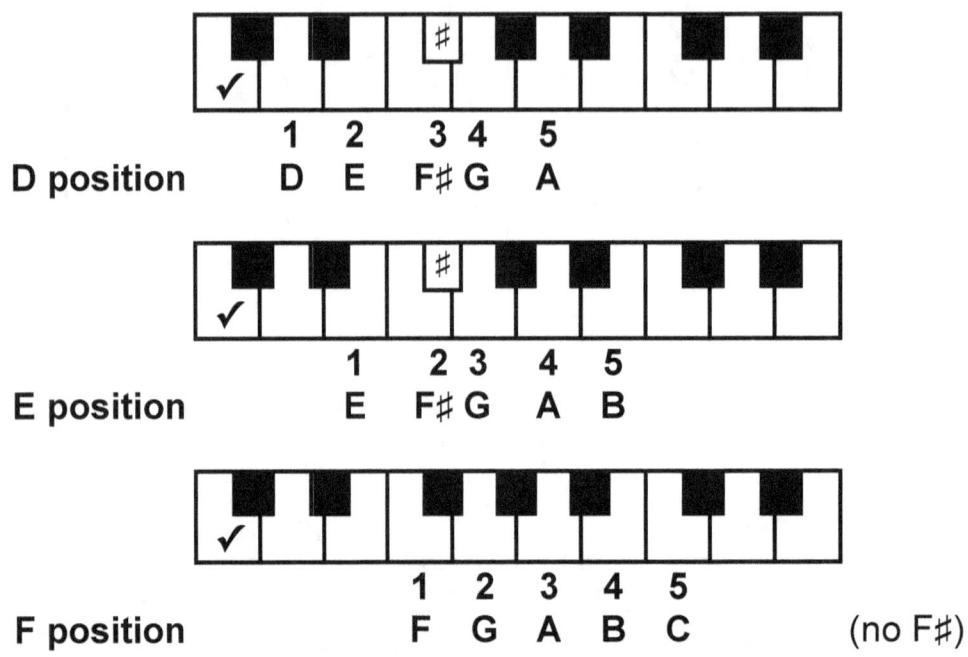

♪ **1: Practice** moving RH from D to E to F positions for **"Aura Lee"** in the Key of G.

2: Aura Lee

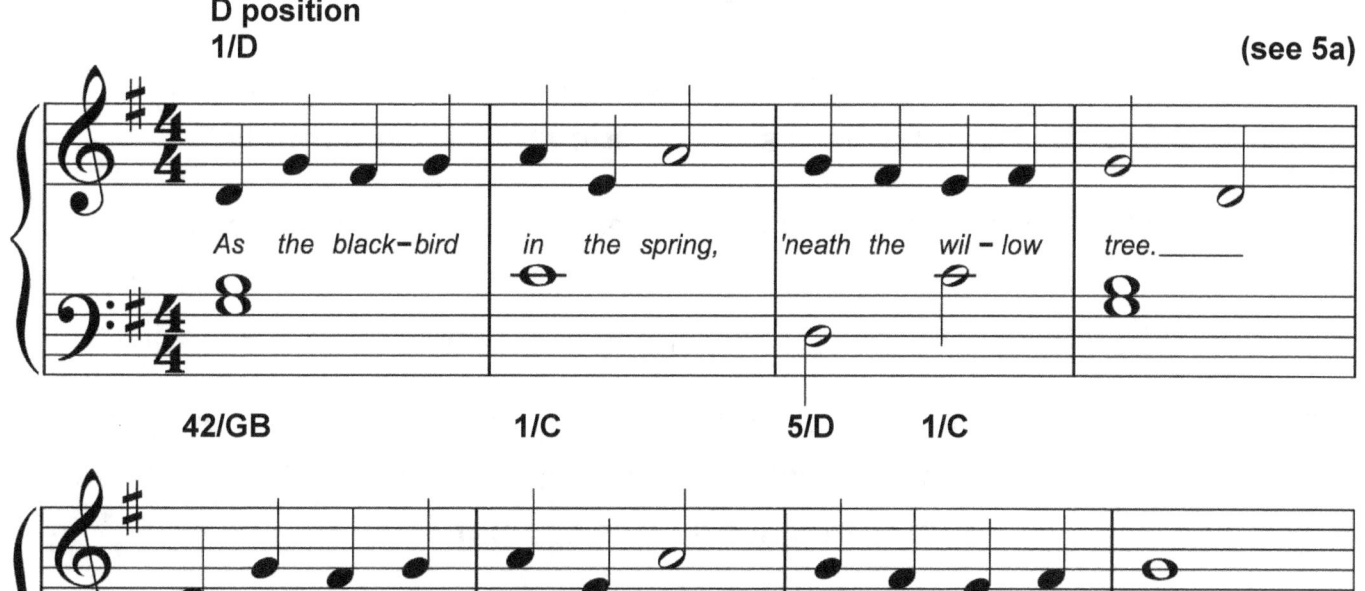
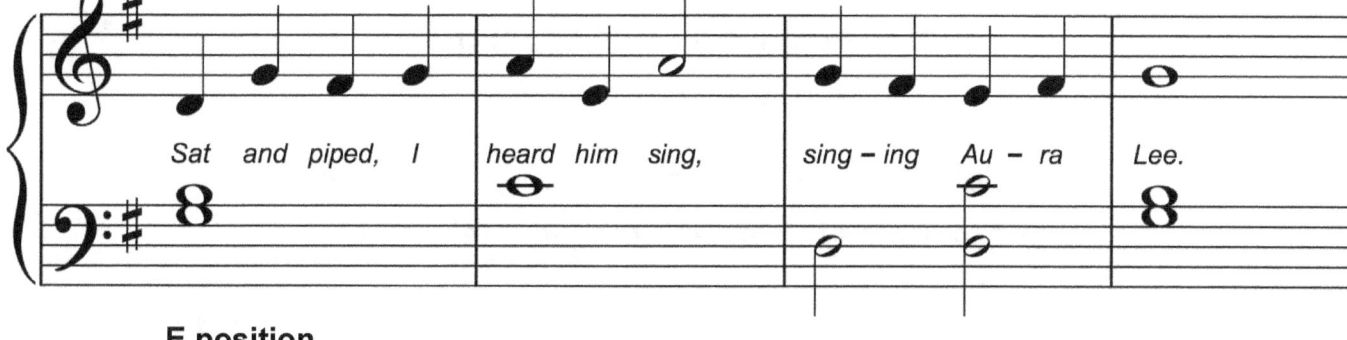
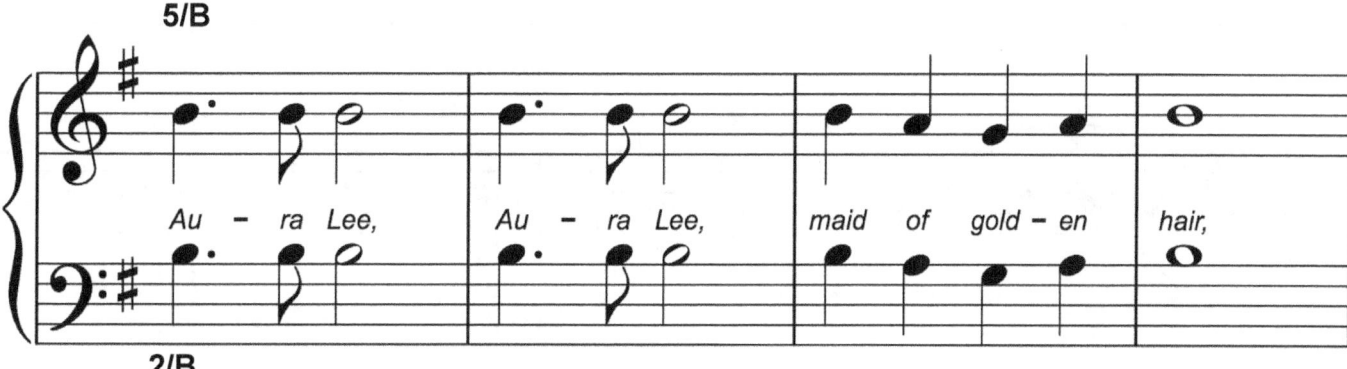
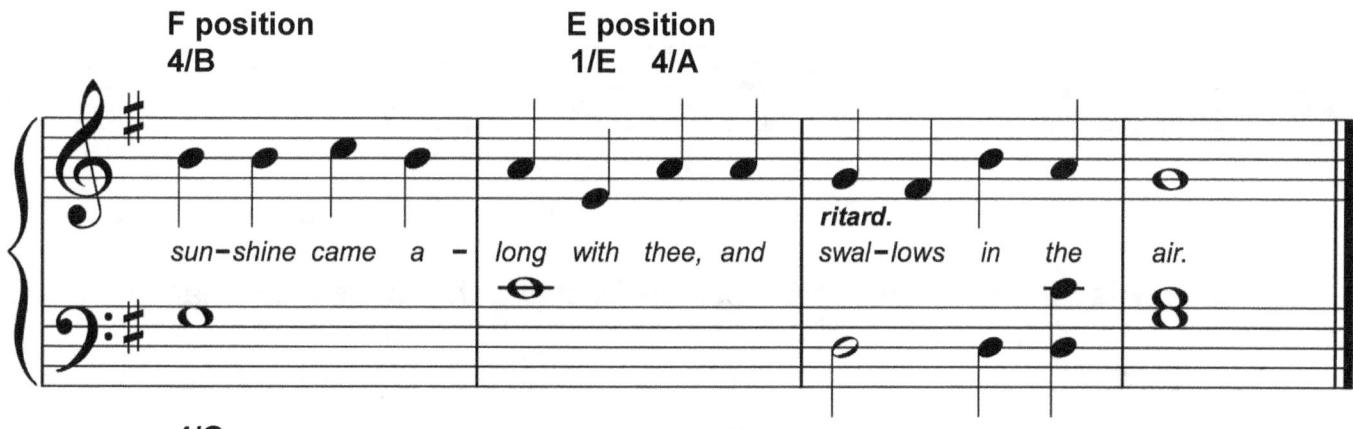

EXPRESSION

Tempo is the slower or faster pace of beats, and is written above the first measure of a piece such as **"Slowly" or "Moderately."**

Volume softness and loudness signs include *"p"* piano for soft, *"f"* forte for loud or *"mf"* for moderately loud. "⊂═══⊃" means **crescendo**, a gradual increase or "⊃═══⊂" **decrescendo**, a gradual decrease in volume.

"Slurs" are curved lines over or under a group of notes. The slur indicates that the notes should be played **legato,** meaning smoothly, connecting the notes. Slurs often divide a piece into **phrases,** like musical sentences.

A dot over or under a note is called **staccato** and indicates to play a detached or short note.

"Pedal_____" or *"Ped._____"* means to hold the pedal down where shown.

♪ **1: Play** the RH notes in G position following the expression marks.

For **"Surfing,"** place the hands in G position an octave apart and play the G~G~D7~G chord progression using broken chords moving from the LH to the RH.

♫ 2: Surfing Progression

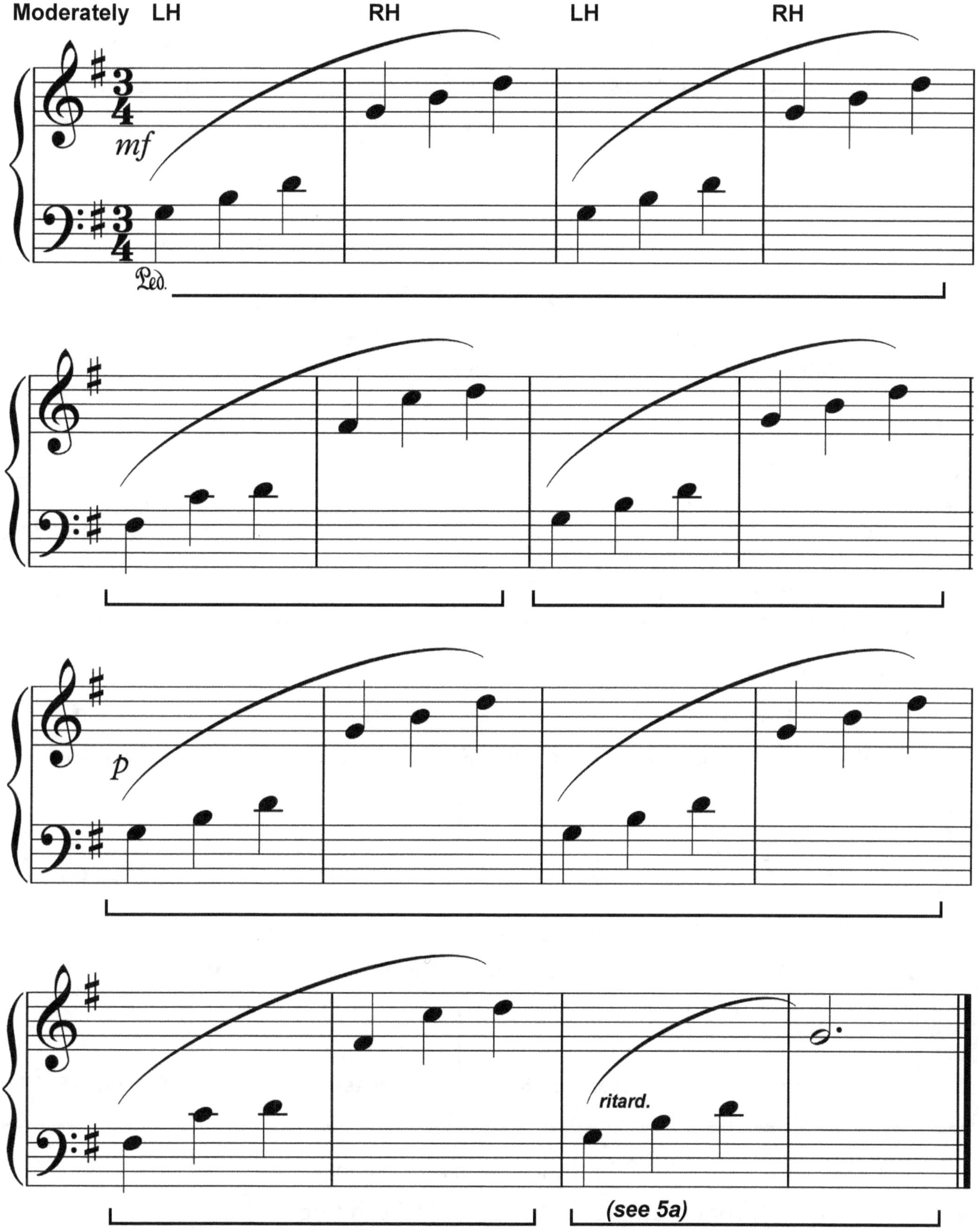

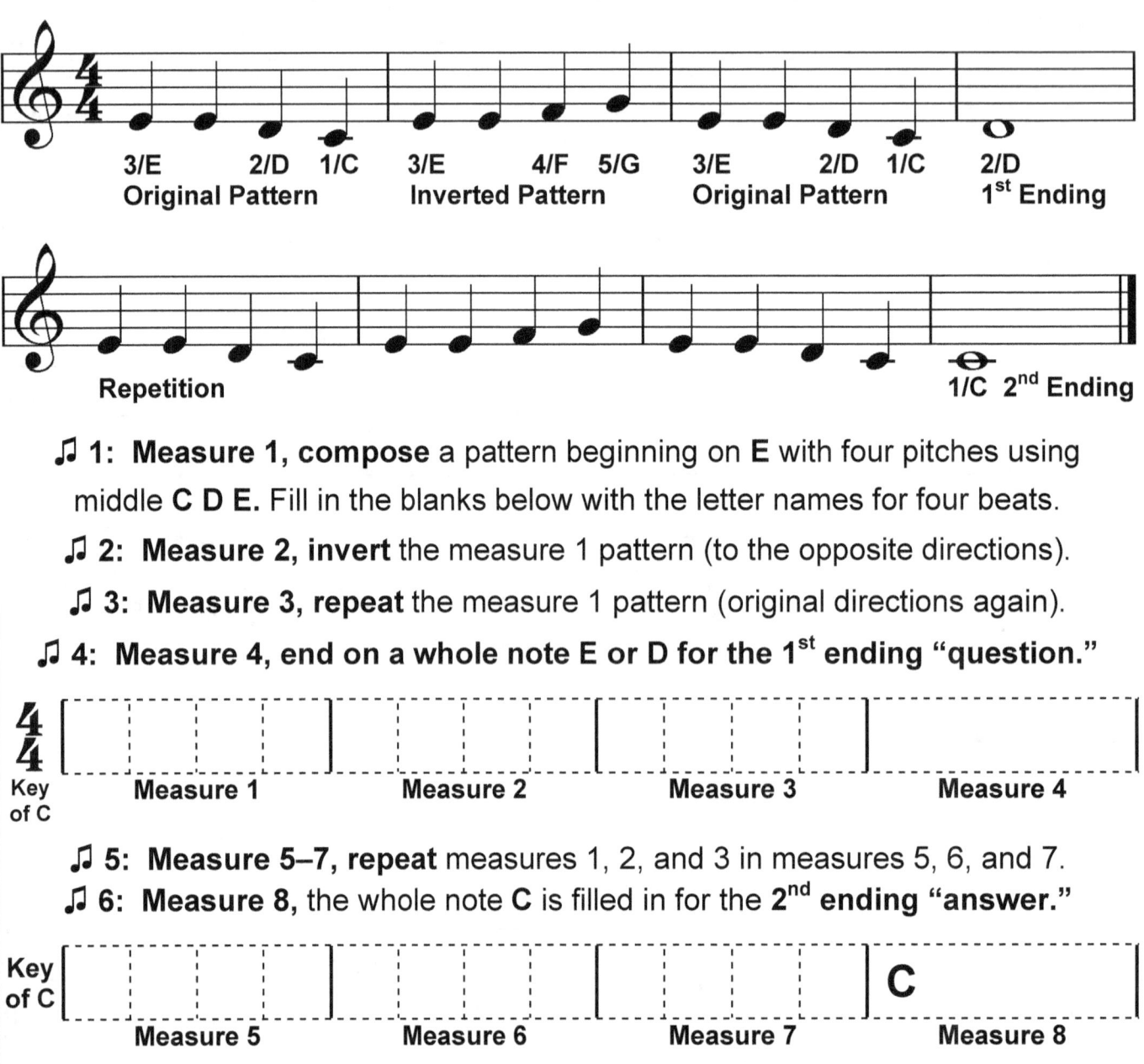

COMPOSITION NINE

♪ **8: Notate the melody** (treble staff). **Choose and notate** a whole note chord, C, F, or G7, in each (bass staff) measure that shares notes with the melody.

Notation Guide ~ Key of C

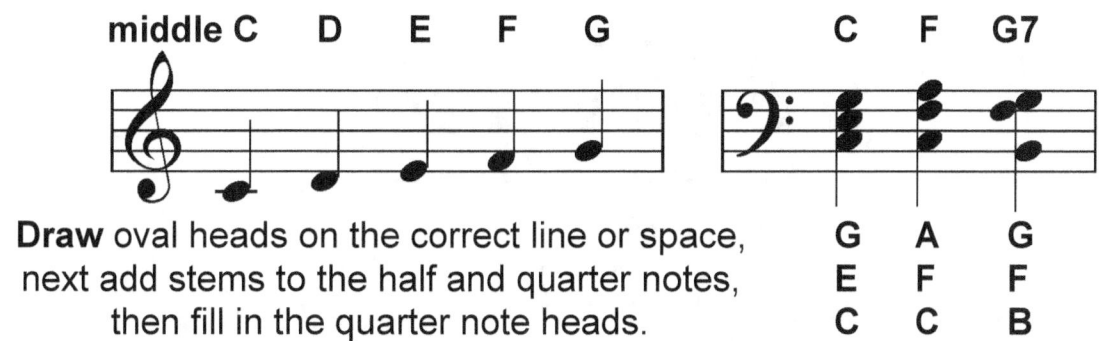

Draw oval heads on the correct line or space, next add stems to the half and quarter notes, then fill in the quarter note heads.

♪ **9: Play and improvise C chord** at the end of the melody, **hold R pedal down.**

♪ **10: Draw a staff;** renotate the melody with chords in the key of G Major.

MINOR ~ 22 a

MAJOR AND MINOR CHORDS

Chords are built out of **two sizes of 3^{rds}** (skips).
A major 3rd (larger, C to E) has **4 half steps** (4 "cracks" between keys).
A minor 3rd (smaller, C to E♭) has **3 half steps** (3 "cracks" between keys).

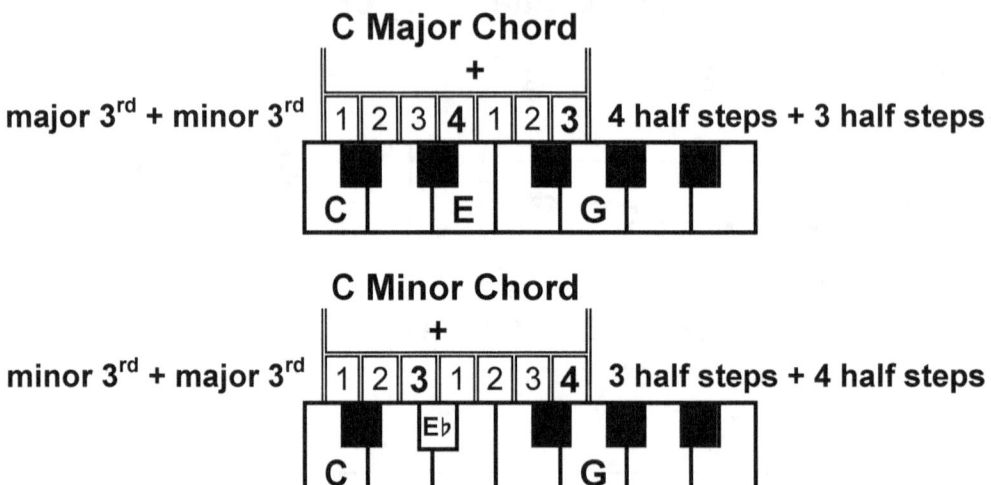

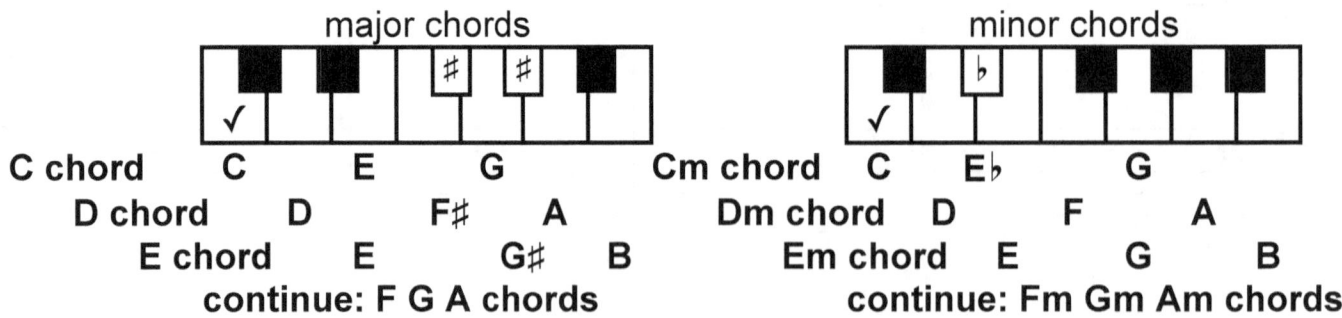

♪ **1: Rotate** between major and minor above (shift finger 3 back and forth).

CHORD SYMBOLS

A plain letter name means **major**; **minor** chords add an "m" or "min" to the letter.
In the key of C: the major chords are C F G, and the minor chords are Dm Em Am.

SCALE DEGREES

```
C D E F G A B
I ii iii IV V vi
```

Major chords are marked with **large numerals**.
Minor chords are marked with **small numerals**.
A diminished chord built on B is explained at 23a.

KEY OF C CHORDS

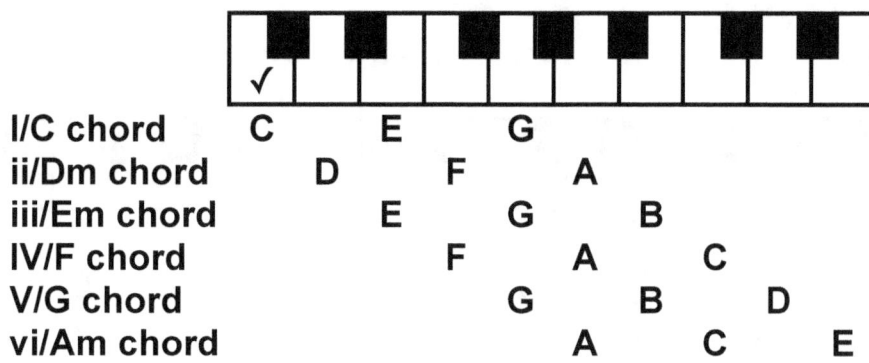

♪ **2: Improvise** each chord in block and broken style with right fingers 135.

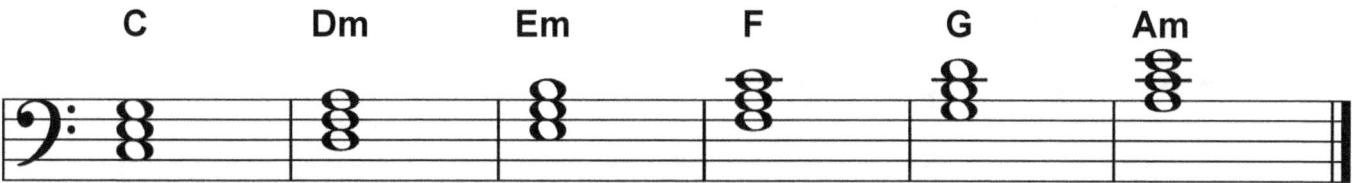

♪ **3: Practice** playing each major and minor chord with left fingers 531.

♪ **4: Improvise** a chord progression (begin and end on the same chord).

Minor chords are often substituted for **major chords** to create variety. Notice that related major and minor chords **share two pitches.**

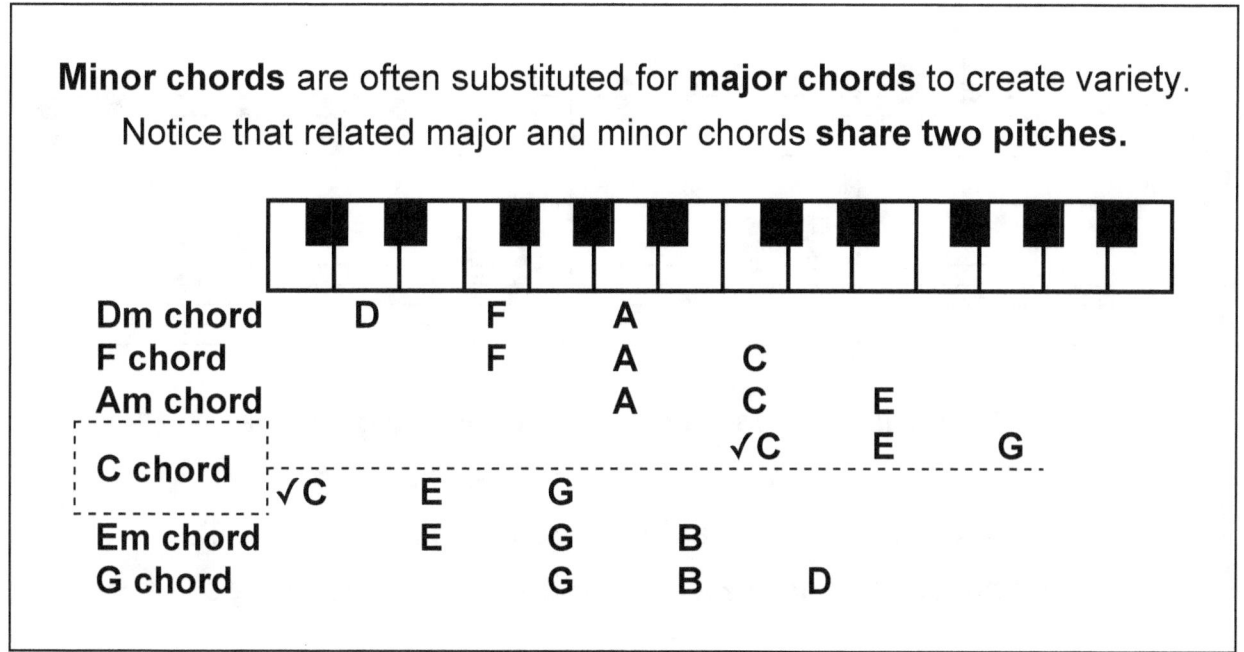

♪ **5: Play** the related major and minor chords above (move the RH 1 up by 3^{rds}).

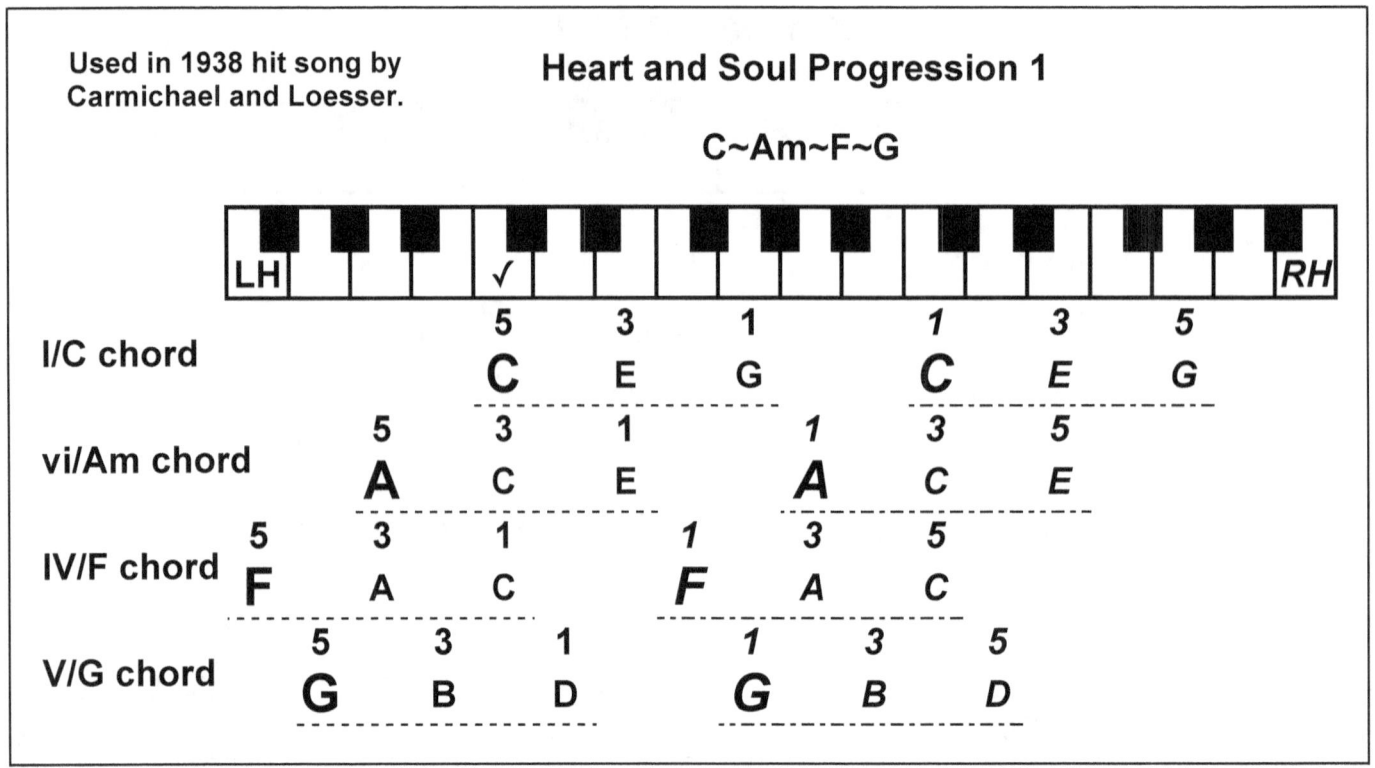

♪ **1: Improvise** the chord progression above
in the block and broken styles with each hand alone
first in C position, next down to A and F positions, then up to G.
Slide the hand to each new chord position before playing.

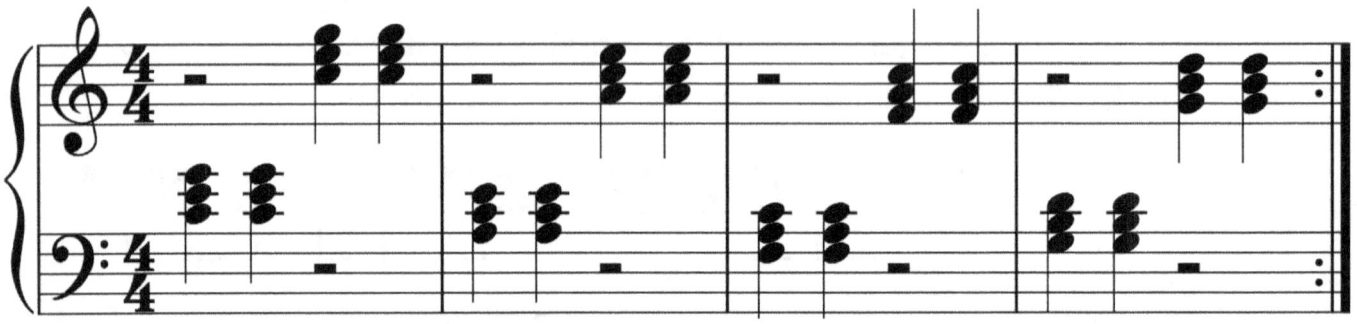

♪ **2: Play** the chord progression in a block style
two times with the LH in middle C position,
then two times with the RH an octave above middle C.
Continue the same way with the Am, F and G chords.

♪ **3: Try** a swing rhythm "Hump-ty Dump-ty" (long~short~long~short, see 8aa)
with each two chords alternating between the left and right hands.

Heart and Soul Progression 2

C~Am~Dm~G7~C

I/C chord		5		3		1		*124 RH*	
root on bottom		**C**		E		G			root + major 3rd + 5th
vi/Am chord		5		3			>1	*125*	
root on top		C		E			**A**		6th + 4th below root
ii/Dm chord			4		2		>1	*135*	
root on bottom			**D**		F		A		root + minor 3rd + 5th
V7/G7 chord	5<				2	1<		*134*	
root on top	B		(D)		F	**G**			6th + 2nd below root
I/C chord		>5		3		1		*124*	
root on bottom		**C**		E		G			root + major 3rd + 5th

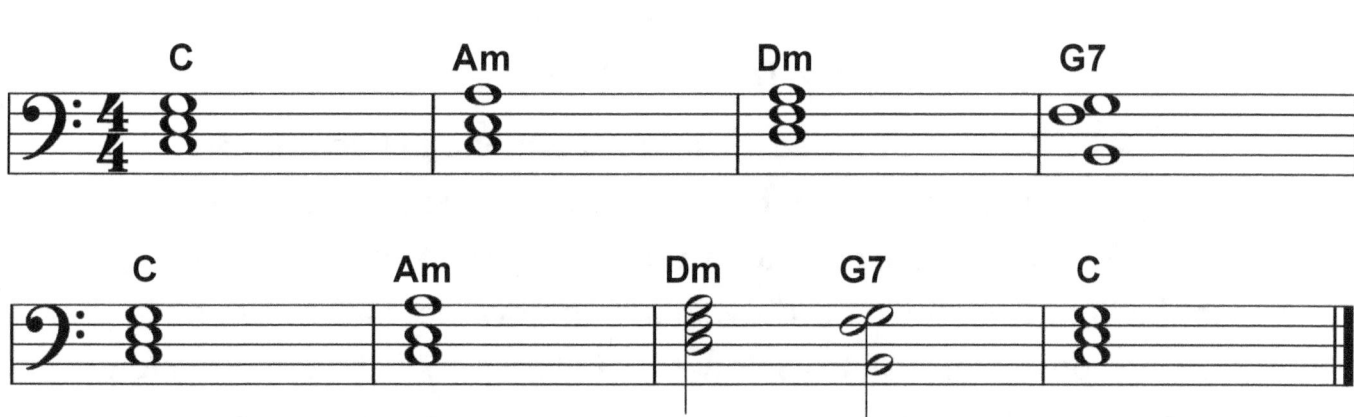

♫ **4: Play** the chord progression **C~Am~Dm~G7~C** with the left hand. Prepare **root pitches first,** then **other pitches,** and finally **play the chord.** LH fingers 5 or 4 play **bottom roots,** 3 or 2 **middle roots,** and 1 **top roots.**

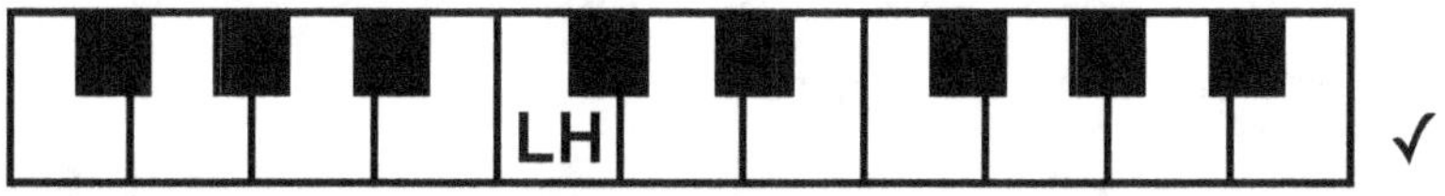

♫ **5: Improvise RH melodic patterns** for the **Heart and Soul Progression 2.**

MINOR ~ 23 a

THREE PITCH CHORDS

Chords built from a root, 3rd and 5th are called **triads.**
There are four types: **major, augmented, minor, and diminished.**
(The chord **built on a B** (BDF) is a diminished triad.)

Triads						Intervals
C	LH 531	C	E	G	135 RH	4 + 3 half steps
Caug/C+	531	C	E	G♯	135	4 + 4 half steps
Cm	531	C	E♭	G	135	3 + 4 half steps
Cdim/C°	532	C	E♭	G♭	124	3 + 3 half steps

♪ **1: Play** the progression
C ~ Caug (CEG♯) ~ C ~ Cm (CE♭G) ~ Cdim (CE♭G♭) ~ C.
Try this progression with the RH.

♪ **2: Improvise** Caug chord or Cdim chord in different octaves holding the pedal.
Notice the "mysterious" quality to the sound produced.

ANY TRIAD, ANY KEY

♪ **3:** To build any triad in any key from **one LH position:**
(a) See or feel **which LH finger** is over, or next to, a root note;
(b) LH 5 or 4, ~ root on bottom + 3rd + 5th (two skips above root);
(c) LH 3 or 2, ~ root in middle with a 4th **below** root / 3rd **above** root;
(d) LH 1 ~ root on top with 6th below + 4th below (or 7th chord **step below**).
(e) RH fingering is the **opposite** of LH, but may need adjusting for ease of play.

Paired interval inversions within an octave

skip or 3rd = 6th	E above/below C
5th = 4th	G above/below C
7th = 2nd or step	B above/below C

♪ 4: Theme from the New World
The Caug chord creates variety in the harmony
when it occurs between the C and F major triads in measure 11.

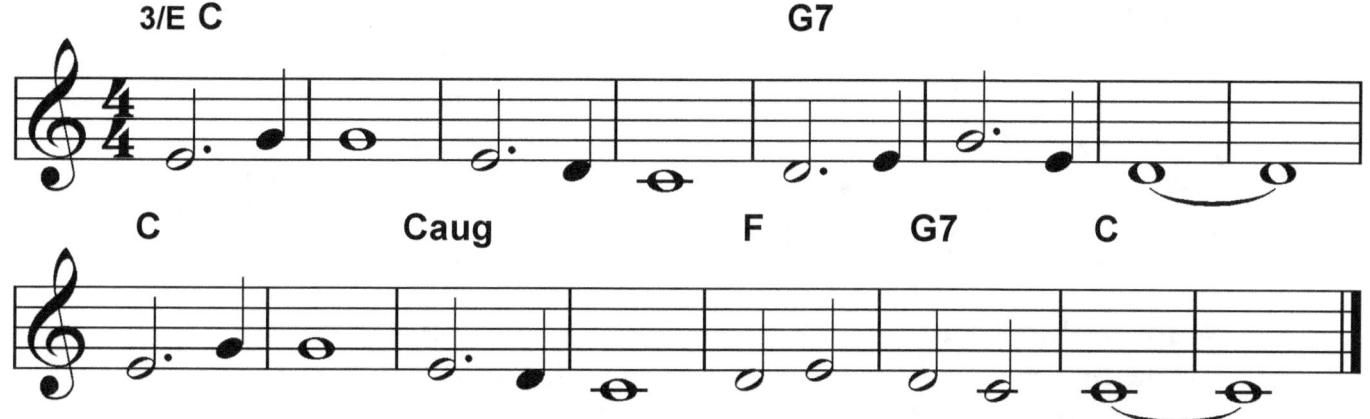

FOUR PITCH CHORDS
A 7th can be added to the root of any triad. Many variations are possible because there are several types of triads and 7th chords.

SEVENTH CHORDS
The seventh chord C7 ~ 4+3+3 (CEGB♭) adds a 7th to a major triad.

This 7th is easily found as a whole-step below the root.

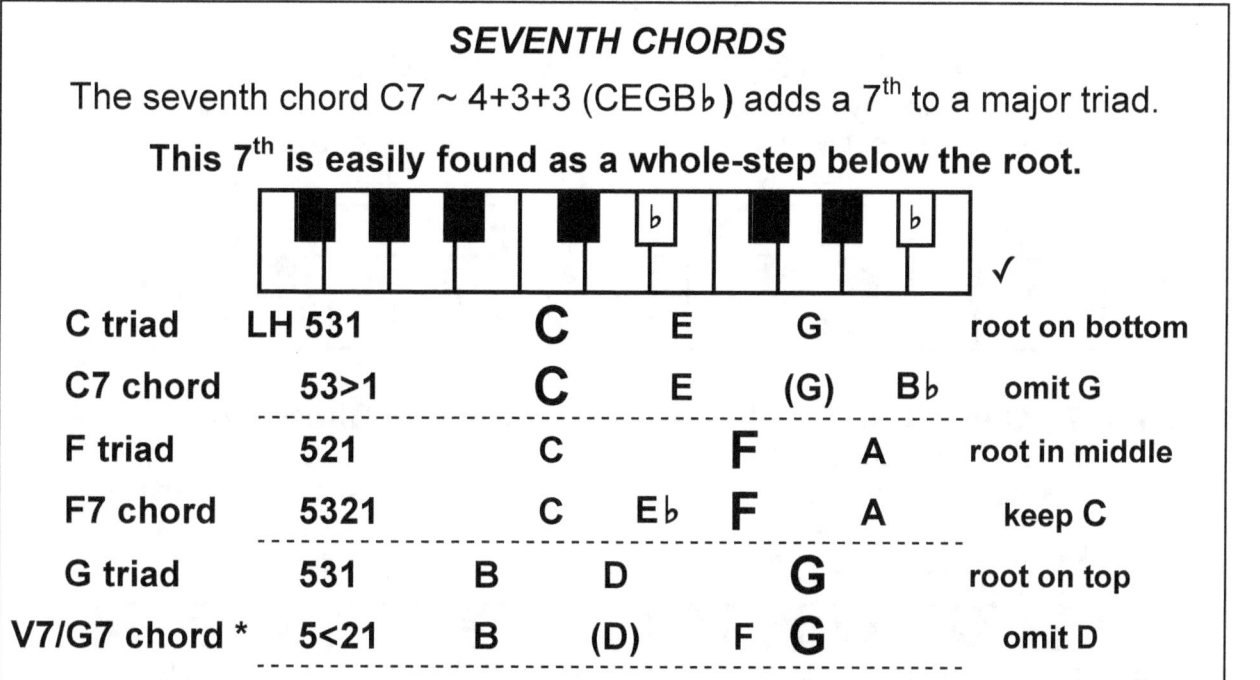

C triad	LH 531	C	E	G		root on bottom
C7 chord	53>1	C	E	(G)	B♭	omit G
F triad	521	C	F	A		root in middle
F7 chord	5321	C	E♭	F	A	keep C
G triad	531	B	D	G		root on top
V7/G7 chord *	5<21	B	(D)	F	G	omit D

♪ 5: **Play** the LH **C~C7~F~F7~C~G7~C** chord progression above in C position.

* DOMINANT SEVENTH
Scale degrees I, IV, and **V** are called tonic, subdominant, and **dominant**.
Dominant seventh chords are 7th chords built on a root that is scale degree V.

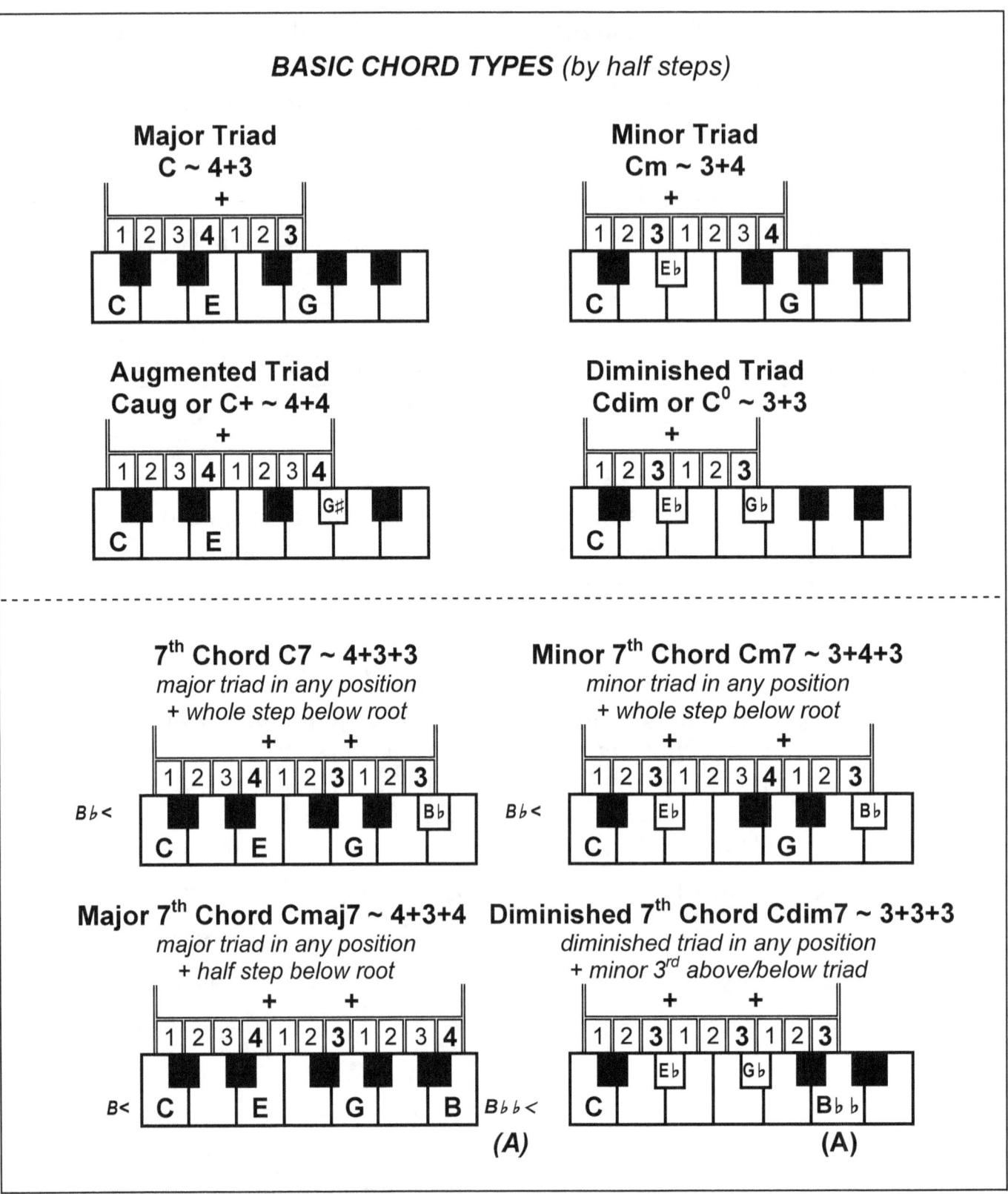

♫ 1: **Practice** building each chord type.

♫ 2: **Try** chords with the 7th below the root.

KEY OF C 7TH CHORDS

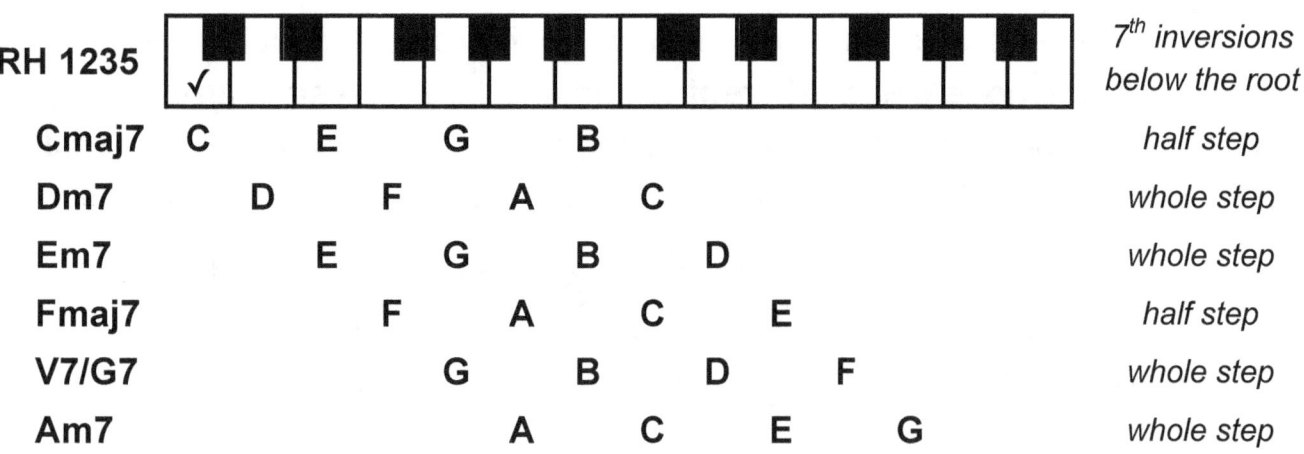

							7th inversions below the root
Cmaj7	C	E	G	B			half step
Dm7	D	F	A	C			whole step
Em7	E	G	B	D			whole step
Fmaj7	F	A	C	E			half step
V7/G7	G	B	D	F			whole step
Am7	A	C	E	G			whole step

♪ **3: Improvise** each 7th chord.

♪ **4: Improvise** a progression of 7th chords.

ALTERED CHORDS

There are many ways to build or alter chords.

A "**/**" between pitches means to play the chord (left letter) with the lowest note (right letter), for example **F/C = CFA**.

A "**6**" adds a whole step to a major or minor chord, for example **C6 = CEGA**.

A "**sus4**" (suspended) means to replace the 3rd with the 4th above the root, for example **Csus4 = CFG**.

A minus sign "**−**" before a pitch **lowers** it a half step, for example **Bm7−5 = BDFA**.

A plus sign "**+**" before a pitch **raises** it a half step, for example **C7+5 = CEG♯B♭**.

MINOR ~ 24 a   107

MAJOR AND MINOR MODES

Modes are scales that can be built on each pitch of the major scale.
Each mode has a different whole and half step structure.
The two most **common modes, 1 and 6,** are called the **major and minor scales.**
The white keys A to A are called the **natural or relative minor of C major scale.**

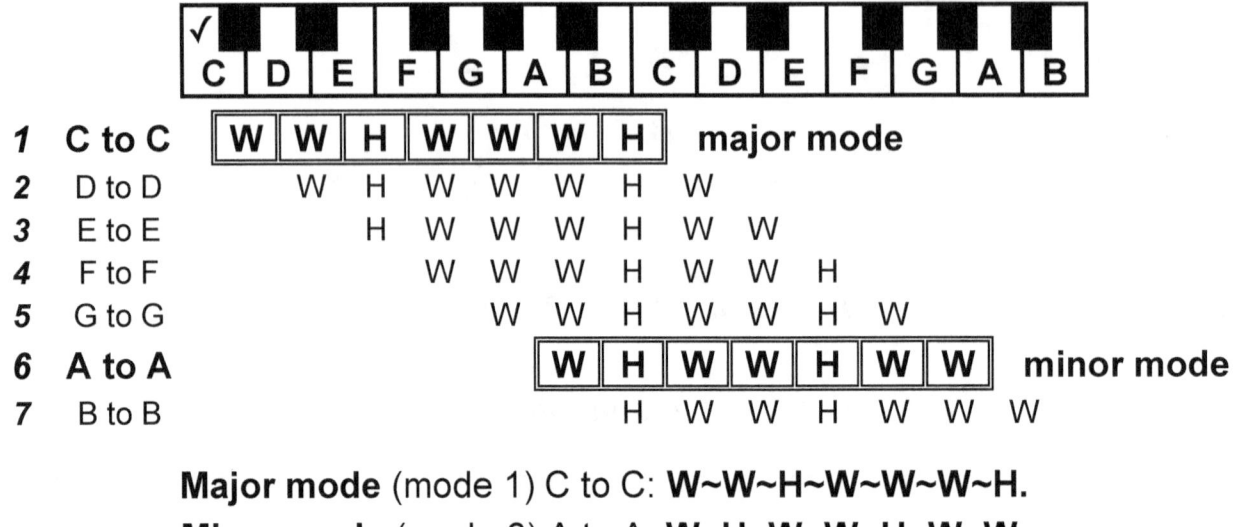

Major mode (mode 1) C to C: **W~W~H~W~W~W~H.**
Minor mode (mode 6) A to A: **W~H~W~W~H~W~W.**

♪ **1:** Starting on the **keynote A** above, **play** the white keys of this scale with the RH 2 ♭, and **say** the **W** and **H** steps: "**A,** whole step **B,** half step **C,**" etc.

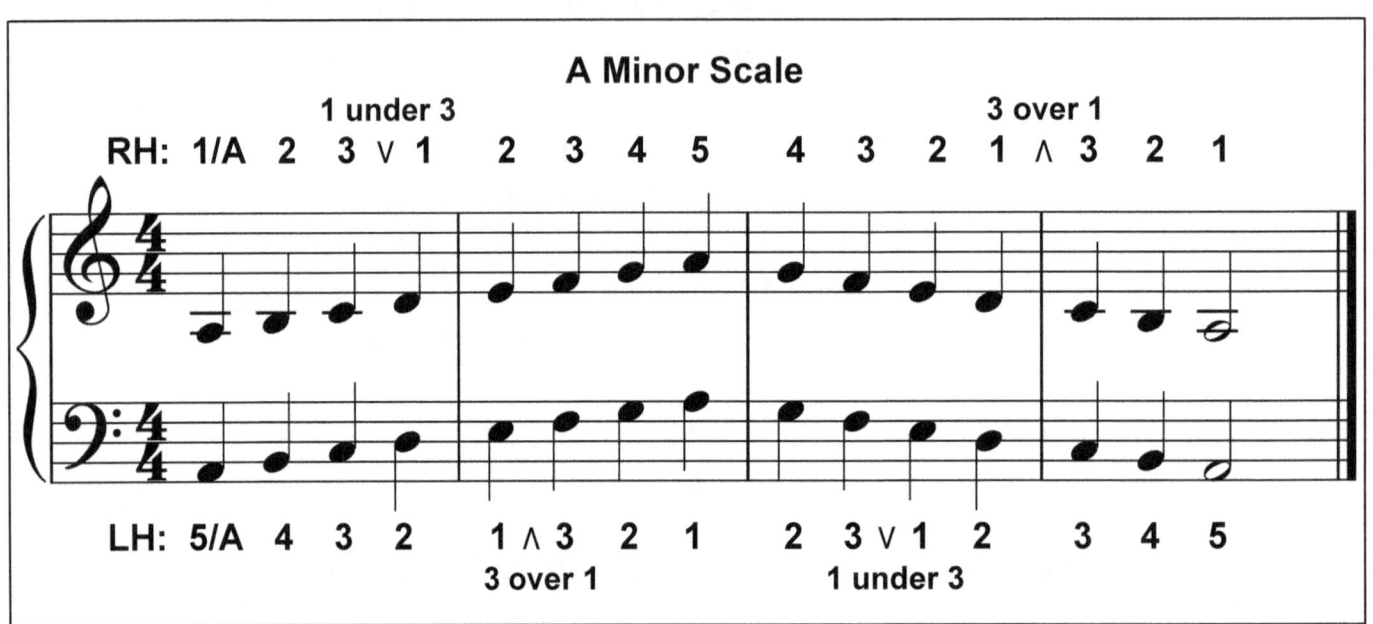

♪ **2: Practice** the A minor scale above.

♫ 3: Song of the Volga Boatmen

Add an Am block chord with the RH (ACE/135) and the LH root note A an octave lower holding down the pedal for a fuller sound after "ho!" and "go."

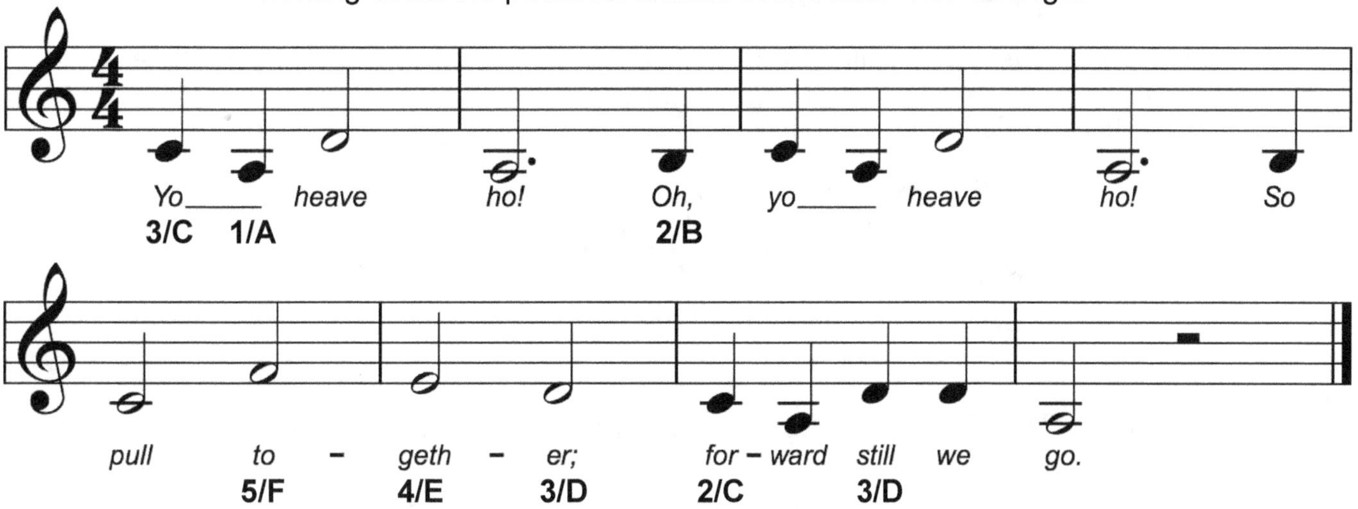
Yo___ heave ho! Oh, yo___ heave ho! So
3/C 1/A 2/B
pull to - geth - er; for - ward still we go.
5/F 4/E 3/D 2/C 3/D

MINOR CHORDS

3 + 4 half steps

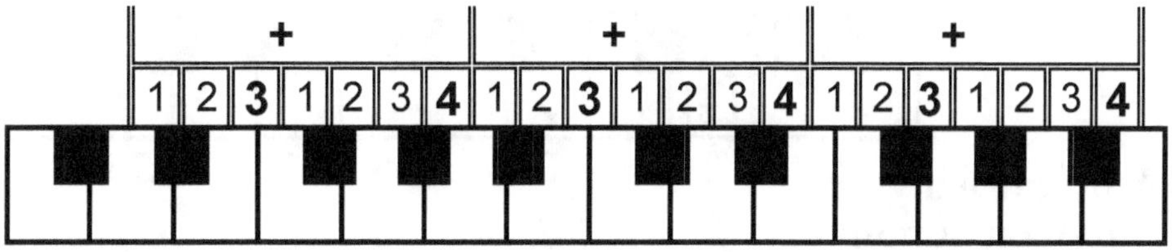
+ + +
1 2 3 1 2 3 4 1 2 3 1 2 3 4 1 2 3 1 2 3 4

iv/Dm chord	**D**	**F**	**A**				
i/Am chord			**A**	**C**	**E**		
v/Em chord					**E**	**G**	**B**
	5th below A subdominant		**keynote tonic**		**5th above A dominant**		

♫ **4: Play and say** the chord numeral and name above: "iv and Dm," etc.

SCALE DEGREES

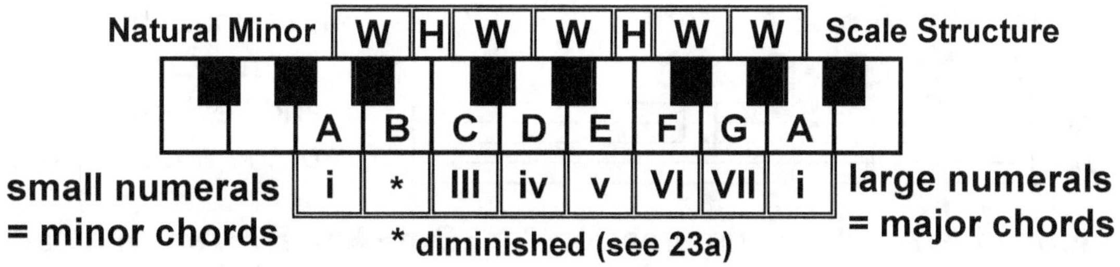
Natural Minor
W H W W H W W
Scale Structure
A B C D E F G A
i * III iv v VI VII i
small numerals = minor chords
large numerals = major chords
* diminished (see 23a)

The **minor chords** are built on the **i** (tonic), **iv** (subdominant), and **v** (dominant).

HARMONIC MINOR SCALE

The **harmonic minor** scale **raises degree VII a half step** from **G to G♯**. This **accidental** must be notated. Em ~ 3+4 (EGB) changes to E ~ 4+3 (EG♯B) and makes the V7 dominant 7th chord E7 ~ 4+3+3 (EG♯BD) possible.

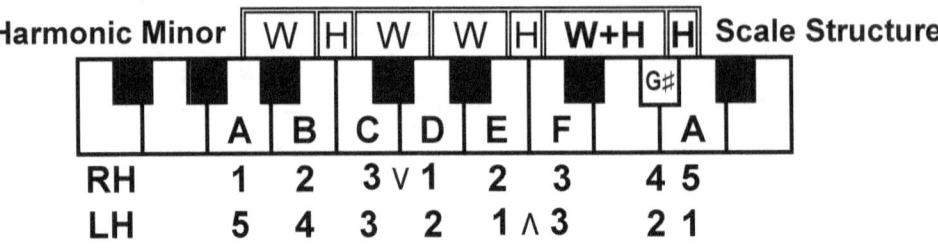

♪ **1: Practice** the A harmonic minor scale with a G♯ above.

Progression Am~Dm~Am~E7~Am

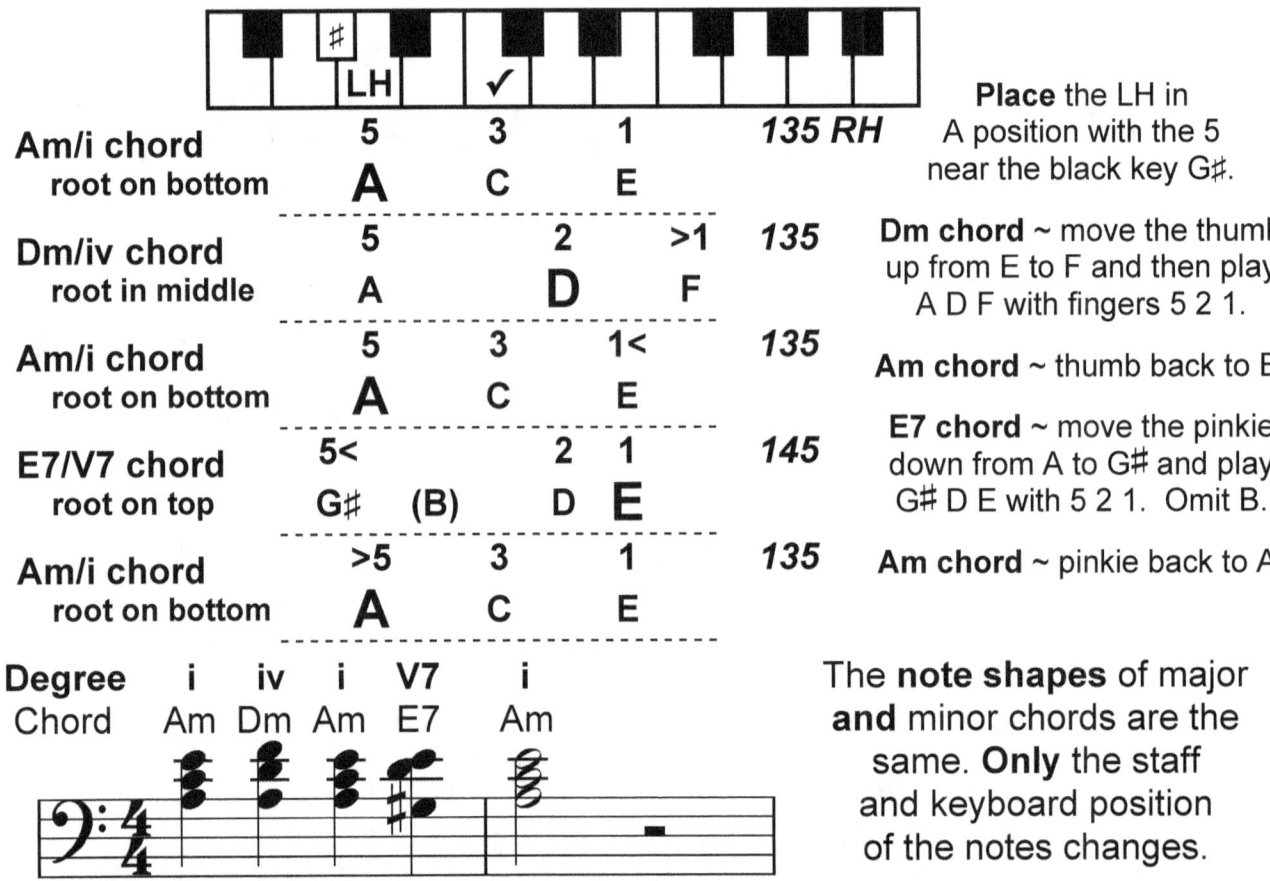

♪ **2: Practice** the A position progression **Am~Dm~Am~E7~Am** with each hand, then **improvise** each chord with hands together in block and broken styles an octave apart.

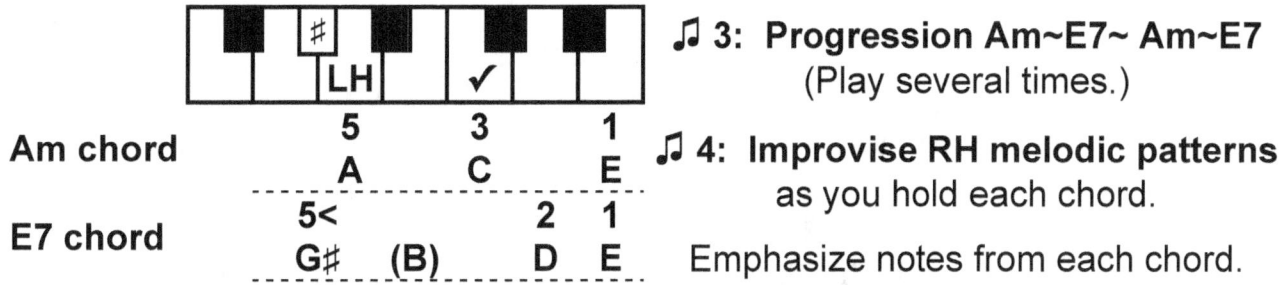

Am chord	5 A	3 C	1 E
E7 chord	5< G#	(B) 2 D	1 E

♪ 3: **Progression Am~E7~ Am~E7**
(Play several times.)

♪ 4: **Improvise RH melodic patterns**
as you hold each chord.

Emphasize notes from each chord.

♪ 5: **Sideshow Tune**

The use of block chords on nearly every beat of the first four measures
and the last four measures supports the strong rhythmic emphasis
of the melody. The single melodic line first in the right hand and
then the left hand in the middle part provides contrast.

From 1893 World's Fair, led to exotic dance forms.

1/A

531/ACE 521/G#DE

4/B

MINOR ~ 25 a

PERFECT FIFTHS
Perfect 5^{ths} have seven half steps.
This is the most important interval in music after the octave.

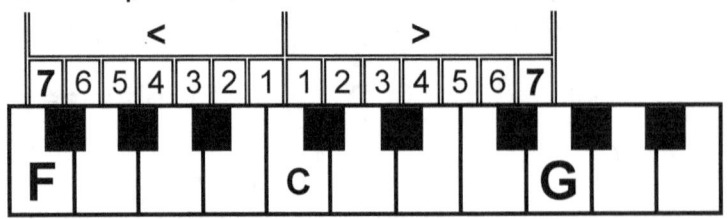

♪ **1: Count** 7 half steps up or down from any pitch to find a perfect 5th.

KEY SIGNATURES
After the key of C (and Am), each key signature adds one sharp or one flat.
These keynotes are a perfect 5th apart.

Sharp keys ~ keynotes are a half step **above** the last sharp in the key signature.

The key signature for the **key of D (and Bm) has 2 sharps, F♯ and C♯.**
Move up a half step above the last signature sharp C♯ to find the keynote D.

Key of D Major

♪ **2: Play** with R 2 ♭.

Flat keys ~ After the key of F major, keynotes are the flat **before** the last flat.

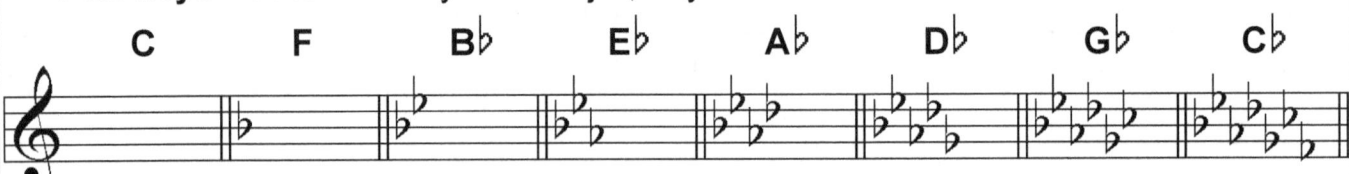

The key signature for the **key of B♭ major (and G minor) has 2 flats, B♭ and E♭.**
The keynote B♭ is the flat in the signature before the last signature flat E♭.

Key of B♭ Major

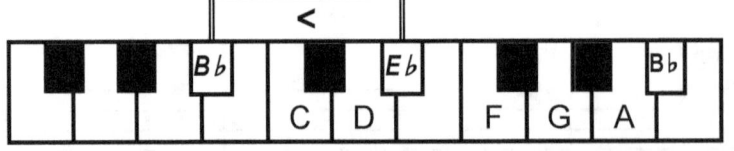

♪ **3: Play** with R 2 ♭.

CIRCLE OF FIFTHS

The circle of 5ths shows the **12 major keys** and the **12 relative minor keys** (the minors begin on major scale degree VI but include the same set of pitches).

Clockwise after C outside (Am inside), **each 5th adds a sharp** to the key signature and **counterclockwise** after C (Am), **each 5th adds a flat** to the key signature.

These 5ths are either white key to white key or black key to black key except clockwise B to F# and B♭ to F.

The key of **C (Am)** = no flats or sharps.

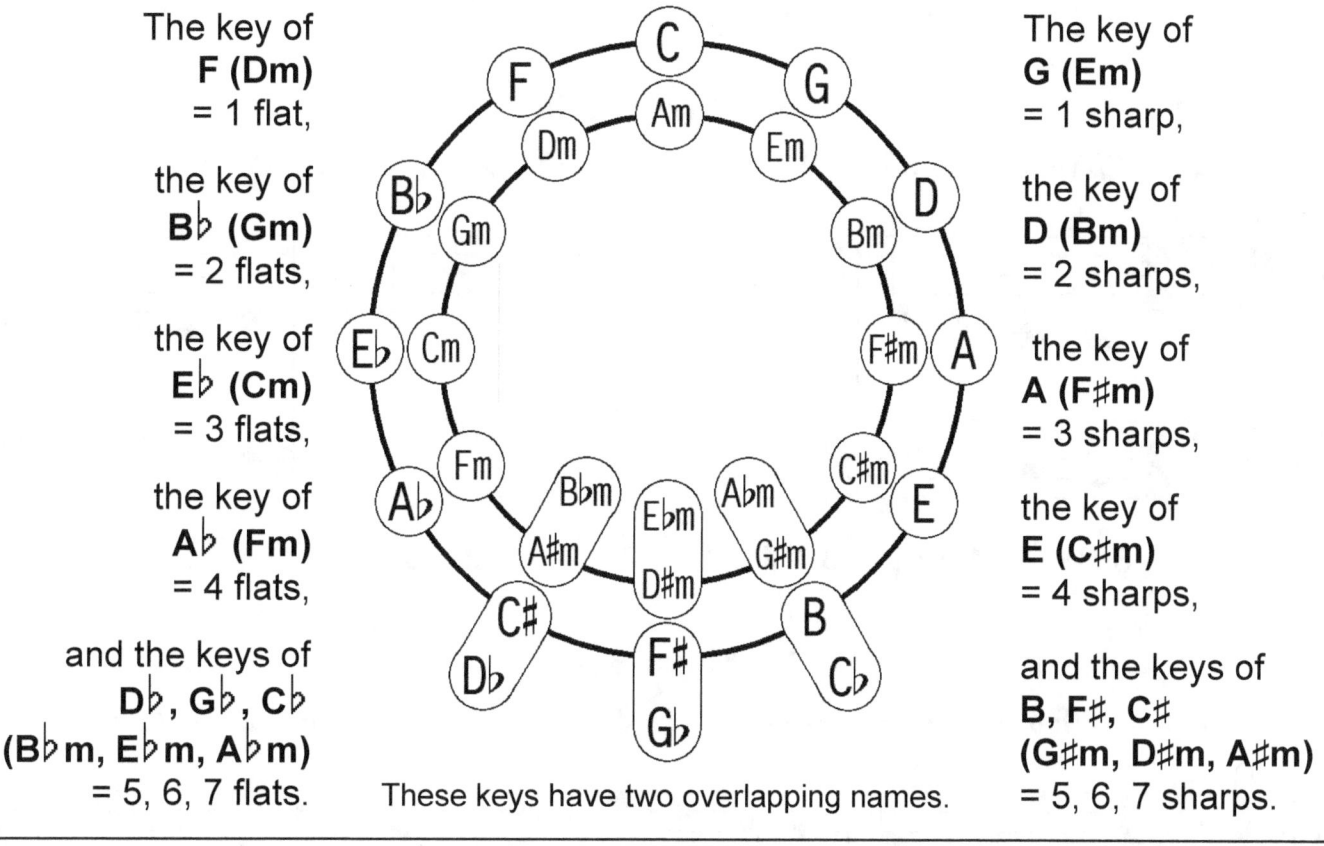

The key of **F (Dm)** = 1 flat,

the key of **B♭ (Gm)** = 2 flats,

the key of **E♭ (Cm)** = 3 flats,

the key of **A♭ (Fm)** = 4 flats,

and the keys of **D♭, G♭, C♭ (B♭m, E♭m, A♭m)** = 5, 6, 7 flats.

The key of **G (Em)** = 1 sharp,

the key of **D (Bm)** = 2 sharps,

the key of **A (F#m)** = 3 sharps,

the key of **E (C#m)** = 4 sharps,

and the keys of **B, F#, C# (G#m, D#m, A#m)** = 5, 6, 7 sharps.

These keys have two overlapping names.

♪ **4: Play** the pitches of the circle of 5ths clockwise from C back to C, **RH 2** ♭ C to G to D to A, etc.; then from C back to C counterclockwise, C to F to B♭, etc.

♪ **5: Improvise** patterns of 5ths such as C-G to D-A to E-B.

♪ **6: Play** alternating major/minor 3rds (4~3~4~3~ etc.) clockwise and counter-clockwise for related chords C~Em~G~Bm~D, etc. and C~Am~F~Dm~B♭, etc.

KEYS WITH FLATS

F Major Scale

B♭ Major Scale

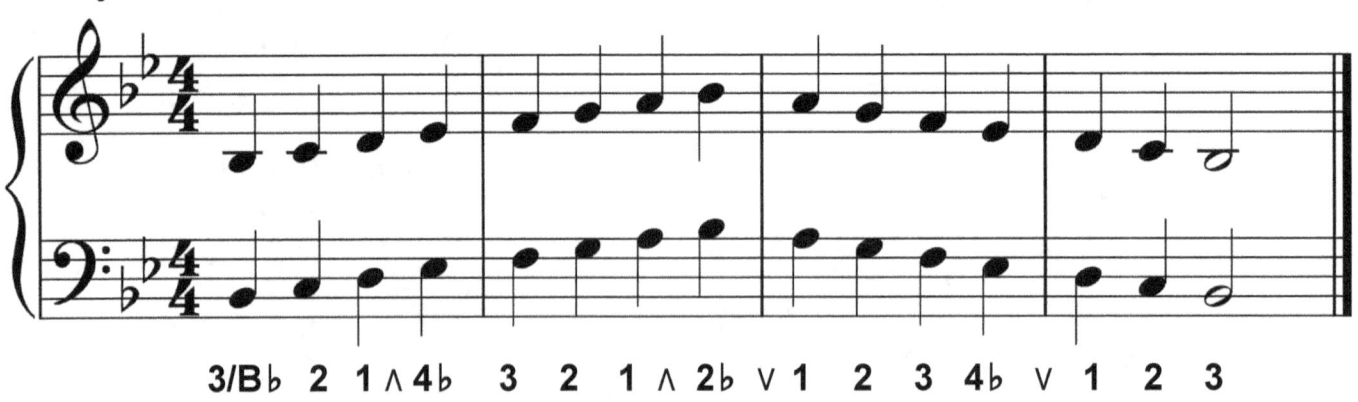

E♭ Major Scale

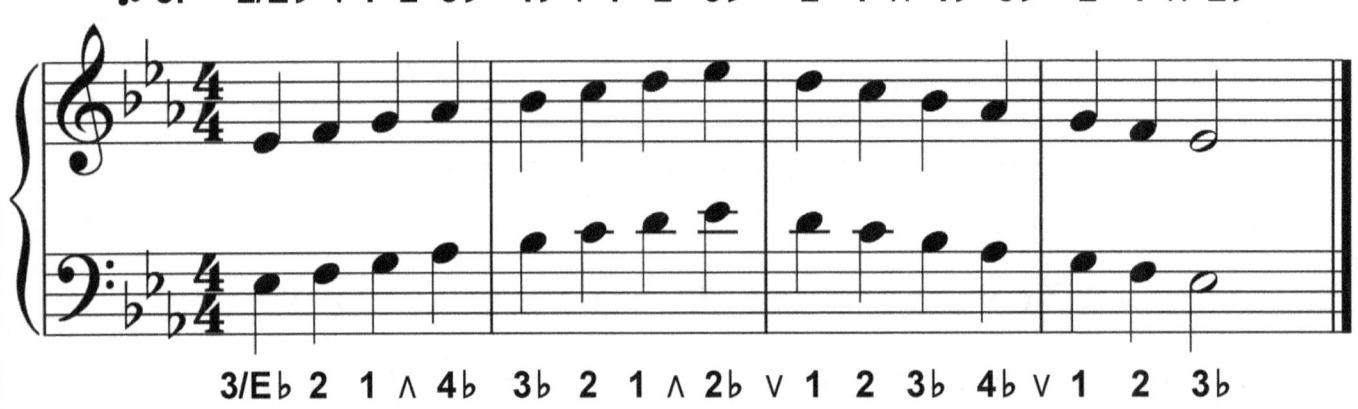

KEYS WITH SHARPS

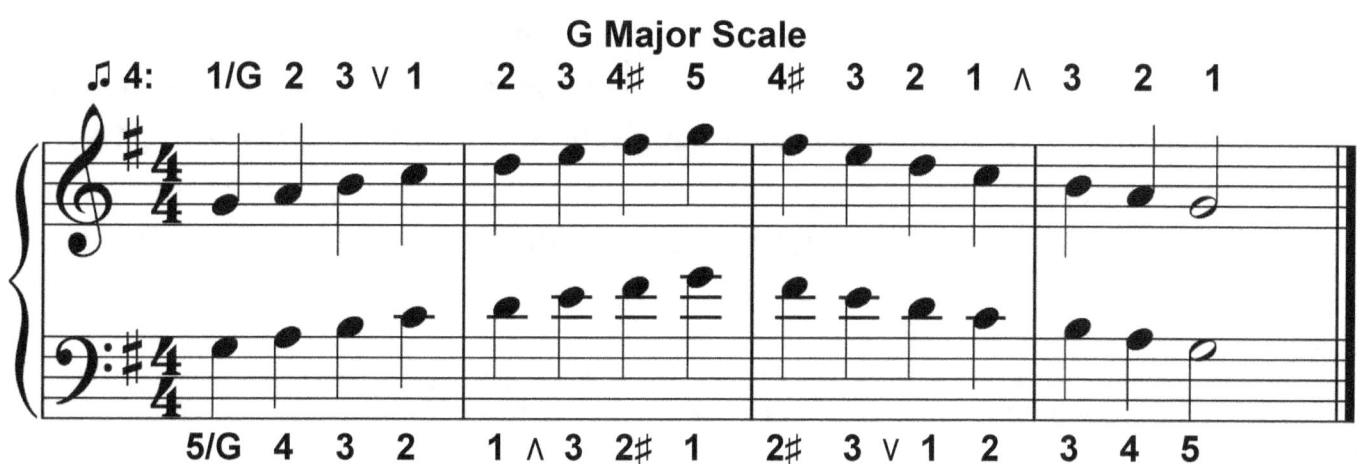

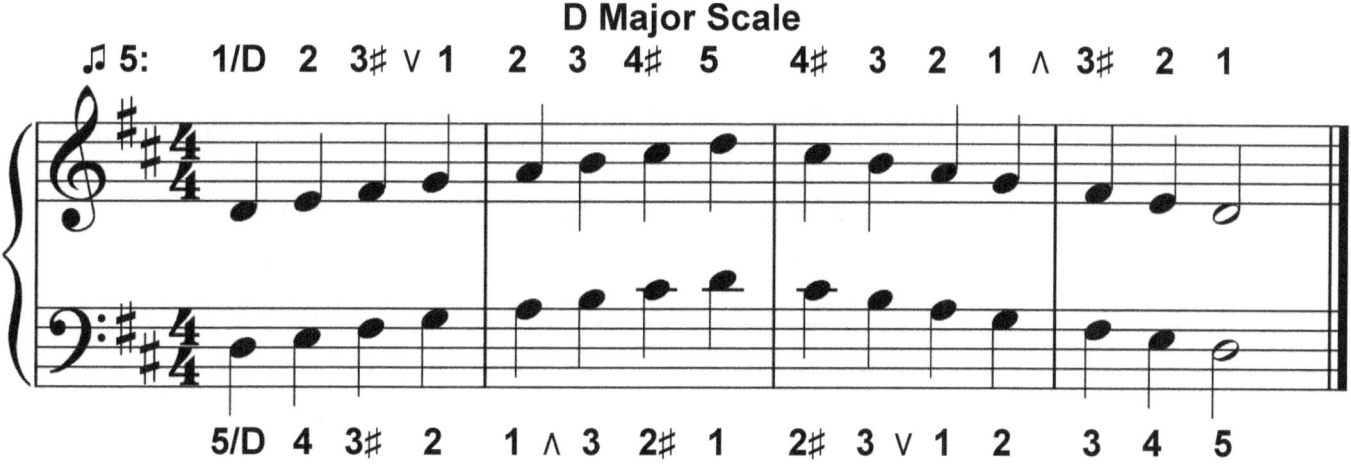

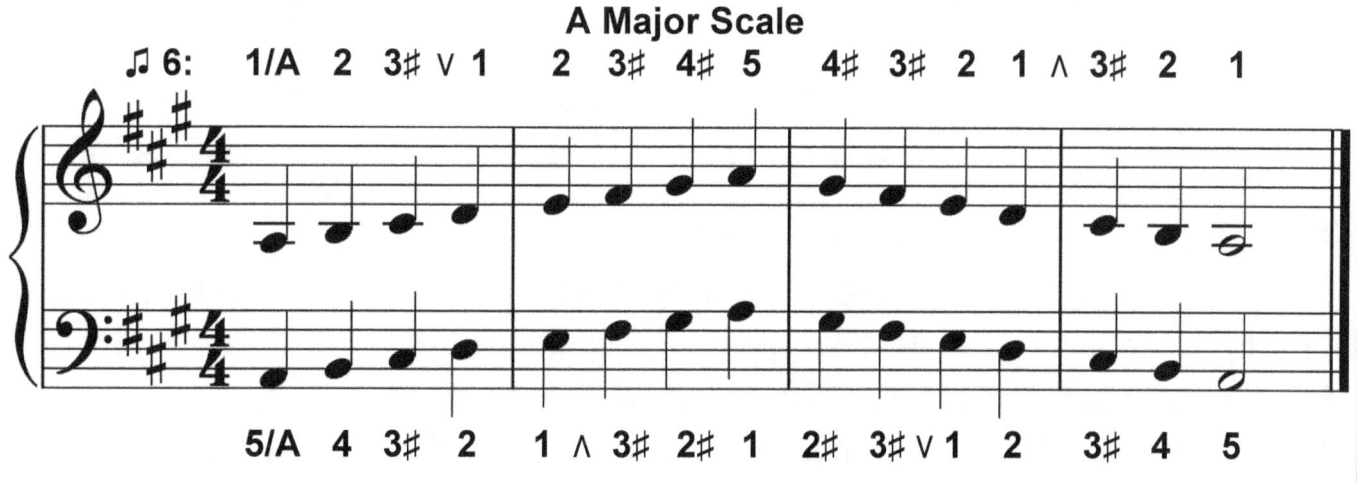

COMPOSITION TEN

♪ **1: Measure 1, compose** a pattern of four pitches using only middle **C D E** (in any order). Fill in the blanks below with the **letter names for four beats**.
♪ **2: Measure 2, retrograde** measure 1 pattern **(same notes backwards, 19b).**
♪ **3: Measure 3, sequence** measure 1 pattern **(raise by 1 or 2 notes, 16c).**
♪ **4: Measure 4, 1st ending,** pause on **whole note E or D** for the **"question."**

A $\frac{4}{4}$ | _ _ _ _ | _ _ _ _ | _ _ _ _ | _ _ _ _ |
   Measure 1   Measure 2   Measure 3   Measure 4

♪ **5: Measures 5–7, repeat** measure 1, retrograde 2, and sequence 3.
♪ **6: Measure 8,** the whole note **C** is filled in for the **2nd ending "answer" (16c).**

A1 | _ _ _ _ | _ _ _ _ | _ _ _ _ | C _ _ _ |
   Measure 5   Measure 6   Measure 7   Measure 8

♪ **7: Measure 9, compose** a 2nd four note **C D E** pattern, start on **E or D.**
♪ **8: Measure 10, invert** the measure 9 pattern **(opposite directions, 21c).**
♪ **9: Measure 11, repeat** measure 9. **Measure 12,** end on **whole note E or D.**

B | _ _ _ _ | _ _ _ _ | _ _ _ _ | _ _ _ _ |
   Measure 9   Measure 10   Measure 11   Measure 12

♪ **10: Measures 13–16: Repeat** measures 5–8 (the **A1** second phrase).

A1 | _ _ _ _ | _ _ _ _ | _ _ _ _ | C _ _ _ ‖
   Measure 13   Measure 14   Measure 15   Measure 16

First phrase, measures 1–4 is called **"A."**
Second phrase, measures 5–8 is called **"A1"** (like A, but ends on the keynote).
Third phrase, measures 9–12 is called **"B"** (contrast).
Fourth phrase, measures 13–16 is called **"A1"** (repetition).
The **A~A1~B~A1** form is common in composition (see **"Ode to Joy,"** 6b).

COMPOSITION TEN

♫ 11: Notate the melody with chords and play (Notation Guide ~ Key of C).

INDEXES

RHYTHM			CHORDS	
accented beats 11	35	33	L/R	C F G
allegretto	88	38	LH	C F G7
bars or measures	54	★ 42	LH	C F G7
D.C. al Fine	21	49	RH	C G7
Dots and Ties	21	60	LH	I IV V7
Dotted Quarters	83	60	LH	F Bb C7
dotted double bars	49	★ 61	LH	F Bb C7
double bar	14	★ 67	LH	F C7
Expression	95	69	RH	F Bb C7
fermata	65	70	RH	F Bb C7 low
Notes and Rests	11	80	LH	G C D7
Partial Measures	23	★ 81	LH	G C D7
Ritard	21	91	RH	G C D7
Rhythm	11	92	RH	G C D7 low
Shorter Notes	25	101	L/R	C Am F G
swing style rhythm		★ 102	L/R	C Am Dm G7
Hump-ty Dump-ty	34	103	L/R	C Caug Cm Cdim
Time Signatures	15	104	LH	C C7 F F7 G G7
triplets	50	105	L/R	Basic Chord Types
um-pah-pah	87	109	L/R	Am Dm E7
		★ 110	LH	Am E7

★ **Improvise RH melodic patterns**

YouTube

Today's students learn when they are able to both hear and see musical performances that reflect diverse historical periods, cultural styles, artists, and ensemble groupings.

With YouTube, you can hone in on whatever you like or need by downloading to a flash drive. You are able to play student preferences in popular music, curriculum repertoire and other relevant pieces to reinforce musical concepts.

For example, students may compare the presentation styles for the "Ode to Joy" theme by Beethoven performed in a church, at the Olympics in Japan, and in the movie *Sister Act II*. Students can identify time signatures in a Strauss waltz, a Sousa march, "Let It Be" by the Beatles, and "Morning Has Broken" by Cat Stevens. The use of the fifth is identifiable in a Gregorian chant, the movie *Chariots of Fire*, and "Love Me Do," also by the Beatles. Other elements of applied theory may be illustrated in this engaging way.

Our Goal

A hands-on understanding of
melodic pattern, harmonic structure,
rhythmic proportion, and basic ensemble.